Idolatry and the Construction
of the Spanish Empire

Idolatry

and the Construction
of the Spanish Empire

Mina García Soormally

UNIVERSITY PRESS OF COLORADO

Louisville

© 2018 by University Press of Colorado

Published by University Press of Colorado
245 Century Circle, Suite 202
Louisville, Colorado 80027

ASSOCIATION
of UNIVERSITY
PRESSES
The University Press of Colorado is a proud member of the Association of University Presses.The University Press of Colorado is a cooperative publishing enterprise supported, in part, by Adams State University, Colorado State University, Fort Lewis College, Metropolitan State University of Denver, Regis University, University of Colorado, University of Northern Colorado, Utah State University, and Western State Colorado University.

∞ This paper meets the requirements of the ANSI/NISO Z39.48-1992 (Permanence of Paper).

ISBN: 978-1-60732-800-1 (cloth)
ISBN: 978-1-60732-801-8 (ebook)
DOI: https://doi.org/10.5876/9781607328018

Library of Congress Cataloging-in-Publication Data

Names: García Soormally, Mina, 1972– author.
Title: Idolatry and the construction of the Spanish empire / by Mina García Soormally.
Description: Boulder : University Press of Colorado, [2018] | Includes bibliographical references and index.
Identifiers: LCCN 2018029735| ISBN 9781607328001 (cloth) | ISBN 9781607328018 (ebook)
Subjects: LCSH: Idolatry—Mexico—History. | Indians of Mexico—Religion. | Catholic Church—Mexico—History. | Mexico—Religion. | Mexico—Religious life and customs. | Mexico—History—Spanish colony, 1540–1810.
Classification: LCC F1219.3.R38 G37 2018 | DDC 972/.01—dc23
LC record available at https://lccn.loc.gov/2018029735

Cover illustrations: "Mar del Nort" by Johannes Jansson, 1650, courtesy of the David Rumsey Map Collection, www.davidrumsey.com (top); "Columbus Taking Possession of the New World," public domain image from Library of Congress (bottom)

To Clark, Amanda, and Olivia,
for their laughter, their hugs, and their patience.

To my parents and siblings, whom I carry in my heart wherever I go.

Contents

Preface

Early spring in Seville. As I type away on my computer, I listen to the horses clacking on top of the cobblestones. Clop, clop, clop, clop; and I suddenly realize that my typing has taken the same cadence, and the carriage is now marking my pace as well. I imagine, since the tall windows of the Archivo de Indias do not give me any other choice, a couple of tourists wearing big straw hats and loud-colored shirts who can't stop smiling while complaining about how hot it is.

The marching bands are already practicing their music for Holy Week while the store owners are getting ready for the avalanche of tourists that come with the good weather. From now on, and for a couple of months, the bottles of water will quadruple their price and McDonald's will house a thousand different languages at a time because, in the heat of Seville, who wants to be adventurous and try the traditional cuisine? But, as I reflect on these scenes I wonder, were we (Spaniards) always this open to foreigners? Did we always welcome other cultures, other lifestyles? Do we now?

While walking in the tangle of quaint winding streets and lovely plazas of the Jewish quarter, one could almost believe all the clichés: the smell of the orange blossoms dominates the air, the busy balconies hide the sky and, if you pay attention, you could probably hear a guitar in the distance. Every -other house sells postcards and cheap T-shirts accompanied by the typical pottery printed with "Recuerdo de Sevilla." But, looking at one of our main sources of revenue—the tourist industry—I have to ask myself, are we really open to foreigners, or just "open for

DOI: 10.5876/9781607328018.c000

business"? In other words, what role does the *other*, foreigners or outsiders, play in our scheme of things? How have Spaniards conceived their own identity throughout modernity?

Early Christianity sought to define who belonged and who didn't, what was accepted or not, in religious terms, setting the boundaries for what was considered the norm, while encoding beliefs and behavior in everyday life—discriminating, therefore, between true and false religion. Following this tradition, Pedro Ciruelo (1470–1548), professor of theology and teacher to Philip II of Spain, when discussing the meaning of false doctrine wrote that, "witchcraft and superstition deserve heavy punishment both from the prelates and by civil judges, as well as expulsion from the lands of Christian peoples as very evil and poisonous things which are known to be extremely prejudicial to the honor of God and very dangerous and hazardous for Christian souls, will be seen as a certainty. In the end, they draw down the anger of God upon the nations, cities and villages where they are tolerated" (1977: 77).

This idea presents a component of inclusiveness/exclusiveness that makes the doctrine the perfect instrument to appeal to the right people. In this way Ciruelo presents the root of true religion while demonizing any ritual not sanctioned by the Catholic Church, establishing who, in his point of view, is in or out, who belongs and who does not.

However, as Christianity expanded and came into contact with other peoples and other forms of worship, it became impossible to keep true and false doctrine so neatly divided. Christian belief and practice thus resulted in an ever-changing dichotomy, playing differently in diverse circumstances, constantly defining and rearticulating the reality that it was trying to label. Encountering the *other* produced a multilayered religiosity that combined orthodox Christian beliefs and pre-Christian rituals; that is, behaviors and beliefs that the Christian authorities would ultimately call idolatry.

Idolatry is a concept that, throughout history, has determined the life or, more accurately, the death of many individuals in Europe and its colonies. But what exactly is idolatry? What characteristics define it? What is its relationship with heresy and apostasy? How was it used at the time the Americas were colonized? How was this concept transformed as a result? These are some of the questions I will address in the following chapters. In them I will show that idolatry does not have a single meaning, but rather it is an ever-changing concept, polyvalent in nature, used and redefined in very different instances and contexts. It is, then, a malleable concept and so are its applications, making it a very interesting point of reference in the Early Modern period. Recovering this concept is of great importance since it speaks of some crucial behavior in particular spaces and times, and it is embedded in the process of socialization itself. It refers both to the nature of those who use it and of those who are labeled by it and reaches deeply into the fundamental mechanisms of hegemony.

The arrival of colonizers in the "new" territories occurred in the midst of a debate over idolatry that was taking place throughout Europe and which later continued in the New World. They were times of self-definition, but the new circumstances made the task that much bigger: it was then Spain's duty to incorporate this "New World" into the known one, to create a place for these "new" peoples in the European scheme, and to establish a relationship with the colonized *other*.

In this crossroad, Spain used the concept of "idolatry" to label not only that which was undesirable, but especially that which was unknown. The self-centered attitude that Spaniards brought with them was not only noticeable in the way they baptized the newly "discovered" as "Indians" but also in the manner they treated their cosmology, culture, religion, and way of life. The "discovery," therefore, not only implied a position relative to the *other* but also a questioning of European concepts never challenged before.

This idea is based in the practice of *othering* and allowed Spaniards to see the colonized subject as the radically different, not only inferior, but also barbarian, and evil. Therefore, it became the "demonic *other*," reproducing models that had already been used in Spain to fight the Moors and the Jews, and that made the conflict with the American idolaters that much more familiar. This idea also assumes that European practices are both seen as superior and universal and that everything that does not belong in this scheme of things can be rejected, replaced, and eliminated.

But this "demonic *other*," barbarian and evil, is not only defined in religious terms: it is also the physically different, the non-white, the subaltern, the colonized. It is the one defined by who the colonizers are not and, therefore, the one with no rights, not even to an identity of its own. It is the *other* who is spoken for and who struggles to assert his own value and to find his own voice. For that reason, they are the target of the campaigns of extirpation by those who want to make disappear not only the idols that they worship but also the culture that supports their very existence.

It is in this confluence of elements that I place my book, tracing the formation of a new ideology on the basis of religious and political conflicts fought in two different battlefronts: the Iberian Peninsula and the Americas, resulting in a modern nation that would become a point of reference for the whole world. In this context my book is a study of the role that the shifting concept of idolatry played in the spiritual and territorial conquest of the Americas, in particular in colonial Mexico, as well as its relation to the subsequent construction of imperial power and hegemony. My research illuminates the theological and practical conquest of the New

World, the creation of otherness, and the emergence of indigenous resistance under the auspices of religion, in an attempt to broaden our understanding of the politics of colonization as conditioned by the particular moment in European history (Catholic reform, Protestant Reformation, and Counter-Reformation) and the previous experience with Judaism and Islam in Spain.

My book offers an interdisciplinary perspective, both in the goal and in the sources used. Although firmly set on a literary basis, my analysis shares concerns with other fields such as history, religion, and cultural studies in order to paint a complex picture of the first incursion of Europeans into the Americas. Varied too are the sources that I use to compose this picture, from evangelization plays and chronicles of the Indies to legislation and literature produced on both sides of the Atlantic Ocean.

In order to access the complexity of the topic, I am following postcolonial theory. Although there are other approaches that would allow me to study idolatry in New Spain during the sixteenth and seventeenth centuries, I think that the contextual component of postcolonial theory is essential. For this reason I do not wish to focus my attention only on the logistics of these campaigns, nor on the study of accusations of idolatry. Instead, I study Spanish colonialism in Spain and New Spain, paying special attention to issues relating to the fight for control, religion, and race. This postcolonial approach also allows me to study cultural practices born in response and in resistance to the Spanish attempts to colonize, like the creation of *otherness* and the issues that arose between the metropolis and the periphery, and amongst the natives themselves.

It is my intention with this study to contribute to bridging the existing gap between European studies and those on the colonies. These two areas of studies have remained mostly separated. This project contributes to the growing field of transatlantic studies and explores the redefinition that was taking place in Europe and in the colonies, not only as simultaneous events but also as necessarily entangled ones.

I also contribute to the field the idea of the "Catholic Atlantic," developed in my second chapter, a concept derived from Felipe Fernández-Armesto's "Atlantic Mediterranean" (a new area of influence that completes itself with the Portuguese Azores in the north, the Spanish Canaries in the south, and the coasts of the Iberian Peninsula and Africa in the east). I would rather refer to this new circle of influence as the Catholic Atlantic, a creation not only in the geographical and political sense, but also, and more important, in the colonial aspect, an area where Catholic values are implanted as a portal to access not only a physical space but also the ways of the European societies and cultures. This "inner sea," created by European sailors as a way to mark the limits of the navigation at the time, the horizons of the known world, became the first oceanic laboratory in which to exercise the cultural and geographical colonization that was still in its early stages of development.

In order to carry out this sort of analysis, I have tried to recover some texts that were lesser-known in the world of colonial literature and some of the debates originating from them. In particular, I look at the indigenous rewrite of a Spanish play and the mechanisms of indigenous resistance that we can see operating in it, and the *Información* initiated by Archbishop Montúfar about the apparition of the Virgin of Guadalupe, which tells us more about how the colonial world worked. My book offers new insights into the lives and the struggles of those who were living in this in-between. Its goal is to recover their voices as free as possible from the otherwise inevitable mediation. In doing so my project gives a voice to the dominated, to the subaltern, and to their search for a space where they could develop according to the ethical and moral values that had centered their culture before the irruption of the "discovery." I explore questions dealing with the imposition of a culture, a religion, and a corpus of moral values over the subaltern and the resulting consequences in the context of the first encounter between the Spaniards and the native population of the Americas.

I have divided my book into four interdependent chapters. The first one offers a corpus of the most necessary definitions when dealing with idolatry in the context of the cultural encounter between the Spaniards and the indigenous peoples of the Americas in the sixteenth–seventeenth centuries. In it I explore the concept of idolatry and heresy, and I relate them to the use of these terms in the Protestant Reformation. I argue that idolatry does not have a single meaning and, though I offer my own definition for this particular context, I emphasize the polyvalent nature of the concept, a feature that allows it to be constantly redefined.

My second chapter looks at the situation of idolatry in New Spain as found upon the arrival of the first bishop, the Franciscan Juan de Zumárraga. It explores the way he faced the fight against idolatry during the process of establishment of the Spanish empire. I follow Zumárraga's transition from inquisitor in Navarra to bishop of New Spain. I also present the first reactions of the *conquistadores* in relation to the religious practices of the indigenous population, and I relate them to the reactions experienced in Spain towards the first *infidels* Spaniards came in contact with (Jews and Moors), and the antecedents in the war of Granada.

The third chapter continues with the study of idolatry in New Spain. I start by making a connection to the Battle of Pavia (1525), and I study the legitimacy of the practice of massive baptisms. From there, based on plays such as *Ejemplo del juicio final* (1533) and *La conquista de Jerusalén* (1539), I explore the role of drama as an instrument at the service of the spiritual conquest of New Spain as a propaganda machine. Finally, I study the mechanisms of repression used in the Spain of the Reconquista (based, mainly, on texts by Alfonso X, Hernando de Talavera, and Ferrán Martínez) and connect these practices with the study of some inquisitorial cases in which Indians were accused of idolatry.

The fourth chapter is a reflection on the use of images in the process of conquest and colonization of New Spain. I am particularly interested in the progression from idolatry to symbol of national identity experienced by the Virgin of Guadalupe and the handling of her apparitions. Also, I juxtapose the use of this image in the process of colonization and evangelization of the transatlantic colonies with its immediate antecedent in the use of the Virgen de Candelaria in the conquest of the Canary Islands and the previous use of the intercession of the Virgin in the process of converting the Jews and Moors in Spain as portrayed in the *Cantigas de Santa María*.

I posit that the conquest of America was presented, in its first instances, as a virtual extension of the Reconquista that had taken place in Spain since 718, and during which Castilians fought to build an empire based, among other things, on the discrimination against others in religious terms. In my opinion, the fight against the peninsular heathens (Moors and Jews) provided the necessary experience and mindset to experiment and practice with the repression of the *other*, making of Spain a cultural laboratory that was transported across the Atlantic Ocean.

There has been some important work done, mostly by historians, on the phenomenon of idolatry, especially in Peru. Nicholas Griffiths, Kenneth Mills, and Sabine MacCormack have worked on campaigns of extirpation. Pierre Duviols has edited previously unpublished trials on heresy, coming directly from the Archiepiscopal Archive of Lima. To his contribution we can add works by Ana Sánchez, Juan Carlos Estenssoro, and Juan Carlos García Cabrera. Specifically, on the topic of New Spain, Serge Gruzinski has done some extensive work on images in relation to the process of conquest. There are also important contributions by Christian Duverger, Robert Ricard, Fernando Horcasitas, Richard Greenleaf, Aracil Varón, and Othón Arróniz. But while some attention has been paid to the description of idolatry, little has been done to link the accusation of idolatry in colonial New Spain and its European counterpart and the issues around the fight against the "original infidels." My book explores the theological and practical conquest of the New World and the creation of otherness in an attempt to broaden our understanding of the politics of colonization as conditioned by the particular moment in European history and the previous experience with Judaism and Islam in Spain.

Before I go any further, I would like to clarify one aspect that will become apparent in the following pages. In developing my comparative approach to the subject of idolatry and the use of the concept, I will be skipping back and forth between Spain and New Spain, not necessarily in chronological progression, in order to develop parallels and contrasts that the simple chronological order might have ~~rendered~~ obscured. To make it easier to follow the chronological order of events, I provide a chart in Appendix D.

My research is deeply connected with religious aspects, especially as they play a part in the political and territorial conquest of the Indies. In my opinion these attempts to carry out the conversion of the New World were part of the process of colonization of the imaginary that took place in the sixteenth and seventeenth centuries, but it is still very much present in the expansion of dominant cultures all over the world. I am particularly interested in looking at questions of interaction with the "infidels" because, although my project studies the Early Modern period, these are issues that today, more that ever, are present in our lives as the current political climate is engaged in battling a different *other*. This is what keeps my project relevant nowadays since I explore questions dealing with the imposition of a culture, a religion, and a corpus of moral values over the subaltern and the different consequences and reactions resulting from this, in the context of the first encounter between the Spaniards and the native population of the Americas.

My interest in the topic began years ago, in the course of working on my first doctoral dissertation for the University of Málaga, Spain. At that time I was working on magic, sorcery, and witchcraft in literary texts in Spain, and the transition to thinking about the same topics on the other side of the Atlantic was not a big leap. On that occasion I studied the relation between society and superstition in some texts of the Early Modern period as a way of approaching the practices that were common at the time and the manner in which those were seen in the contemporary literary texts. So, beyond the literary analysis, I looked at the socioeconomic aspects that are so intimately related to sorcery, especially in the Celestinesque tradition. I proposed the role of the go-between as that of a social agent, as the protagonist of the struggle that women of the time had to go through in order to have access to positions of authority, to vindicate their own voices. This research was published by Renacimiento in Seville, in 2011, under the title *Magia, hechicería y brujería: Entre La Celestina y Cervantes*. Similarly, in the study of some of Cervantes's works, my aim was to present the portrait of the witch and the sorceress in the social context of the time and to emphasize their marginal condition. I concluded that both Rojas and Cervantes create a parallel society to the institutional: a periphery, whether in the form of an animal, of a different identity, or under the disguise of craziness or sorcery. In this periphery, outside of the center of power, a subaltern reality creates a tension that is destroyed under the label of witchcraft. In this situation witchcraft, therefore, provides a space in which those members of society marginalized because of their race, religion, or gender find the possibility of flirting with the idea of being included, of acquiring the public recognition that seems impossible any other way. Nevertheless, it becomes evident in all these stories that this hope, disguised in the form of a spell, is nothing more than an empty illusion.

Acknowledgments

Before I let you immerse yourself in the following pages I would like to thank my dear advisor, Margaret R. Greer, for her wise comments, her patience, and her friendship over the years; Walter Mignolo and Thomas Robisheaux for their warmth and generosity; and Carlos Eire for believing in me from very early on. Thank you all for your support of this project and your collaboration.

My gratitude also goes to the Duke Graduate School and the Department of Romance Studies, which became my home away from home and taught me to see the world in a new light.

Elon University has a very special place in my heart for the number of great people and great experiences it has put me in contact with. I especially want to thank Tim Peeples and Gabie Smith for their support and the smiles on their faces when they heard the news about this book and, of course, my wonderful colleagues in the Department of World Languages & Cultures at Elon who have always supported my initiatives.

Very special thanks go to my working group: Melissa Figueroa, Glenda Nieto-Cuebas, Tania de Miguel Magro, and Erin Cowling. These dear friends have renewed in me my love for research, have taught how to work collaboratively and, more important, how to share the journey, the ups and the downs of the American academia.

Last but not least I want to thank my dear friends Ignacio López, Nina Namaste, Shereen Elgamal, Shannon Tennant, and Samuele Pardini, who have always been there for me, helping me all along the way, and sharing innumerable coffees. But my biggest thanks go to my family: my parents and siblings in Spain who keep cheering me on in all my adventures and, of course, Clark and my beautiful girls, Amanda and Olivia, who mean everything to me.

Idolatry and the Construction
of the Spanish Empire

1

The Limits of Idolatry

Downtown is packed. There are thousands of chairs aligned all over the city, and the population has doubled again this year. As the *nazarenos* process, the spectators eat their sandwiches and enjoy the parade. Suddenly, silence takes over the street as the first image shows up far, far away. The marching bands stop playing, and the sandwiches find their way back into the plastic bags as we all make an effort to see over everybody's heads. A white shadow approaches and, as it comes closer, the spectators become practitioners, a category that includes everybody, if only this week. The sepulchral silence is suddenly broken as a loud applause fills the air.

"Está andando, está andando!"[1]—somebody screams as he follows the wave in the tunic of the image as it is rocked right in front of us. And *el Cautivo* passes by, in his white robe, followed by an estimated 5,000 people who rely on this image to heal a relative, get out of bankruptcy, or even pass final exams, since nothing is too difficult for this image of Christ which is said to be the most miraculous one in the Holy week in Málaga.[2] Not the ones in front or behind, not the ones still to come in the following days (it is only Monday of Holy Week), but this very one, this image

---

1 "He is walking, he is walking."
2 The image of the Cautivo is one of the most famous in the Holy Week in Málaga, Spain. It presents the image of Christ standing and with his hand tied up as he has been *captured*. He is wearing a crisp white robe that, moved by the rocking of the throne and the breeze from the Mediterranean Sea, makes him look like he is actually walking himself. He is surrounded by 800 *nazarenos* and carried by 240 men who, joined by the thousands of spontaneous petitioners and the throne of María Santísima de la Trinidad, make for an eight-hour walk around the main streets of the city.

DOI: 10.5876/9781607328018.c001

that seems to walk over the crowd. And, what to say about the images of the Virgin, processed all over the city followed by people screaming": "¡Guapa!"?

These scenes are repeated year after year in southern Spain where, for a week, the general public establishes a relationship with these figures that only a small percentage maintains during the rest of the year. The images become real. They are cared for, dressed, and adorned with special devotion. They walk the streets; they become the object of our prayers and songs, of our devotion, our affection and the source of our rivalries, since the member of the other *cofradías* will always say that their images are the best looking this year. And, in the view of this spectacle that forms part of some of my dearest memories, I wonder: am I an idolater? Is this paganism happening in the core of the very Catholic Spain? What would Erasmus, Luther, or Calvin say if they saw this? How would Spaniards have reacted if, instead of the Virgen del Rocío it had been Pachamama on that throne; that is, if the Incas were celebrating like this? Would they have been punished for idolatry? And if so, why are we not?

The goal of this chapter is to offer a corpus of the most necessary definitions when dealing with idolatry in the context of the cultural encounter between the Spaniards and the indigenous peoples of the Americas in the sixteenth–seventeenth centuries, and I aim to answer a number of simple but underexplored questions: What is heresy? What is its use in the period around the "discovery" of America?[3] How is this concept transformed because of the "discovery"? What is the relationship between heresy and idolatry? What is the significance of the concept of "idolatry" in Europe in the period around the "discovery"? How was it used and to whom did it refer? To anticipate my conclusion, I argue that idolatry does not have a single meaning and, though I make an effort to offer my own definition in relation to the context of colonial Mexico in the moment of the first encounter with the Spanish invaders, I really want to emphasize the polyvalent nature of the concept, a feature that makes it possible to be used and redefined constantly, in very different instances and contexts. It is a malleable concept and so are its applications, making it a very interesting point of reference that crosses the main debates of the period. Therefore, in my opinion, recovering this concept not only speaks about some crucial behavior that was taking place in a particular space and time, but it is also embedded in the process of colonization itself. It refers both to the nature of the "Indians" and to that of their colonizers, to the Catholic understanding of the nature of God himself and his worst enemy, and reaches very deeply into the fundamental mechanisms of hegemony and coloniality.[4]

---

3   I prefer to use discovery in quotes since those territories had already been populated for years. The event of 1492 only incorporates them to the Western world, but it is not a discovery in the pure sense of the word.

4   From now on and throughout the whole book, when I mention God free of qualifiers, it will have to be understood that I am using this term from the Catholic, Christian perspective.

TRUE VERSUS FALSE RELIGION

Christianity has tried to define what is true versus false religion, what is accepted or not and, therefore, who belongs and who doesn't, setting the boundaries for what is considered the norm in a particular context, while encoding beliefs and behavior in everyday life. Following this tradition, Pedro Ciruelo (1470–1548)—professor of theology, author of *A Treatise Reproving all Superstitions and Forms of Witchcraft* (1538), and teacher to King Phillip II of Spain—when discussing the meaning of false doctrine wrote that "what superstitions teach is false and deceitful and it is not the teaching of God, who abhors superstitions: rather, it is the devil, the father of lies (as Christ said), who takes delight in vain superstitions" (1977: 90–91). But this idea was completed by including a component of inclusiveness/exclusiveness that makes the doctrine the perfect instrument to appeal to the *right* people: "That witchcraft and superstition deserve heavy punishment both from the prelates and by civil judges, as well as expulsion from the lands of Christian peoples as very evil and poisonous things which are known to be extremely prejudicial to the honor of God and very dangerous and hazardous for Christian souls, will be seen as a certainty. In the end, they draw down the anger of God upon the nations, cities and villages where they are tolerated" (77).

This way the root of his concept of true religion is presented at the same time that he demonizes any ritual not sanctioned by the Catholic Church, establishing who, in his point of view, is in or out, who belongs to it and who does not. But as Christianity expanded and it came in contact with other peoples and other forms of worshipping, it became impossible to keep realities so neatly divided into what was true or false doctrine, and acceptable levels of syncretism seemed a much more difficult goal to attain.[5] Christian religion and its practice thus resulted in an ever-changing reality, playing differently in diverse circumstances and constantly defining and rearticulating the reality that it was trying to label. This process of encountering the *other* normally results in the coexistence of a multilayered religiosity that combines orthodox Christian beliefs together with pre-Christian rituals; that is, with other behaviors and beliefs that the Christian dogma would end up labeling as "superstition," "heresy," "idolatry," and so on. This dichotomy—which can be seen as an expected differentiation between an "official religion," defended by the Christian authorities, and a "popular religion" that collects the excess—the native rituals not contemplated by the Christian norm, has not always coexisted in peace but rather has resulted in animosity and persecution.[6]

---

5 I understand "syncretism" as the process by which different practices are combined into one religion. It can take the form of fusion or, in more extreme cases, of assimilation when elements of one religion are absorbed by another one that becomes dominant. In those cases, it might not be a process of fusion, since one religion may almost eliminate the other; therefore syncretism can develop in different degrees.

6 For an extended study on the meaning of "popular religion," see Carlos Eire's (2005) article: "The concept of popular religion" in *Popular Religion in Mexico*.

Heresy and idolatry are two concepts that, throughout history, have determined the life and, more accurately, the death of many individuals in Europe and its colonies. Understood differently in different parts of the world at different times, these two concepts were closely interwoven in the discourses about imperialism and construction of hegemony that were developing in the times around the "discovery" of America, a period when the position relative to these terms could close the distance between life and death.

But what exactly is heresy, according to Catholic dogma? What are the characteristics that make it unique? What is the relationship between heresy, apostasy and idolatry? What was its use in the period around the "discovery" of America? And how was this concept transformed because of the "discovery"? These are some of the questions that I will attempt to answer below.

Etymologically, the term heresy means *choice*; that is, it refers to the possibility of choosing to believe in things other than what a particular faith establishes and, therefore, in the eyes of that established faith, heresy is seen as erroneous in such a way that the believers should try to separate themselves from the heretic and that the church, as a whole, ought to create a distance from all who *choose* differently (Eimeric and Peña 1983: 57). It is important to take into account that we are not talking about a decided abandonment of a particular religion but rather a *deviation* in some aspects of that faith, a choice about what dogmas to believe in and what not within that religion. This is, therefore, the main difference between "apostasy" and "heresy" in that whereby the believer accepts the whole deposit of dogmas as proposed by the church, the heretic accepts only the parts of it that meet his own approval, and the apostate abandons the faith altogether. Ciruelo relates these terms when talking about the ill influence of spells, or *ensalmos*:

> Any man or woman who seeks a cure through spells tacitly accepts a return to health with the aid of the devil and thus makes a pact of friendship with the enemy of God and man. This pact is a most serious sin of *idolatry*; it violates the first commandment. It is also apostasy from the virtue of Christian religion sealed at baptism. *Apostasy* calls down the wrath and anger of God upon such an individual and his household. One day he will experience punishment at God's hand, and that punishment will be an affliction much greater than the one healed by the devil by means of the lips and hands of the enchanter. (208, my emphasis)

Nevertheless, in all cases, for these deviations to take place it is necessary that the heretic be a previous believer; that is, he needs to belong to structured religion such as the Catholic Church before he can distance himself from it; in other words, in this case baptism becomes a necessary requirement for becoming a heretic and also the main ingredient that differentiates heretics from idolaters, as understood in the New World, since the latter had not been baptized when they worshipped a god other than the Catholic one and, therefore, could not choose to deviate from the doctrine.

This emphasis on choice has been stressed in the Catholic inquisitorial literature for a long time, and Nicholas Eimeric's *Directorium Inquisitorum* (1376) dwells heavily on it. Eimeric (1320–1399) was a Catalan Roman Catholic theologian and inquisitor general of the Inquisition of the Crown of Aragón in the latter half of the fourteenth century. In his best-known work, the *Directorium Inquisitorum*, he placed the heretic between the total sum of truths revealed in the true doctrine and the perverse and erroneous version of it chosen by the sinner (Eimeric and Peña 57). Heresy, thus, is presented as an intellectual error perhaps motivated by pride or exaggerated trust in one's own insight, the illusions of religious purity, the attractiveness of political or ecclesiastical power, or the relationship with material interests and personal status. According to Eimeric, it isolates the person or group that falls in it and weakens the community as well as the church that has to fight it. The *Malleus Maleficarum* (1487), the most famous treatise against heresy and witchcraft and the most widely circulated all over the Catholic world, shares this point of view and defines heresy, in relation to witchcraft, as the infidelity carried out by a person already baptized ("Quienes tratan de inducir a otros a realizar tales maravillas de malvada índole son llamados brujos o brujas. Y como la infidelidad en una persona bautizada se denomina técnicamente herejía, esas personas son lisa y llanamente herejes"[7] (Kramer and Sprenger 1975: 21), stressing the intellectual aspect of heresy and the importance of free will after baptism in this religious deviation.[8]

---

7   My translation: Those who try to induce others to perform wonders of an evil nature are called witches. And, since the infidelity of a baptized person is technically called heresy, those people are plainly and simply heretics.

8   This same emphasis on infidelity is present in the *Treatise on Superstition and Witchcraft*, the manual compiled by the Spanish friar Martín de Castañega in 1529 and in which the relationship between Catholic idolatry (or more accurately, infidelity to the Christian God and demonic cult) is firmly established. Castañega explains that the basis for this diabolic practice is the inversion of the rituals associated with the Catholic religion and so, instead of "sacraments," he talks about "execrements" for the heretics and conceives of a religion that, taking the Catholic practices, turns everything upside down. Castañega defines this church as follows: "La yglesia diabólica es generalmente toda la infidelidad que está fuera de la yglesia católica, la qual no es propiamente una porque no creen ni adoran un dios verdadero, ni confiessan una fe católica y verdadera, ni reciben ni tienen sacramento que aproveche y valga" (Martín de Castañega 1946: ch. 2). (The diabolic church is generally every infidelity that is found outside the Catholic Church, and it is not really a church because they do not believe in one true god, neither do they profess the Catholic faith nor receive or have any sacrament that is worthy. My translation.) Of course, Martín de Castañega gives this definition in a context that is specifically dealing with the heretics that people were concerned about in the Spain of the time and, therefore, with no intention of referring to the situation taking place in the New World, but, if we consider that he is writing at the same time that Hernán Cortés is incorporating a vast number of Amerindians into the Western imaginary, this definition could be looked upon differently. For one, that idea of the diabolic church could also be used to refer to the practices of the Indians, since they were outside of the Catholic Church as well; they did

But this is not necessarily true in all cases, and in other contexts heresy is devoid of that emphasis on free choice and becomes, instead, the result of ignorance of the true creed, erroneous judgment, or imperfect apprehension and understanding of dogmas, leaving pride to one side to simply becoming the victim of a misinterpretation and not an agent of deviation or religious disagreement. A situation like this is what can be said to have occurred in the Spanish colonies in America where, once baptized, the Indians developed a mixture of their native rituals and the newly learned ceremonies of the Catholic cult, resulting in a syncretic combination that was considered, by the Spaniards, heretical. But, whereas in these cases preaching and deeper understanding of the doctrine could potentially alter and eventually eliminate the mixture, in the case of heresy by pride, obstinate denial or rejection of some aspects of the creed seem to be much more difficult to eradicate and can even turn into the seeds of schism.

Because of its main characteristic—that is, introducing doubt within the dogmas of an established church—heresy has frequently been punished with the total expulsion of the subject from that religion; that is, with permanent Catholic excommunication and, in most cases, the confiscation of his possessions.

But there was a time when even dreaming about things contrary to the Catholic religion was enough to be considered an infidel, since it was believed that it was the Devil himself who put these thoughts in the minds of the already confused practitioner. Therefore, whoever thought of things such as witches flying was just as guilty as if they had committed a heresy themselves and was as heretical as the flying witches they had imagined. This text, then, provided no defense for those accused of imagining heresies since who can prove what one does or does not think about? But, at the same time, this text reduced all the witches' universe, so in vogue at the time (*Sabbaths*, night flights, metamorphosis, etc.) to mere illusions, imaginations engineered by the Devil with no existence beyond the heretic's mind.

This attitude of fear and persecution was helped along by Pope John XXII, who, fearing himself victim of *maleficia*, decided to give the inquisitors in Toulouse and Carcassonne an incentive to fight diabolic acts and worked on a number of letters and decrees (in 1323, 1326, 1327, and 1331) in which he pushed for the prosecution of these crimes against the Catholic doctrine. Undoubtedly, one of the main measures that were attributed to this pope was contained in the bull published in 1318 in which he allowed, for the first time, the trial of dead heretics who, from

---

not believe in one god only (leaving aside the question about whether any of the gods they worshiped was true or not in the eyes of the Spaniards); and they had no sacraments at all. In that sense, and according to Martín de Castañega's definition, the practices of the Indians had to be considered diabolical, and they themselves would constitute the Church of the Devil, even when the cosmovisions of the different groups did not include the Devil or were even developed in ways similar to Catholicism.

then on, would be tried in effigy and submitted to the same treatment as their living equivalents.

But if that were not enough, in 1326, Pope John XXII published his bull entitled *Super Illius Specula*, a document in which he asserts the reality of diabolic acts, making them change from the status of mere illusions, imagined or dreamed, as they had been taken since the *Canon Episcopi*, to become a pagan reality, something whose existence no one could deny since it had affected the pope himself (Robbins 1991: 345–46).[9] Needless to say, all these facts put together in a very short span of years started an avalanche of trials against heresy in general, and witchcraft in particular, a type of heresy considered so abominable that it seemed to justify the machinery that had been created to fight it.[10]

But Pope John XXII was not the only one who took interest in the fight against heresy. The attempts to fight it extended long after this initiative and, in the latter part of the fifteenth century, Pope Innocent VIII published his *Summis desiderantes affectibus* in which he specifically addressed the matter. In this bull he ratified the undoubted existence of witches and *Sabbaths* and, therefore, recognized the need to intensify the persecution. To better develop this important task, Innocent VIII gave more jurisdictions to the inquisitors. As a result of this petition formulated in 1484, the inquisitors Heinrich Kramer and Jacobus Sprenger answered three years later with their *Malleus Maleficarum*, or *Hammer of the Witches*.

This work was very popular during the sixteenth and seventeenth centuries, just the period that we are looking at, the period around the imperial moment, just following the "discovery" of America. This inquisitorial handbook, supremely misogynist, follows the path started by Eimeric's work and opposes the *Canon Episcopi* in the affirmation of the reality of heresy and witchcraft, especially as performed by women. It even goes on to say that since several popes had established the existence of witches, it would be heretical *not* to believe in it, because the negation of a reality asserted by the maximum authority of the church becomes heresy in itself. The *Malleus* shows the first authorized uses of torture in the fight against idolatry, since it considers it "the first of all superstitions" (Kramer and Sprenger 1975: 39) and one that needs to be fought as harshly as possible. It is not surprising that in this atmosphere of obsession with the worst maleficia, Pope Innocent VIII appointed

---

9 In 1320, Matteo and Galeazzo Visconti were accused in a trial of having conspired to kill Pope John XXII. They had made a silver statuette reproducing the features of the pope and bearing his name. Later, they exposed the statue to the elements for seventy-two nights. It was considered a proof of witchcraft, and that same year the pope issued the second of his bulls directing prelates to deal with the problems of heresy and witchcraft (Freedberg 1989: 266).

10 I dealt with this topic in my book entitled *Magia, hechicería y brujería: Entre La Celestina y Cervantes* (2011). It is an interdisciplinary study of witchcraft and sorcery in Early Modern Spain, drawing on Inquisition manuals and socioeconomic studies as well as literary texts.

Tomás de Torquemada to be Grand Inquisitor of Spain, precisely the same year that the famous manual was published.

From then on, every important inquisitorial manual was based on the same two premises: First, witchcraft existed and was a reality which nobody could deny any more; and second, it was based on idolatry; that is, on the worship of a god other than the Catholic one, in this case, the Devil himself, with whom the witches established an explicit pact, denying God the required obedience. In this line we can find the *Reprobación de las supersticiones y hechicerías* (1529), by Pedro Ciruelo; *Tratado muy sotil y bien fundado de las supersticiones y hechizerias y vanos conjuros* (1538) by Martín de Castañega; and the *Disquisitionum Magicarum Libri Sex* (1599), by Martín del Río, particularly his second book.

But all these texts introduce one more term that needs to be clarified in relation to the ones we have already talked about: superstition. In his *Summa Theologica* (1265–1274), St. Thomas Aquinas refers to it as: the vice of over-doing religion either by superstition or giving God honor in unfitting ways, extending honor to other creatures, worshiping them (idolatry) or looking to them for knowledge (divination and fortune-telling) or guidance (magical practices) (Question 92. I, 409–10). Therefore, superstition sins by excess; that is, it constitutes worship to an improper god or to the right God in improper ways, according to the Catholic Church. From this point of view, there are four species of superstitions of which idolatry, the worship of idols, is only one. It is accompanied by improper ways of worship of the true God such as divination and vain observances, which include magic, witchcraft, and all the occult arts.[11] All of these behaviors are heretical and superstitious and have been fiercely fought throughout the history of Catholicism.

As we have already seen, idolatry is a superstitious act and, therefore, a form of heresy, but let us become a little more familiar with the full meaning of this concept. The reason why I choose to concentrate on this term rather that any other (such as "superstition" or "heresy") is because, although they are very closely related, idolatry, rather than any other manifestations of religious deviation, was the central focus in the eyes of the doctrinal colonizers. This is the way the Spaniards decided to refer to the native religion which, because it worshipped idols not known by the Catholic conquerors, was considered idolatry. Also, this label was used to define the Indians in opposition to the newly arrived who chose to call themselves Christians, as is reflected in their accounts at almost all times.

---

11 Some of the most famous superstitions include astrology, the use of amulets, chiromancy, necromancy, spiritism; oneiromancy, omens or prognostics of future events; the use of lucky and unlucky days, numbers, persons, things, actions; the evil eye, spells, incantations, ordeals, and so on.

IDOLATROUS "NEW" WORLD

The word "idolatry" is formed from two Greek words: *eidōlon*, "image" and *latreia*, "adoration;" so, from a purely etymological point of view, "idolatry" means "adoration of images" (Eliade Vol. 7, 72–81). In the same line, the *Diccionario de autoridades* (1964) describes idolatry as "the worship or cult that the Gentiles give to creatures or statues of false idols" (my translation), understanding Gentiles to mean "non-Jew" and, eventually, all pagans. Idolatry, therefore, as described above, is the worship of a creature instead of God, but it also implies in some cases the adoration of idols made by man, who is himself a creature, so it puts the creation of man above that of God Himself, as it is emphasized by Isaiah 44:9–18.

It seems fitting that in order to fully understand the way the concept of idolatry was used by Spaniards in the context I am interested in—that is, in colonial Mexico—it is necessary to go back to the main source, the Bible, from which the concept was taken before it evolved in the aforementioned context.

There are several places where idolatry takes center stage in the Bible. The passage that first comes to mind is the adoration of the golden calf (*Exodus* 32), where the Israelites worship a calf made of gold while in the desert after fleeing from Egypt. On this occasion, God orders the killing of many among them, the same punishment that he imposes when the Israelites succumb to idolatry again, lured by the women of Mō'ab (*Numbers* 25:1–5).

On no few occasions, the Bible incites the reader to fight idolatry. Its formal condemnation is found in *Exodus* 20:3–5:

> You shall not make for yourself an idol, whether in the form of anything that is in
> heaven above, or that is on the earth beneath, or that is in the water under the earth.
> You shall not bow to them or worship them; for I the Lord your God am a jealous
> God, punishing children for the iniquity of parents, to the third and the fourth
> generation of those who reject me.

To this reference we can add *Deuteronomy* 4:15–19,[12] *Wisdom of Solomon* 14:27–31,[13]

---

12 "Since you saw no form when the Lord spoke to you at Hō'reb out of the fire, take care and watch yourselves closely, so that you do not act corruptly by making an idol for yourselves, in the form of any figure—the likeness of male or female, the likeness of any animal that is on earth, the likeness of any winged bird that flies in the air, the likeness of anything that creeps on the ground, the likeness of any fish that is in the water under the earth. And when you look up to heavens and see the sun, the moon and the stars, all the host of heaven, do not be led astray and bow down to them and serve them, things that the Lord your God has allotted to all the peoples everywhere under heaven."

13 "For the worship of infamous idols is the reason and source and extremity of all evil. For they either go mad with enjoyment, or prophesy lies, or live lawlessly or lightly forswear themselves. For as their trust is in soulless idols, they expect no harm when they have sworn falsely. But on both counts shall justice overtake them: because they thought ill of God and devoted themselves to idols, and because they deliberately swore false oaths, despising piety. For not the might of those that are sworn by but the retribution of sinners ever follows upon the transgression of the wicked." This book, the *Wisdom of Solomon* is part

and *I Corinthians* 10:19–22 where, for the first time, a connection is established between idolatry and the worship of demons.[14]

Saint Thomas of Aquinas does not share this demonic concept that, by the fifteenth century, was fully accepted.[15] Actually, the fight against idolatry had been the focus of many efforts born from the Council of Trent as we saw from the interventions of Pope Innocent VIII. So, if for Kramer and Sprenger idolatry was the first of all superstitions, for the Spaniard Pedro Ciruelo[16] idolatry was a vice, a sin, and an error by which "man denies Him [God] the obedience He requires and gives to Satan the honor due to Him" (76).

In dealing with the Spanish colonies, we can clearly appreciate two opposing movements. On the one hand, we can recognize those who, based on the Old Testament, think that idolatry is a sin that needs to be fought and, therefore, becomes one of the main reasons why preaching by Spaniards and tremendous efforts in pursuing the evangelization of the Indians are required.[17] On the other hand, there are those

---

of the standard Catholic *Bible*, but it is generally included in the *Apocrypha* in the English Protestant Bible (King James Version).

14 "What do I imply then? That food sacrificed to idols is anything, or that an idol is anything? No, I imply that what pagans sacrifice, they sacrifice to demons and not to God. I do not want you to be partners with demons. You cannot drink the cup of the Lord and the cup of demons. You cannot partake of the table of the Lord and the table of demons. Or are we provoking the Lord to jealously? Are we stronger than he?"

15 He understands it as the practice of "offering divine worship to idols . . . In itself, idolatry is the most serious of sins since it sets up another god in the world, diminishing God's primacy" but leaves out the diabolic component that other thinkers, like Acosta, would see as an essential part of this behavior (St. Thomas Aquinas 1989, Question 94.I, 410).

16 The complete title is *A treatise reproving all superstitions and forms of witchcraft: very necessary and useful for all good Christians zealous for their salvation.*

17 Ginés de Sepúlveda (1494–1573) participated in this idea, defending what he thought was the legitimate right of the Spanish empire to conquer, or colonize and evangelize, the so-called New World. In doing this, he opposed Bartolomé de Las Casas in the famous Valladolid Controversy developed in 1550 and concerned with the justification of the Spanish conquest of the Indies during the reign of Charles V. Sepúlveda sustained the position of the colonists, claiming that the Indians were "natural slaves" as defined by Aristotle in Book I of *Politics.* Aristotle starts by comparing the barbarian and the slave in terms of their nature and then observes that "barbarians have no class of natural rulers." Finally, he defines the slave as follows: "One who is a human being belonging by nature not to himself but to another is by nature a slave, and a person is a human being belonging to another if being a man he is an article of property, and an article of property is an instrumental for action separable from its owner . . . For he is by nature a slave who is capable of belonging to another (and that is why he does so belong), and who participates in reason so far as to apprehend it but not to possess it; for the animals other than man are subservient not to reason, by apprehending it, but to feelings. And also the usefulness of slaves diverges little from that of animals; bodily service for the necessity of life is forthcoming from both, from slaves and from domestic animals alike. The intention of nature is therefore to make the bodies also of freemen and of slaves different—the latter strong for necessary service, the former erect and unserviceable for such occupations, but serviceable for a life of citizenship" (Aristotle 1932: 19, 23). Therefore, he portrays the slave as an inferior human being whose only asset is his physical might and who needs to be ruled by others. For his part, Sepúlveda, in his *Tratado sobre las justas causas de la guerra*, stated that "con perfecto derecho los españoles imperan sobre estos bárbaros del Nuevo Mundo é islas adyacentes, los cuales en

who, following Saint Thomas, think that idolatry is not a sin but merely misguided practices that do not justify the presence of Spaniards in America.

Among the latter, Vitoria stands out in considering that the idolatry among the Indians was not a sin but rather a calamity, and concludes that neither the pope, nor his Christian representatives on earth (in this case, the king of Spain) had the right to use violence to fight the behaviors of those who were not their subjects, though he did not go as far as to propose that the Spaniards leave the New World altogether.

Bartolomé de Las Casas, the famous Dominican friar and later bishop of Chiapas, insists on this point and suggests that idolatry is a natural occurrence. According to his opinion, all men have a natural thirst for finding a superior being, a primary reason for everything, and he believes that when this natural desire is not well guided, the Devil sometimes takes advantage of the situation and pushes people to worship false idols. Therefore, in his opinion, idolatry is nothing more than a badly oriented desire to know God and, because of this, is both natural and universal: "La idolatría, supuesta corrupción de la naturaleza humana, sin tener guía de doctrina o de gracia de Dios, es natural, porque aquello que todas las gentes o la mayor parte dellas sin ser enseñadas, usan y hacen y acostumbran, aquello parece y es natural" (Las Casas 1967: 381).[18]

He bases this idea on the episode in the Garden of Eden, and he considers that once man betrayed God, there was a breakage in the direct communication with the divine. From that point on, revelation could only occur via learning from man to man; that is, only when man reaches a particular degree of learning through the teaching of other men can he connect with God, but the natural drive has to be there first. In this sense, Las Casas establishes a link between the degree of idolatry in a particular group of people and its degree of civilization, implying that native Indians are living in a more primitive state than the Spaniards who found them and that, necessarily, civilization brings Christianity with it.

Francisco de Ávila, priest in the Peruvian province of Huarochirí and one of the most active instigators of the auto-da-fé in Lima (1609), basically agrees with this approach, though he introduces some essential variations. He starts by establishing a difference between Andean peoples and Incas, and, if he admitted that the former

---

prudencia, ingenia, virtud y humanidad son tan inferiores á los españoles como los niños á los adultos y las mujeres á los varones, habiendo entre ellos tanta diferencia como la que va de gentes fieras y crueles á gentes clementísimas, de los prodigiosamente intemperantes á los continentes y templados, y estoy por decir que monos á hombres." (Sepúlveda 1941: 101) (To paraphrase, he says that the natives are "as children to parents, as women are to men, as cruel people are from mild people and as monkeys to men").

18 My translation: Idolatry, supposed corruption of human nature without guide for the doctrine or the grace of God, is natural because that which all or most people do without having being taught seems and is natural.

only sinned out of ignorance and therefore should not be treated as harshly, he did not reserve the same privileges for the latter. He articulates it as follows:

> Que todos quantos avia desde el mismo Inga, hasta el Mitazo, estaban en la red, i lazo del menio; Y todos dexado a su criador, veneraban, i adoraban lo que no debian, los Ingas al Sol, como si fuera su criador, i para sujetar las pueblos, i gentes primero hazian saber a todos, que debian adorar al Sol porque esse (dezian) nuestro padre, i criador de los Ingas.
>
> Y la demas gente vulgar, que no adoraba? Adoraba al Sol, Luna i Estrellas: Y aunque adorar a estos es gran pecado, no estan culpables, *Sed in his minor est querela. Sap.* 13:6.[19]

In this passage, while admitting the idolatry of the Andeans and their worship of Sun, Moon, and Stars, Ávila is willing to recognize their innocence because they were misguided and trapped by the Devil while trying to look for God, but in the case of the Incas he is not as forgiving. He believes that they venerated the Sun, not because they did not know better but because they chose to worship it instead of God and, to make things worse, they imposed this cult over other peoples who had been conquered by them. So, not only did they sin but forced other people to follow their idolatrous ways in the name of colonization. Idolatry, thus, did not only conquer the souls of the colonized, but also their physical territory. So, according to Ávila, the Incas, as rulers of the Andes, worshipped the Sun not as a mistake due to ignorance or due to a lesser degree of civilization, as Las Casas would have argued, but they used this practice being fully aware of its implications, in order to manipulate religion for a political purpose, that of expanding their empire.

Therefore, in establishing a connection between idolatry and territoriality, Las Casas adopts an interesting approach. If, as we have seen, Ávila thinks that, in the case of the Incas, expansionist ambition leads to the spread of idolatry, the Chiapas bishop adds a twist and states that idolatry goes hand in hand with isolation of human groups and linguistic diversity. In his opinion, thus, and since the Garden of Eden, the word of God can only be passed directly from man to man, but the

---

19 This passage is taken from a sermon by Ávila, written for the vigil of the Epiphany (Lima, 1646–48). (Monten and Collier 1999: 98–99 in the Spanish version and page 91 in English).

The biblical sentence it refers to is the following: "But yet, for these the blame is less; For they indeed have gone astray perhaps, though they seek God and wish to find him"

My translation: All, from Inca to Mitazo, were ensnared in the traps of the Devil. All had forsaken their creator. The Incas venerated and worshipped that which they shouldn't have (the Sun), as if it were their creator. And, in order to subjugate the villages and the people, first they made them realize that they should worship the Sun because they said it was their father, the creator of the Incas.

And the various other people, what did they worship? They worshipped the Sun, Moon, and Stars. Still, although the worship of these was a great sin, they weren't as guilty—Sed in his minor est querela [*Wisdom of Solomon* 13:6].

fragmentation of groups and the distance between them makes this task very difficult. This is the reason why, according to Las Casas, the native peoples of the colonies have not been in contact with the Christian doctrine. Also, the division of languages after the episode in Babel makes this transmission that much more difficult, allowing idolatry to rule over the Americas (Las Casas 1967: 383).

In relation to this, Cristóbal de Molina, a Spanish friar who wrote a chronicle (*Fábulas y mitos de los Incas; Fables and Myths of the Incas*) around 1573, believes that there is a relationship between idolatry and writing, asserting that if the Incas had been peoples of writing, they would not have fallen in the deep abyss of idolatrous thinking: "Causóse todo esto demás de la principal causa que hera no conocer a Dios y darse a los vicios y ydolatrías, no ser jentes que usavan de escritura, porque si la usaran no tuvieran tan ciegos y torpes y desatinados herrores y fábulas, no obstante que usaban de una cuenta muy subtil de unas ebras de lana de dos nudos, y puesta lana de colores en los nudos, los quales llaman *quipos*" (Molina 1989: 57–58).[20] Following this thought, it should not be surprising that *quipus* were ordered to be destroyed as soon as possible, since they were believed to be receptacles of superstition in general, and idolatry in particular.[21] Of course, this action did not take into account that, together with what Spaniards thought superstitious, they were also destroying infinitely valuable information about the Incas' way of life and, ironically, also testimonies of their progressive acceptance of Christian doctrine, since some of the *quipus* contained information in this regard.

More and more, and for a long period of time, idolatry became the face by which America was recognized and a synonym of the innate inability of the Indians. A sample of this can be found almost a century later in some of Calderón de la Barca's plays that deal with the Indies and the issues around evangelization. In *La aurora en Copacabana*, America appears as the landscape of idolatry par excellence though, in the end, it is also the place where change is possible and there is a successful shift

---

20 All this is caused, in addition to the main cause which is not knowing God and abandoning themselves to vices and idolatries, by not being peoples of writing, because if they had used it, they would not have had blind, awkward, and foolish errors and fables, although they used a subtle system of woolen threads with two knots and with colored wool in the knots, which are called quipos (my translation).

21 The third Council of Lima, which took place in 1582–83, decreed the destruction of quipus because of their supposed relationship with idolatry. (Lisi 1990: 191)

"Capítulo 37: Y como entre los indios, ignorantes de las letras, había en vez de libros ciertos signos de diferentes cuerdas que ellos llaman *quipos* y de éstos surgen no pocos testimonios de antigua superstición en los que guardan el secreto de sus ritos, ceremonias y leyes inicuas, procure los obispos destruir por completo todos estos instrumentos perniciosos."

And since among the Indians, ignorant in terms of writing, there were, instead of books, certain signs of different threads that they call quipos and from them no few testimonies of superstition originate where they keep the secrecy of their rites, ceremonies and iniquitous laws, bishops should try to completely destroy all those destructive instruments"

toward Catholicism (Calderón de la Barca 1994: 128). It is important to remember that the character of "Idolatry" is portrayed dressed like an Indian: in black and covered with stars which represent its object of worship. In the same line, in *Mística y real Babilonia*, also by Calderón, Idolatry shows up on stage dressed as in the previous play: in black, covered with stars, and also like an Indian, with multiple feathers (Calderón de la Barca 1979: 113). America then, becomes associated with idolatry.

But, going back to the sixteenth century, the most definitive shift in the evolution of the concept of idolatry takes place at the end of the decade of the 1560s and the beginning of the 1570s, coinciding with the rebellion of the *taquiongos*. This movement, whose name literally means "dancing sickness" or the "disease of the dance," constituted one of the first attempts of organized Native American resistance. It preached the total rejection of Spanish religion and customs and, instead, it proposed their return to the teaching of their predecessors, to the worship of the Sun, their *huacas* (sacred entities or places) and their *mallquis* (the mummified remains of their ancestors. The leaders of the Taki Onqoy, the most important being Tupac Amaru, claimed that they were messengers from the native gods and preached that a pan-Andean alliance of native gods and peoples would come together to destroy the Christians.

This movement was met by the brutal repression of the *visitador* Cristóbal de Albornoz and the viceroy Toledo, who decided to exterminate this possible focus of distress before it really became a threat, and Tupac Amaru was publicly beheaded in 1572.[22] However, what is most relevant in terms of the evolution of the concept of idolatry is that this event, the repression of the Taki Onqoy, marks the final moment in the progression that we saw above. Idolatry, once considered some misguided practices with no evil intentions, now definitely becomes a major sin, one that puts at risk the supremacy of the Spanish empire and that has to be fiercely fought.

This final shift that insists on the diabolic nature of idolatry finds in José de Acosta (1540–1600) its main supporter. Acosta was a Jesuit missionary and theologian who spent most of his life in Peru.[23] He was elected provincial in 1576. Aside from his publication of the proceedings of the provincial councils of 1567 and 1583, Acosta is best known as the writer of *De Natura Novi Orbis* (1596), *De promulgation Evangelii apud Barbaros* (1588), *De Procuranda Indorum salute* (1588)

---

22 See Duviols (1977); and Albornoz's *Instrucción para descubrir todas las Guacas del Piru y sus camayos y haziendas*, found in Cristóbal de Molina (1989). In that text, and in reference to this movement of Taki Onqoy, Albornoz attributes the discovery to himself (192–93). See also Guamán Poma's reflection and warnings in relation to the Taki Onqoy phenomenon (1956: 66).

23 The Jesuits arrived to the New World some thirty years after the other orders. They sought areas abandoned or unclaimed by the previous missionaries. They expanded rapidly and, by the end of the XVI century until their expulsion in 1767, had between 450 and 520 members in Peru. They proved to be extremely resourceful and successful at learning the language, teaching in the vernacular, trading goods, and demonstrating a nonviolent European presence, proving that the only alternative to slavery was evangelization mission and integration through church and school (Lynch 2012: 48).

and, above all, the *Historia natural y moral de las Indias* (Seville 1590), where he provided a detailed description of the geography and culture of the "newly-discovered" territories of the Indies. In that work he assures his readers that the main causes from which idolatry originates are the arrogance of the Devil and the mortal hate that he has toward men (Acosta 1894: 3–4):

> Que la causa de la idolatría ha sido la soberbia y envidia del demonio. Es la soberbia
> del demonio tan grande y tan porfiada, que siempre apetece y procura ser tenido
> y honrado por Dios: y en todo cuanto puede hurtar y apropiar á sí lo que solo al
> altísimo Dios es debido, no cesa de hacerlo en las ciegas naciones del mundo, á quien
> no ha esclarecido aun la luz y resplandor del santo Evangelio.[24]

For Acosta, therefore, idolatry was neither natural nor innocent, but diabolic and manipulative. Described as such, the definition now serves a double purpose. On the one hand, it continues the atmosphere of fear that developed in Europe during the witch-hunt period. On the other hand, defining all these peoples from "the blind nations of the world" as idolaters allows Acosta and his followers to formulate a concept of opposition. It integrates the unknown into a known system, that of the opposition between good and evil, while unifying the *other* in a group against which Spaniards can fight.

But at the same time, and perhaps this came as surprising collateral damage, the fact that Spaniards insisted on the association of the Indians with the Devil backfired on them. This insistence on the Indians' diabolic way of life gave them the possibility of using this very strong alliance for their own cause and, for the first time, if Spaniards adopted the flag of Christianity, they handed Indians the flag of the Devil. Therefore, that which had been different, exotic, or strange in the first encounters is now armed with a diabolic force that the Indians did not even know could be used for their own advantage. In this way Spaniards created their own struggle and an enemy to reproduce the ones that they were used to combating, and the ones that they were comfortable with, the ones that belonged to their self-centered way of looking at what was happening in the Spanish colonies.

This idea is based on the practice of *othering* and allows us to see the colonized subject as the radically different, conceived not only as inferior but also as savage, barbarian, and evil. Therefore, it becomes the "demonic other" reproducing models that had already been used in Spain to fight the Moors and the Jews and that made

---

24 My translation: The cause of idolatry has been the arrogance and envy of the Devil. The arrogance of the Devil is so great and so stubborn that he always wants and tries to be honored as God, whenever he can steal and take for himself that which is only due to Most High God, he does not stop doing it, especially in the blind nations of the world that have not been illuminated by the light and the splendor of the Gospels.

the conflict with the American idolaters that much more familiar. This idea also assumes that European practices are superior and universal and that everything that does not belong to this scheme of things can be spared, rejected, replaced:

> En tiempo de los Ingas, y aun antes que los vuiera, todos por sus ayllos, y por sus divisiones teniendo sus Idolos, para aver de adorarles, y hazer sus fiestas un mes, y aun dos meses antes que llegase la fiesta de su Idolo mayor se disponian para ella. Y el gran Sacerdote solia dar noticia, y apercibir, que para tal dia lo estuviessen: hiciesen su chicha, y todo lo demas, porque ya llegava, dezia, el dia de nuestro gran Padre. Y Tambien les mandaba, que ayunassen, no comiendo con sal, ni agi, y que los varones, y mugeres se abtuviessen entre si. Y deste manera dezia abeis de ayunar: y sino lo hizieredes assi serà gran pecado, y caereis en enfermedades, y trabajos, se os claran los sembrados, y moriràn vuestros hijos; y diziendo esto los amendrentavan, y hazian ayunar, sin dormir toda la noche. No os digo la verdad?
>
> Mirà hijos mios, todo esto es engaño del Demonio; porque el Demonio maldito sin cessar esta siempre pensando, y desseando hazerse señor, y que los hombres lo adoren como a Dios, y por esto anda remedando a Dios. No aveis visto un mico, ò mono como, mirando lo que haze la persona, el lo imita? Deste modo el Demonio remeda a Dios, como mono de Dios. Y como los Padres en las Iglesias cantan alabando a Dios; el Demonio haze que a el le canten, adorando los cerros, las nieves y las piedras; y si nuestra madre la Iglesia nos haze ayunar en la Cuaresma, y Vigilias; el Demonio de la misma suerte haze a los que le siguen ayunar, y los trabaja, y lo mesmo haze en otras muchas cosas, engañando a los que poco saben.[25]

As we can see from this passage, Ávila not only thinks that the Indians have not reached the degree of civilization that the Spaniards have but also links this fact with their foolishness, with their barbarism, which inevitably has diabolic roots. But not only that: if the Devil is the monkey of God and the Incas are ruled by

---

25 This passage is taken from a sermon by Ávila, written for the vigil of Nativity (Lima, 1646–48; Monten and Collier 1999: 55), in the Spanish version and page 49 in English. "In the time of the Incas, and even before their time, each allyu [*sic*] and area had idols, so that they might adore them and celebrate their monthly festivals, sometimes preparing for two months in advance for the major ones. The high priest used to announce the day so everyone would prepare chicha and all the rest for the quickly-approaching holiday of our father. He also told them, both men and women, to abstain from salt and ají? (pepper) [*sic*]. In this manner they fasted. If they did not, it would have been a grave sin. And they would have fallen sick, and their crops would have died. Thus he frightened them, and made them stay up all night. Do I not tell you the truth?

Look, my children, all this is a trick of the Devil. The wicked Devil always tries to make himself God, and he wants men to adore him as they do God. Thus he imitates God. Have you not seen a monkey, trying to act like a human? Thus the Devil tries to imitate God: like a monkey of God. And as the priests in temples sing for God, the Devil makes them sing to him adoring mountains, rocks and snow. Just as our mother the Church has us fast during Lent and during Vigils, the devil makes those who follow him fast; he does the same in many things, tricking whose who know little."

him, in what position does this leave them? However, the preacher is careful not to call them monkeys because the negation of human nature would immediately be interpreted as the lack of capacity to reason and, therefore, would have aborted the process of evangelization.

The struggle against the supposed idolatry of the Indians missed a crucial point. It did not consider the fact that what Spaniards saw as idolatrous was embedded in every single aspect of the Indian way of life. It not only affected the idols that were worshiped but also the way they related to one another, their sexual relationships, the crops they grew, their division of time, and so on. This way of life was not questioned or even questionable, but part of the established order and, because of this, almost impossible to eliminate. Gruzinski goes on to say that

> La idolatría aporta no sólo una respuesta a la desgracia biológica y social, a la precarie-
> dad de las condiciones de vida sino que, mucho más todavía, inculca una manera de
> ver y de actuar en contextos tan distintos y complementarios como la ancestralidad, la
> producción y la reproducción, el cuerpo enfermo, el hogar, el vecindario, los campos,
> el espacio más lejano del monte adonde va uno a cazar el venado y a recolectar la miel
> silvestre.[26]

Idolatry, thus, is not only a way of dealing with the world; it becomes the world for those who live it, a way of knowing what surrounds them but also to know their own selves, a way of preserving the past and looking into the future, a spiritual code as well as the law.

At this point I would describe idolatry, in the context of the first Spanish colonies in the New World, as *those beliefs and practices of the natives that do not conform to those of Catholicism and become, for this reason, the target of the Spanish colonizers. It is that irreducible excess of indigenous culture that persists in spite of imperialistic efforts, the remains of a subjectivity that, once colonized, becomes sinful, erroneous and false.*

Idolatry, taking this approach, is used as part of the huge machinery that Spaniards put together with the intention of developing their plans for imperial expansion. Among the functions it performs, it is used by the colonizers to alienate the *others* and unite them in an artificial category defined by what Spaniards were not. Idolaters in colonial Peru and Mexico are, therefore, those who eat what Spaniards do not, worship what they do not, look different from the colonizers,

---

26 Gruzinski (1993: 158): "Idolatry not only brought an answer to biological and social unhappiness, to the precariousness of conditions of life but, even more, inculcated a manner of seeing and acting in contexts as distinct and complementary as ancestrality, production and reproduction, the sick body, the domestic hearth, the neighborhood, the fields, and the more distant realm of the *monte* where one went to hunt deer and gather wild honey."

speak something that is unintelligible to them, and so forth. But the creation of this heterogeneous group creates an enemy to attack: their diabolic nature which, by the mere virtue of its existence, gives purpose to the hundreds of friars who were sent to the colonies, the innumerable soldiers who accompanied them, and what is more important: the birth of a diluted, nonconcrete, invisible enemy that guarantees and justifies the maintenance of a policy of expansionism in Spain that otherwise might have been impossible to sustain. Also along these lines, the characteristics of the enemy make him one that will never be fought enough, one that the colonizer can never be sure is destroyed, one that can scare populations for indeterminate periods of time, and one that can always be blamed for all kinds of excesses. The fight, therefore, has long moved away from the mere discussion of religious matters and has developed into hegemonic terms: it is embedded in the process of colonization itself and shapes the reality of the dominant group as well as that of the invaded.

But, at the same time that the concept of idolatry was being defined in the "New World," those who were defining the purest orthodoxy in the colonies, that is, the Spanish, the Christians par excellence, were being called "idolaters" back in their own continent, producing an ironic situation that runs parallel in many ways to that in America.

EARLY MODERN EUROPEAN RELIGIOSITY

The origins of what was happening in Western European religiosity during the sixteenth century can be partially explained by the events that took place in the previous two centuries, and of which I offer just a brief overview. In general, during the fourteenth and fifteenth centuries, dissatisfaction with the church could be found at all levels. The Avignon papacy first (1305–1378) and the Great Schism later (1378–1414) contributed a great deal to a crisis in the religiosity of late medieval Europe and a sense of unrest that discredited the authority of the pope and harmed the reputation of the monastic system. This breakdown opened the doors for the great cultural debates about religious reforms and values that were to take place during the sixteenth century and that resulted in the Protestant and Catholic Reformations.

The Roman Church started to be noticed because of its excessive wealth during the period; the poor resented the wealth of the papacy, and the very rich were jealous of it. But it was the poor moral example that provoked the biggest reaction since the lax discipline in many monasteries and nunneries in Europe had reached almost epidemic proportions. Some of the abuses of the Catholic Church included the sale of indulgences (certificates to forgive sins) and of high-church offices (simony), which contributed to the wealth of the church but also to its bad reputation. The clergy had become lax, corrupt, and immoral, and the church was in desperate need of a reform (Mullett 1999: ch. 1.).

The Renaissance and the development of humanism brought a fresh air of intellectual freedom that finally stirred both the Catholic and the Protestant Reformations (increasing debates on religious values, personalized interpretations of the Bible, the search for a more personal spirituality, etc.), but also brought a renewed attention to pagan antiquity, a neopaganism that, although it influenced the arts greatly, both in form and in content, was fought from the spiritual point of view in the search for an evangelical purity that had been lost somewhere along the way.

Erasmus of Rotterdam (1466–1536) was a reknowned scholar who took upon himself the task of using his learning in the search for the purification of the doctrine while criticizing the vices of the Catholic Church. He despised the laxity the Catholic Church had fallen into because, according to his opinion, it perpetuated ignorance, superstition and obscurantism. He intended to supply the remedy, starting by pointing out what other educated men of his time barely dared articulate. This way, Erasmus delivered a message that was heard all over Europe and that had great influence on many Spanish intellectuals, such as Cervantes himself.[27] But it was not Erasmus's mission to establish change, but rather to open this possibility to others that would follow, as well as to increase awareness about the abuses that were taking place within the Catholic Church. Therefore, Erasmus thought of a church within, a personal and accessible religiosity and, in order to achieve this goal, in 1516 he translated and published a German version of the Greek New Testament so that everyone could read the Gospel in their languages, a gesture that was a way of challenging the mediation as understood by the Catholic Church.[28]

But he grew impatient and angry with the superstitious ways of the Catholics, especially in dealing with the cult of statues, the devotion to the relics of the saints, pilgrimages to visit different Virgins, worship saints, endowment of masses, and so on. He thought that the people cultivated a religion of external acts, of appearances, rather than practicing an introspective and personal devotion; that was his idea of *true* religion, free from the weight of the Middle Ages and from its dependence on visible things: "You should always try to advance from things visible, which are for the most part imperfect or of a neutral status, to things invisible. This precept is so pertinent to the matter that when they either neglect it or do not understand

---

27 On Erasmus in general, and in his effects in Spain, the classic work is still Bataillon (1966). Also see Eire (1986).

28 Continuing his attacks on Catholic ways of worshipping, Erasmus added the following: "To work miracles is primitive, obsolete, and out of date; to teach the people is a drudgery; to interpret the Scriptures is pedantry; to pray is futile and lazy; to shed tears is weak and depressing; to live in poverty is base; to be excelled is shameful, and scarcely worthy of one who will hardly allow the greatest king to kiss his sacred foot; and finally, to die is unpleasant, to die on the cross a disgrace" (Erasmus 1953: 112).

it, most Christians are merely full of credulous wonder, not devout, and except for using the *name* of Christ are not far removed from the superstition of pagans."[29]

In his attacks against superstition, he defines it as "a misplaced faith in the external forms of religion" (Eire 1986: 37) that causes an inadmissible fragmentation of the deity. Therefore, even when Erasmus saw nothing evil or sinful in these practices, he would much rather have seen a shift from a visual religion to an internal one, since for him the dangers implicit in these erroneous ways of worship were far too great. But, although he stressed the importance of the spiritual life over the cult of the material, Erasmus never denied the value of the external religious symbols and he never fought to see them abolished.[30] In his opinion, the use of material elements in the cult was then limited to serving as aid for the weak but was not advised. So, if we go back to my first example of the Holy Week in Málaga (Southern Spain), I would dare say that Erasmus would not have considered it evil, heretical, or sinful, but probably, and according to his teachings, it would have been too close for comfort to idolatry, too dangerous, foolish, and totally unnecessary: "As for stone and painted images, I am not so foolish as to demand what stands in the way of worship. The stupid adore such substitutes in place of the saints themselves, who are finally crowded out altogether" (Erasmus 1953: 87). In these lines Erasmus asks his followers to become the monitors of their own worship and, instead of relying on the vigilance of the institutions, such as the church or, even worse, the Inquisition, he suggests that each individual take control of his own practice and be ready to take the consequences, good or bad, derived from it. In this sense he insists on distinguishing between the theory and the practice of religion, that is, in talking about the contrast between the ideal of the Bible and the reality practiced in everyday life, which he sees as infected by the corruption of the Catholic Church:

---

29 This passage belongs to Erasmus's description of the fifth rule for Christian living as presented in his *Enchiridion Militis Christiani*, written during the first years of the sixteenth century, where he continues as follows: "Unless this kind of worship is restored to Christ and detached from any consideration of creature comforts or inconveniences, it is actually not Christian at all. It is not much different from the superstition of those who in earlier times used to prime Hercules a tenth of their goods in the hope that they might get rich, or offer a cock to Aesculapius that they might recover from an illness, or slaughter a bull to Neptune that they might have a safe voyage. The names have changed, of course, but the purpose is the same" (Erasmus 1963: 99)

30 In his *Enchiridion*, Erasmus ties his reflection on the use of images with his concern about the corruption of the church and, more important, with its effects in the common folk: "Will they not say, then, 'Do you forbid the worship of saints, in worshipping whom you worship God?' As a matter of fact, I do not so much censure those who do these things out of a kind of ingenious superstition as I do those who, with an eye to their own profit, parade certain observances, which may perhaps be tolerable, as if they represented the highest and purest devotion, and for their own gain encourage the ignorance of the common people, of which not even I am entirely critical ... To do things of this sort, therefore, is not so blameworthy as it is destructive to come to a halt with them, and to lean upon them" (Erasmus 1963: 100).

If wisdom should come to Popes, what comforts it would deprive them of! Did I
say wisdom? Even that grain of sense which Christ speaks of would do it. It would
deprive them of all wealth, honor, and possession; all the triumphal progresses, offices,
dispensations, tributes, and indulgences; the many horses, mules and retainers; in
short, it would deprive them of all their pleasures. These few words comprehend a
multitude of worldly goods. In their place wisdom would bring vigils, fasts, tears,
prayers, sermons, studies, sighs, and a thousand similar trials. And think the hard-
ship on all those copyists and notaries, all those advocates, promoters, secretaries,
muleteers, grooms, bankers, and pimps—I was about to add a softer but, perhaps, a
naughtier name. In short, all those who bring shame—I mean fame—to the Roman
See would have to beg for their bread. This would be terribly inhuman, and, even
worse, those very princes of the church and true lights of the world would be reduced
to a staff and a wallet. (Erasmus 1953: 111)

Nevertheless, for Erasmus, the unity of the church was a fundamental characteristic
and, in this sense and in many others, he disagreed with Martin Luther.

The Protestant Reformation began in 1517 when Luther (1483–1546), an Augus-
tinian monk and professor at the University of Wittenberg, published his ninety-
five theses on the door of the Wittenberg Castle's Church and collected in one
document the general dissatisfaction that had been felt for a long time in many sectors of the Catholic Church. These ideas, helped by the birth of the printing press,
made their way throughout Europe very quickly and provoked a major schism for
Christendom (Aranguren 1957: ch. 1).). Because his teachings cover many issues, I
will only concentrate on Luther's words on idolatry, a concept that he understands
as follows:

All manner of religion, where people serve God without his Word and command,
is simply idolatry, and the more holy and spiritual such a religion seems, the more
hurtful and venomous it is; for it leads people away from the faith of Christ, and
makes them rely and depend upon their own strength, works, and righteousness. In
like manner, all kinds of orders of monks, fasts, prayers, hairy shirts, the austerities of
the Capuchins, who in Popedome are held to be the most holy of all, are mere works
of the flesh; for the monks hold they are holy, and shall be saved, not through Christ,
whom they view as a severe and angry judge, but through the rules of their order.
(Luther 1878: CLXXI, 69)

As we can see in the lines above, the concept of idolatry shifts considerably in Luther's
imaginary from the one that had been established up to that moment. Therefore,
idolatry remains the worship of a creature instead of God, but instead of referring to
those beliefs and practices performed by a distant and unknown *other* (as happened

in the context of the conquest of America), now the idolaters are those of us who are corrupted, who sin by excess in the ritual and from whom Protestants want to gain independence. The Catholics, now called the "papists," are the new idolaters in a time when, ironically, they were evangelizing the Indies and implementing what the Spanish Catholics considered the purest of orthodoxies. But, according to Luther:

> The papists took the invocation of saints from the heathen, who divided God into numberless images and idols, and ordained to each its particular office and work. These, the papists, void of all shame and Christianity, imitated, thereby denying God's almighty power, every man, out of God's Word, spinning to himself a particular opinion, according to his own fancy; . . . The invocation of saints is a most abominable blindness and heresy; yet the papists will not give it up. The pope's greatest profit arises from the dead; for the calling on dead saints brings him infinite sums of money and riches, far more than he gets from the living. But thus goes the world; superstition, unbelief, false doctrine, idolatry, obtain more credit and profit than the upright, true, and pure religion. (Luther 1878: CLXXVIII, 73–4)

Therefore, although Luther's main interest was not the extermination of idolatry or even the organized fight against it, he stated that the pope and his followers were nothing more than worshippers of idols and servants of the Devil,[31] and in this light, he feels forced to redefine some concepts:

> Saint Augustine and others distinguish thus between heretics, schismatics, and bad Christians: A schismatic is one that raises divisions and dissensions, professing the true faith of the Christian church, but not at union with her as to certain ceremonies and customs; an evil Christian is he that agrees with the church both in doctrine of faith and ceremonies, but therewithal leads an evil life, and is of wicked conversation. But a heretic is one that introduces false opinions and doctrines against the articles of the Christian faith, contrary to the true meaning of Holy Scripture, and stubbornly maintains and defends them. The papists do not call me a heretic, but a schismatic; one that prepares discords and strives. But I say, the pope is an arch heretic, for he is an adversary to my blessed Saviour Christ; and so am I to the pope, because he makes new laws and ordinances according to his own will and pleasure, and so directly denies the everlasting priesthood of Christ. (Luther 1878: CCCCXCV, 217)

For Luther, then, the idolatry of the papists is far from being an error, either committed by ignorance or out of carelessness, but a deliberate deviation from the *true*

---

31 "The Pope and his crew are mere worshippers of idols, and servants of the devil, with all their doings and living; . . . The devil has shown him the kingdoms of the world, and made promise to him as he did to Christ. This makes him condemn and scorn our sermons and God's service, by which we are beggars, and endure much, while for his doctrine he get money and wealth, honour and power, and is so great a monarch, that he can bring emperors under his girdle" (Luther 1878, CCCCXLIX, 201).

religion by which the pope is honored as a god and becomes the idol of a group that trusts in the institution more than in Christ himself, and who seems to have lost the North in their devotion.

But not everything was lost for Luther, who proposes preaching over imposed destruction of images, a process of learning and convincing rather than a frontal attack, a strategy that was vindicated in the Indies right at the same time.[32] Therefore, Luther believed that if a person was well grounded in his or her faith, the images could do no harm, but if that was not the case, and the faith was not very well rooted, the presence of images could lead to an idolatrous use of them. So the images themselves were not dangerous, but it was the *use* that they were given that could become idolatrous. In this case they should be destroyed and, in any case, as prevention, Luther stated that the images were unnecessary.[33]

---

32 Luther, The Third Sermon, March 11, 1522 Tuesday after *Invocavit*: "You read in the Law (Exod. 20 [:4]), 'you shall not make yourself a graven image, or any likeness of anything that is in heaven above, or that is in the earth beneath, or that is in the water under the earth.' There you take your stand; that is your ground. Now let us see! When our adversaries say: The meaning of the first commandment is that we should worship only one God and not any image, even as it is said immediately following, 'You shall not bow down to them or serve them' [Exod. 20:5], and when they say that it is the worship of images which is forbidden and not the making of them, they are shaking our foundation and making it uncertain. And if you reply: The text says, 'You shall not make any images,' then they say: It also says, 'You shall not worship them.' In the face of such uncertainty who would be so bold as to destroy the images? Not I. But let us go further. They say: Did not Noah, Abraham, Jacob build altars? [Gen. 8:20; 12:7; 13:4; 13:18; 33:20]. And who will deny that? We must admit it. Again, did not Moses erect a bronze serpent, as we read in his fourth book (Num. 22 [21:9])? How then can you say that Moses forbade the making of images when he himself made one? It seems to me that such a serpent is an image, too. How shall we answer that? Again, do we not read also that two birds were erected on the mercy seat [Exod. 37:7], the very place where God willed that he should be worshipped? Here we must admit that we may have images and make images, but we must not worship them, and if they are worshipped, they should be put away and destroyed, just as King Hezekiah broke in pieces the bronze serpent erected by Moses [II Kings 18:4]. And who will be so bold as to say, when he is challenged to give an answer: They worship the images. They will say: Are you the man who dares to accuse us of worshipping them? Do not believe that they will acknowledge it. To be sure, it is true, but we cannot make them admit it. Just look how they acted when I condemned works without faith. They said: Do you believe that we have no faith, or that our works are performed without faith? Then I cannot press them any further, but must put my flute back in my pocket; for if they gain a hair's breadth, they make a hundred miles out of it. Therefore it should have been preached that images were nothing and that no service is done to God by erecting them; then they would have fallen of themselves. That is what I did; that is what Paul did in Athens, when he went into their churches and saw all their idols. He did not strike at any of them, but stood in the market place and said, "You men of Athens, you are all idolatrous" [Acts 17:16, 22]. He preached against their idols, but he overthrew none by force. And you rush, create an uproar, break down altars, and overthrow images! Do you really believe you can abolish the altars in this way? No, you will only set them up more firmly. Even if you overthrew the images in this place, do you think you have overthrown those in Nürnberg and the rest of the world? Not at all" (Luther 1999).

33 Luther's Third Sermon, March 11, 1522, Tuesday after *Invocavit*: "But now we must come to the images, and concerning them also it is true that they are unnecessary, and we are free to have them or not, although it would be much better if we did not have them at all. I am not partial to them."

Parallel to events in Germany, a movement began in Switzerland under the leadership of Ulrich (or Huldreich) Zwingli (1484–1531). Zwingli prepared sixty-seven propositions strongly attacking Catholic positions and, basing his arguments on scriptural authority, he claimed that "true religion, or piety, is that which clings to the one and only God" and added that "true piety demands, therefore, that one should hang upon the lips of the Lord and not hear or accept the word of any but the bridegroom ... So piety is not piety unless you trust with all your heart the Lord who is the spouse of the soul, fix your eyes on Him only, and lend your ear to none but Him" (Zwingli 1981: 92).

In contrast, Zwingli sees *false* religion as the conjunction of two different aspects: on the one hand, the human arrogance in trying to look for God with the skills of the intellect and, therefore, not letting the works of the revelation go through us;[34] and, on the other hand, the love for the created above the Creator, that is, Zwingli identifies *idolatry* and false worship as one of the two main aspects of which false religion consists: "It is false religion or piety when trust is put in any other than God. They, then, who trust in any created thing whatsoever are not truly pious. They are impious who embrace the word of man as God's" (97–98). From these words we can imagine that although Zwingli's main concern was not the eradication of idolatry, he put a great deal of energy into defining what it is that made idolaters (in his opinion, Catholics) different from him and into offering an alternative that, in the end, never became a new reformed church.

Zwingli was inspired by Martin Luther and followed him in rejecting the authority of the pope in Rome as well as in considering Christ the sole mediator between God and men and also excluding the sacred role that the Virgin Mary has for Catholics. But the two reformers disagreed on several key points of doctrine. Zwingli and Luther met at Marburg in 1529 in a vain attempt to unite the two movements (*Marburg Colloquy*) but, although they agreed in fourteen out of the fifteen issues that they discussed, they could not agree over the meaning of the Lord's Supper. Both of them rejected the Catholic concept of transubstantiation, but Luther maintained that Christ was physically present in the bread and wine of the Eucharist, while Zwingli understood Christ's words, "this is my body," in a symbolic way. He insisted that the celebration of the Lord's Supper was a remembrance of what happened in Christ's last supper, not a new sacrifice, but Luther rejected categorically this metaphorical explanation.

---

34 "It must be admitted that only by God Himself can we be taught what He is. For, according to the view of Paul, I Cor. 2:11, as no one 'knoweth the things of a man, save the spirit of the man, which is the man himself, even so all are ignorant of the things of God save the Spirit Himself of God.' We may well call it the rash boldness of a Lucifer or a Prometheus, if any one presumes to know from any other source what God is than from the Spirit Himself of God" (61–62).

Zwingli went even further, and where Luther purged from worship only those Roman Catholic practices that were against the principle of being justified by faith alone, Zwingli ruled out anything lacking explicit biblical sanction, including removing all music from churches. Actually, he saw the whole mass as a form of idolatry and wanted it abolished and replaced by a simple observance of the Lord's Supper.

As for the images, Zwingli also wanted to abolish them and move the altar from the platform to the floor, making it a simple table where he could celebrate a religious service in which the scripture and the sermon would take center stage, and the rest of the elements would disappear. In the same line, Zwingli also advocated the elimination of all holy days except Christmas, Good Friday, Easter, and Pentecost Sunday. Therefore, he radicalizes Luther's position and, in an attempt to see people free from idolatrous and superstitious ways, he does away with many of the elements that were an integral part of the Catholic ritual, identifying Catholicism with false religion, mass with idolatry, and images with superstitious elements.

Finally, John Calvin (1509–1564) sought to define a middle ground between Luther and Zwingli on the issues surrounding communion. In his opinion, Christ was spiritually—not physically—present in the elements of the Eucharist. The core of Calvinism is the Zwinglian insistence on the literal reading of Christian scriptures. Therefore, anything not contained explicitly and literally in these scriptures had to be rejected; and, in the same line, anything that was written in the Bible needed to be followed strictly and exactly. It is the latter point where Calvin went further than Zwingli, since he wanted to reorganize, not only the religious life and beliefs but also the church, the political organization, and society itself so that they would be modeled by the literal reading of the sacred texts.

This emphasis on the written word and the literal interpretation of the same brought Calvin to despise the physicality of representations as an improper way of referring to the divine—that is, he believed that the visible could not contain the invisible, or the material in the spiritual—and he joined the attack on images that had been started by Luther and radicalized by Zwingli:

> We think it unlawful to make any visible figure as a representation of God, because he hath himself forbidden it, and it cannot be done without detracting, in some measure, from his glory . . . If, then, it be not lawful to make any corporeal representation of God, much less will it be lawful to worship it for God, or to worship God in it. We conclude, therefore that nothing should be painted and engraved but objects visible to our eyes: the Divine Majesty, which is far above the reach of human sight, ought not to be corrupted by unseemly figures. (Calvin 1844: 108)

Therefore, Calvin does not reject the value of art (which he considers gifts of God), not even in its application toward the church, but he does reject the efforts made in trying to represent God, basically because he does not trust human nature. He argues that idols "were forbidden to the Jews because they were prone to superstition" (99), and, from there, he develops a lack of trust for men that makes him try to reduce the dangers that he could encounter as much as possible, including, of course, the use of images in worship because

> since the whole world has been seized with such brutal stupidity, as to be desirous
> of visible representations of the Deity, and thus to fabricate gods of wood, stone,
> gold, silver and other inanimate and corruptible materials, we ought to hold this as
> a certain principle, that, whenever any image is made as a representation of God, the
> Divine glory is corrupted by an impious falsehood. Therefore God, in the law, after
> having asserted the glory of Deity to belong exclusively to himself, when he intends
> to show what worship he approves or rejects, immediately adds, "Thou shalt not
> make unto thee any graven image, or any likeness." In these words he forbids us to
> attempt a representation of him in any visible figure . . . God compares not idols with
> each other, as though one were better or worse than another; but he rejects, without
> a single exception, all statues, pictures, and other figures, in which idolaters imagined
> that he would be near them. (98)

Therefore, the erection of images of God or, for that matter, any representation of him, is not only idolatrous and superstitious but also goes against the main principle that rules Calvin's doctrine: having the whole creation glorify God by worship and obedience, since the images would be in direct conflict with Calvin's reading of the scriptures.

But, along with the corrupt nature of humankind, Calvin found another subject toward which to direct his blame and, just as Erasmus did years earlier, Calvin singles out the Catholic Church and the papists as responsible for the spread of idolatry all over the Christian world:

> If the papists have any shame, let them no longer use this subterfuge, that images are
> the books of the illiterate; which is so clearly refuted by numerous testimonies from
> Scripture. Yet, though I should concede this point to them it would avail them but
> little in defense of their idols. What monsters they obtrude in the place of Deity is
> well known. But what they call the pictures or statues of their saints—what are they
> but examples of the most abandoned luxury and obscenity? . . . Whom, then, do the
> papists call illiterate, whose ignorance will suffer them to be taught only by images?
> Those, truly, whom the Lord acknowledges as his disciples; whom he honours with
> the revelation of his heavenly philosophy . . . In fact, those who presided over the

churches, resigned to idols the office of teaching, for no other reason but because they were themselves dumb. (103–4)

Calvin nostalgically remembers a time when the Catholic Church had no images and when the delivery of the doctrine was not as corrupt, but since then, he observes a pattern by which any new convert could keep his pagan activities under the disguise of Christian themes, a practice that, we must consider, was probably taking place as he spoke, though not with the permission of the Catholic *conquistadores*.

To give a more rounded idea of how much idolatry and false worship upset Calvin, I would like to give one more example, this time directly related to his own life (or rather, death). In 1564, debilitated by a series of illnesses, Calvin died in Geneva. But he took the time to specify in his will that he wanted to be buried in an unmarked grave *to avoid any possibility of idolatry*, in a last attempt to be consistent with his theology, which humbles man and exalts God above all.

But Erasmus, Luther, Zwingli, and Calvin were not the only ones who realized that Christianity needed reform. Catholics themselves started a movement within, even before the Protestant Reformation as such was on its way, which culminated in the Council of Trent (1545–63), a turning point in the efforts of the Catholic Church to respond to the challenge of the Protestant Reformation and a key part of the Counter-Reformation. Because of the circumstances in which it was born, the council first reacted against Protestantism and then, as a consequence of it, reshaped Catholic doctrine. So it refused any concessions to the Protestants and, in the process, codified Catholic dogma far more than ever before. It opposed Protestantism by reaffirming the existence of seven sacraments, transubstantiation, purgatory, and clerical celibacy, and decrees were issued in favor of relics, indulgences, and the veneration of the Virgin Mary and the saints. Therefore, tradition was contemplated as one of the elements that constitute the Catholic way of life and worship, but, at the same time, the council took steps to eliminate many of the major abuses within the church that had partly incited the Reformation.

PARALLEL PATHS

Even when the two processes that I have presented until now seem so far one from another—that is, the incorporation of America into the European imaginary and the Protestant and Catholic Reformations—it is important to realize that they were not isolated events. Both processes were taking place at roughly the same time, but the coincidences do not stop there. I think it is remarkable that at the very same time that Hernán Cortés and his men were encountering *idolatry* in the New World, in 1521, Germans began to define Catholic symbols and rituals as idolatrous with nearly identical language.[35] But it is not only through chronology that these two key events are related. In fact, they are interwoven, and the two are expressions of the same phenomenon. The concern for idolatry is, at the bottom, a late medieval development and a part of a new system of ethics. Therefore, it was not a concept invented for Europeans to refer to the *other* in the colonies, and though it was applied in this situation, the concept of idolatry was created by Europeans to refer to themselves, to other Europeans who had gone beyond the set boundaries and, thus, the plasticity of the term. It was created to discover the enemy within, either by confession or other methods, and it was only convenient to reshape it in order to describe the *other*, though that was not the primary goal of this concept. I think it is essential to point out these connections and to them I will devote the remainder of this book.

As we have seen, Zwingli was very thorough in presenting the differences between true and false religion as a way of creating a distance between reformed protestants and old-fashioned Catholics, but this distinction can also be found in the chronicles of Bernal Díaz del Castillo, a soldier in Cortés's army who, when confronted with the reality of New Spain, cannot help but marvel at the expressions of false religion that fill the "new" territories: "Lleváronnos a unas casas muy grandes, que eran adoratorios de sus ídolos y estaban muy bien labradas de cal y canto y tenían figurados en unas paredes muchos bultos de serpientes y culebras y otras pinturas de ídolos, y alrededor de uno como altar, lleno de gotas de sangre muy fresca; y a otra parte de los ídolos tenían unas señales como a manera de cruces, pintados de otros bultos de indios; de todo lo cual nos admiramos, como cosa nunca vista ni oída" (Díaz del Castillo 1999: 69).[36] In this description, there is an obvious correlation

---

35 Gruzinski reflects on this point in his *Images at War*, where he recognizes a number of parallels: 'But how could one not note certain chronological coincidences? American idolatry was not unique during the sixteenth century. Indeed, the Mexican iconoclasm reigning from 1525 to about 1540 was contemporaneous with the European one, a movement that condemned the worship of saints and banned their representation. While the Franciscans were launching their first expeditions around the lagoon, Farel, the Reformer, was throwing St. Anthony's statue into the Aleine River in Montbéliard (March 1525), and fomenting raids against altars and images. In the following years idolatry was solemnly 'removed' in the Swiss towns that had been won over to the Reformation. In 1536 King Henry VIII had St. Edmund's two shrines in Suffolk destroyed 'for avoiding the abomination of idolatry.' The same year, 'following the example of the good and the faithful kings of the Old Testament, 'the council of Bern gave the order 'to suppress all idolatries, all images and idols. 'As if there were transoceanic echo, the emperor Charles the Fifth enjoined his Mexican viceroy in 1538 to have the 'cues [sanctuaries] and the idols' temples thrown over and suppressed' and to 'seek out the idols and burn them.' While the Spanish were undertaking the purging the entire continent of its idols, Tudor England was progressively destroying its own images as the Reformation became more radical. Churches were even whitewashed, as the pyramids had been in Mexico' (2001: 63).

36 They took us to very big houses, that were chapels for their idols and where very well carved in lime and had in their walls carved many shapes of snakes and serpents and other paintings of idols, and around one of them, there was an altar, full of drops of fresh blood; and, on the other side of the idols, they had

between the images of the pagan idols and the symbols that Catholics relate to the Devil (like snakes) and, in spite of the true admiration that all that fine work produces in the Spaniards, the viewing of the temples is accompanied by a negative judgment of the Indians. In this case they are presented as civilized enough to build marvelous places of worship, an intellectual capacity that will be necessary in the process of being evangelized; but on the other hand, these places are not consecrated to the *right* divinity, but rather to the symbols of the Devil, including the infamous serpents.

At this point I would like to pause for a moment and introduce a reflection about the so-called Indian idols I have been referring to. I have been using this word (idol) to refer to an image or object that is worshipped as opposed to the worship of God as defined from the Catholic point of view. This is also the way I understand this word to be used in the writings of Bernal Díaz del Castillo and others who witnessed the moment of the first encounter (even when Bernal himself wrote about his experiences years after they happened). Nevertheless, as Gruzinski points out, "Columbus . . . took care to avoid the word 'idol,' denying idolatry to instead denounce the fraud of the caciques handling the *cemíes*," which he conceives different than idols and defines as follows:

> Unlike idols representing the devil or false gods, the *cemíes* were essentially things, endowed or not with a life: "dead things shaped of stone or made of wood," "a piece of wood that appeared to be a living thing," objects that recalled memories of the ancestors. They were stones to relieve birthing pains; or whose use brought rain, sun, or the harvests, like those Columbus sent to King Ferdinand of Aragón: or yet similar to those pebbles the islanders kept wrapped up in cotton inside little baskets and that "they feed what they eat." (Gruzinski 2001:11)

Therefore, the concept of "idol" is not a universal one but rather a quite relative term that characterizes the gaze of the one looking as much as the object described:

> Idol and image belonged to the same mold, that of the West. Endowed from the very beginning with a demonic identity, function and form, the "evil and lying," "dirty and abominable" idol could only exist in the gaze of the one who discovered it, was

---

some signs like crosses, painted with other shapes like Indians, all of which we admired like something we had never seen or heard of before (my translation).

It is important to remember that Bernal Díaz del Castillo began writing his history in 1568, almost fifty years after the events described during the first arrival of the Spaniards, and in response to an alternative history written by Cortés's chaplain, who had not actually participated in the campaign. This is the reason why he called his book *Historia de la verdadera conquista de Nueva España*, that is, "True History of the Conquest of New Spain." Also, because of this chronology, it is possible that his descriptions of the Mexican idols and pagan temples had been affected by the debate about idolatry already omnipresent in Europe.

scandalized by it, and destroyed it. It was a creation of the spirit touched by the
Western vision of things ... The idol also designated, as much as it condensed and
interpreted, a selective perception of native cultures, an understanding centered
on figurative and anthropomorphical representations (statues, paintings) that the
Spanish used as one of their keys in their interpretation of the adversary ... But
what did idols become in the eyes of the Spanish? Faked objects, illusion-machines
designed to facilitate fraud; but also devils, "evil things we call devils" (which explains
why the idols were afraid of the Christian images), or even objects into which a
demon had been inserted ... This demonic "possession" was not only how the
conquistadors saw matters: even the most learned clerks confirmed that "the Spanish
believed it, and that was as it must have been." (Gruzinski 2001: 42–43)

In this situation, Díaz del Castillo shows the Spaniards as taking charge of the
process of eliminating *idolatry*, presenting the *true* religion, and incorporating the
Indians to the Western imaginary all at once: "Los españoles aceptan gustosos el
regalo, pero exigen que los indios abandonen sus cultos y abracen el cristianismo.
Pese a la fuerte resistencia local, los españoles destruyen los ídolos, construyen un
altar con una cruz y una imagen de la Virgen y bautizan a los indios"[37] (1999: 174).
As we can see, we are witnessing a process of substitution of symbols: the Spaniards
take down the snakes and put up the image of the Virgin, while there is no mention
of any attempt to educate the Indians. Even more, sometimes the symbols are the
same, as happens in the case of the crosses (the Indian replaced by the Catholic),
and it is only the meaning attached to it that is in question. But in my view, the
meaning of the second cross does not stress the triumph of Christianity over paganism, or the spreading of the evangelization, but rather the change of hegemony. It
is, therefore, a campaign based on the visibility of the symbols, not on doctrine,
obsessed with erecting large crosses as a sign of the Spanish colonial power in order
to show their increasing territories, a gesture that leaves the Christian creed in a secondary position. Religious identity in the Early Modern Americas is constituting
itself as a particular confluence of interactions with foreign landscapes, native tribes
and complex indigenous civilizations, and new models of community and social
interaction (Kirk and Rivett 2014: 6).

Therefore, if idolatry was understood by Las Casas and St. Thomas of Aquinas
as excessive devotion—that is, as a misguided thirst to connect with a superior
being—there were numerous opinions to the contrary such as the ones voiced by
Zwingli, Bernal Díaz, Luther, Calvin, Acosta, and Francisco de Ávila, and so on,

---

37 Spaniards happily accept the gift, but they demand that the Indians abandon their cults and embrace
   Christianity. In spite of the strong local resistance, Spaniards destroy idols, build an altar with a cross and
   an image of the Virgin, and baptize Indians (my translation).

who cannot separate idolatry from its superstitious roots and who link it to the diabolic. In the first group, the deviation in the natural drive to find God is due to a number of factors that include, above all, ignorance, a crucial element that would exonerate Indians from guilt and put it on the one who takes advantage of this ignorance, that is, the Devil. According to Garcilaso, the Andeans (pre-Inca empire) were in this situation: they were idolatrous, but not by choice, a state that can be easily remedied through preaching. This is the same position that Erasmus would adopt in relation to the Catholics, since he thought that their corruption was based on lax, ignorant ways, but never on a servitude to the Devil himself.

The difference with the second group is considerable, since in the latter it would be the corrupted and devilish nature of the Incans themselves that would consciously open a door to the actions of the Devil. Therefore, Acosta, as did the reformers, believed in the diabolic and manipulative nature of the corrupted natives, an element that made the evangelization that much harder and that, in the context of Europe, meant the schism of the church.

In relation to this, Luther saw the pope as the greatest worshipper of idols, since he adored the Virgins and saints, and the reformer attributes this *fragmentation of deity* to his corrupt ways. This same phenomenon takes place in the Indies, where the Andeans, just like the Catholics, have many *idols* that, as the saints or Virgins, are used for specific purposes. For these reasons, Zwingli and Calvin want to abolish and destroy the images, and though, in principle, Bernal Díaz agrees, in his case he differentiates between pagan images and Christian ones. This distinction had no place in the reformers' mindset, since for them the visible could not contain the invisible, and therefore no material could even attempt to represent the divine without corrupting it, but both the natives Indians and the Catholics thought otherwise.

Luther argues that the images are not corrupt in themselves, but their use is, so he insists on the power of preaching rather than that of the destruction of the idols, an idea that is reflected, at roughly the same time, in the thoughts of Las Casas. But Calvin observes that the pagan rituals are sneaking into the Christian universe, disguised as Christian themes that were in reality only occult pagan beliefs, a situation that, as we will see in the following chapters, was also happening in the New World as a product of an impossible synchronism.

As we can see, the dialogue between Protestant Europe and the Indies was well established, and the points of debate were numerous. The matters that were being treated in the two poles were parallel and, though they referred to very different realities, the search for establishing a true religion seemed to have *idolatry* as its core.

At this moment, I would like to step back and take some distance in order to paint a much more general picture. This perspective allows us to see that, indeed, *idolatry* and no other religious crime was common to all these groups. It was part of the way Protestants saw Catholics, as it was present in the way Catholics related to the native population of the Americas, but, moreover, it had also been at stake in the relations that governed the interactions between Catholics, on the one side, and Moors and Jews, on the other, while in the context of the Spanish Reconquista that I propose as an antecedent for the transatlantic enterprise. Therefore, taken one by one, we can establish the idolatrous ways that Protestants saw in the Catholic practice, one that they considered too invested in the material, the visible, and not so deeply committed with the spiritual, the invisible.[38] At the same time, the Spanish Catholics were charging the Indians with the same crime they were being accused of—idolatry—since the newly arrived saw the different native religiosities as cults to idols, things created, with no regard for a divine being. The final stage of this itinerary takes us to the situation of the Moors and Jews in the soon-to-be Spain, in the process of the Reconquista. They were also accused of idolatry, an accusation that could appear shocking being that neither Moors nor Jews include images in their worship. Nevertheless, to the eyes of the Catholics of the time, they too were named idolaters since their worship was to a god other than the Catholic one (seen as the only true one from the perspective of the dominant group), a god that was not Father, Son, and Holy Ghost but rather an invention, a new god created to their specifications, manufactured to their taste: an idol. "Quien tiene falsa creencia en Dios hace y adora ídolos y por eso los judíos y sarracenos, que no creen que Dios uno es Padre, Hijo y Espíritu Santo sino sólo Dios uno, se hacen un ídolo y dios nuevo, que no es Padre ni Hijo ni Espíritu Santo, y por eso adoran un ídolo al hacerse un dios que no es Padre etc."[39] Therefore, even if somebody argued that the God of the Catholics and the Jews is the same, the lack of the two other *personae* in the latter makes them of a completely different nature.

---

38 By contrast, from the Catholic point of view, Protestantism is indeed heretical since it proposes a new dogma based on a deviation from the Catholic one. Nevertheless, the Catholic Church nowadays tends not to refer to Protestantism as such. Modern usage favors referring to Protestants as a "separated brethren" rather than "heretics."

39 This statement belongs to St. Vicent Ferrer's sermons (1350–1419). He was a Dominican preacher (Orden de Predicadores) from Valencia, Spain, who played a critical role during the events of the late 1300s and early 1400s that led to the forced conversions of thousands of Jews and the massacres of others (Ferrer 2002: 104). Vicent Ferrer became an invaluable source in the party of Benedict XIII (born Pedro Martínez de Luna, one of the Avignon popes who was antipope from 1394 to 1409) who, lacking the support he desperately needed for his papal candidacy, sent the Dominican friar on a campaign to evangelize the Jews of Spain. It is possible that the Avignon pope, Spanish in origin, thought that by converting the Spanish Jews, he would get the support from all the Catholic countries, but it is unlikely that he was so candid on the matter. My translation: Whoever has a false belief in God, makes and worships idols, and that is why Jews and Saracens, who do not believe that one God is Father, Son and Holy Ghost but only God, make an idol and a new god that is not Father, nor Son, nor Holy Ghost, and that is why they worship an idol, in making a god that is not Father, etc.

This same author, Saint Vicent Ferrer, in his defense of the Christians argued that

Las imágenes no son adoradas por los cristianos sino la causa del recuerdo en la repre-
sentación, y de esto no deben extrañarse los judíos porque todo el templo de Salomón
estaba lleno de figuras, esto es, de ángeles y de otras representaciones, como se con-
tiene en Éxodo, 25 ... Y advierte que Abraham no adoraba tres figuras sino a un solo
Dios que es tres personas y así judíos, ¿por qué os admiráis si nosotros creemos que la
Trinidad es un solo Dios, puesto que Abraham no lo dijo en plural sino en singular? etc.
También de modo parecido los moros dicen que nosotros adoramos las imágenes etc.,
pero es la ignorancia la que se lo hace decir, pues ellos en sus mezquitas adoran dirigié-
ndose a la pared y, sin embargo, no adoran la pared sino a Dios. También los judíos,
cuando leen la ley de Moisés en la sinagoga y mueven todos las cabezas hacia la escritura,
no la adora sino a Dios representado en ella, y por eso dice Moisés según Éxodo, 20: *No
adorarás ni venerarás*, y no dijo: "No tendrás," sino *no adorarás*.[40] (575)

In this sense, and under this concept of idolatry, it is easy to bring the native Indians
within the same category and accusation of idolatry since, no matter whether anybody thought that there was a god or a spirit within a particular *huaca*, for instance,
it would have been considered the wrong god (meaning not the Catholic one, from
their point of view), and the worship of a false deity would have also been seen as
idolatry (in the case that the Spaniards had actually believed that the *huaca* was a
representation and not the deity in itself).

As we can see, the attempts at defining idolatry, understanding it, and fighting it
occupied a good number of centuries, but the questions could be reopened today,
as I tried to point out in my description of the Holy Week in Málaga (Southern
Spain). Therefore, the answer about my idolatrous ways (or not) will depend on the
approach taken on this superstitious act. As I have tried to show, idolatry does not
have a single meaning, but it is a term full of plasticity that refers back to a heterogeneous reality and, this is the aspect that fascinates me, defines the point of view
of that who approaches as much as the practices themselves. It defines the observer
even more than the observed practices, and in doing that, it places itself in the center of the debate about identity and the struggles between the dominant and the

---

40 My translation: Images are not adored by Christians, but the remembrance in the representation, and
this should not be odd to Jews because the Temple of Solomon was full of images, that is, angels and
other representations, as it is written in Exodus, 25 ... And Abraham warns that he did not worship
images, but a true God that is three persons and so Jews, why do you marvel if we believe that the Trinity
is only one God, since Abraham didn't say it in plural but in singular? etc. The same way, the Moors say
that we worship images etc., but it is ignorance that makes them say so because, in their mosques, they
worship looking at the wall but they do not worship the wall, but God. Also the Jews, when they read the
Law of Moses in the synagogue and they all bow their heads towards the writing, they don't worship it,
but God represented in it, and that is why Moses writes in Exodus 20: "You will not adore nor worship,"
and he did not say: "You will not have," but rather you will not worship.

subaltern, the colonizer and the colonized. But some questions remain such as how did Spain react to the first "infidels" they came in contact with: Jews and Moors? How did this experience shape the first contact that Spaniards established with the transatlantic *other*? These are some of the questions that I will be addressing in the next chapter, in which I will take my analysis to the first years in New Spain.

COMPACT SUMMARY
ON THE EVOLUTION OF THE
CONCEPT OF IDOLATRY
FROM THE MIDDLE AGES
TO THE AMERICAS TO THE
REFORMATION

INTERESTING THAT A
DOCTRINAL NOTION BECAME
A HEGEMONIC NOTION AS
A GENERAL CATEGORY FOR
THE NATIVES

THE IRONY OF OTHERING
INTERESTING THAT THE
NOTION OF IDOLATRY IDENTIFIES
THE OBSERVER MORE THAN THE
PHENOMENON BEING OBSERVED

2

Idolatry in New Spain and the Peninsular Laboratory

Salieron al campo á dar la batalla el ejército de los Españoles, los cuales en buena órden se fueron derecho á Jerusalem, y como el Soldan los vió venir, . . . mandó salir su gente al campo para dar la batalla; y salida, era gente bien lucida y diferenciada de toda la otra, que traian unos bonetes como usan los Moros; y tocada al arma de ambas partes, se juntaron y pelearon con mucha grita y estruendo de trompetas, tambores y pífanos, y comenzó á mostrarse la victoria por los Españoles, retrayendo a los Moros y prendiendo algunos de ellos, y quedando otros caidos, aunque ninguno herido . . . En esto entró Santiago en un caballo blanco como la nieve y el mismo vestido como le suelen pintar; y como entró en el real de los Españoles, todos lo siguieron y fueron contra los Moros que estaban delante de Jerusalem, los cuales fingiendo gran miedo dieron á huir, y cayendo algunos en el campo, se encerraron en la ciudad; y luego los Españoles la comenzaron á combatir, andando siempre Santiago en su caballo dando vueltas por todas partes, y los Moros no osaban asomar á las almenas por el gran miedo que tenían.[1] (García Icazbalceta 1971a: 89–93)

---

1 My translation: The army of the Spaniards got out to the battlefield and orderly, they went straight to Jerusalem, and since the Soldan saw then coming, . . . he ordered his people out to battle; and out, they were good-looking and different from others, because they had caps like the Moors use; and called to battle, they all fought with loud screams and racket from trumpets, drums, and fifes, and the victory of the Spaniards began to show, backing up the Moors and loosing some and falling others, although leaving none injured . . . At that moment St. James entered on his snowy white horse and dressed as he is typically depicted; and as he entered all the Spaniards followed him and they went against the Moors

DOI: 10.5876/9781607328018.c002

This dramatic battle could have been considered paradigmatic at any point during the Moorish domination of the Iberian Peninsula. Within this long period, extending for almost eight centuries, there was repeated confrontation between Christian forces and the Moorish armies, from the first battle in Covadonga in 722 to the final resolution in Granada, 1492. But if we look closely at the scene above, we could actually discern that the people on stage are not really Spaniards or Moors, and the performance is not taking place in the Old Continent. Rather, we are in the presence of a group of Indian actors performing this scene in the middle of Tlaxcala, Mexico, and, although this Moorish-Christian confrontation with reports of Santiago's miraculous leadership could have taken place in any battlefield in Spain during the Reconquista, in reality the narration corresponds to Fray Toribio Motolinía's account of several performances taking place not long after the first arrival of the Spaniards in Mexico.[2]

But, wouldn't this representation be against the best interest of the participants and their communities? Why would the Indians portray the victory of the Spanish *conquistadores* over any other enemy? And if I were to say that the performance was part of the celebration of the Corpus Christi, would this add any significance to the general message? That is, why would the Indians try to evangelize their own people rather than advocating for the maintenance of their own religions and rituals? And how does this presentation of the Moorish-Christian struggle relate to the charge that American indigenous peoples were demonic idolaters? These are some of the apparent incongruities that were taking place in New Spain in the first years after the encounter.

These are times of transition and adaptation, of improvisation beyond theatrical settings, of building utopias that would crash into pieces upon contact with reality. But in those yesteryears, as well as today, theater and plays were used as a point of contact, as a vehicle for spreading messages intended as universal.[3] They were used

---

that stood in front of Jerusalem who, faking fear, fled (some falling on the field) and locked themselves in the city; the Spaniards then, started to attack it, St. James always on his horse all over the place, and the fearful Moors did not dare peek in between the crenels.

2   Fray Toribio Motolinía (born Toribio de Benavente): Franciscan missionary, born at Benavente, Spain, at the end of the fifteenth century. He died in the city of Mexico in 1568. As he and his companions on their way to the city of Mexico passed through Tlaxcala, the Indians, seeing the humble aspect and ragged habits of the religious, kept repeating to each other the word *motolinia*. Fray Toribio, having asked the meaning of this word and learned that it was the Tlaxcalan for *poor*, adopted it as his name from then on. He introduced Christianity in the lands of current Mexico, Guatemala, and Nicaragua. His most famous work is *Historia de los Indios de Nueva España*. (*Diccionario enciclopédico Espasa* 1978, 8, 24–25)

3   See, for example, an article that appeared in the Raleigh edition of *The News and Observer* on November 18, 2005: "Theatre provides catharsis of Mexican troupe." This article deals with the representation of Lorca's drama *Bodas de sangre*, or *Blood Wedding*, in a Mexican bullring. On that occasion the artistic director, María Alicia Martínez Medrano, had decorated the bullring to look like a rural Indian village and, from that scenery, tried to convey messages that she felt to be universal and that, according to the director, would provide a good opportunity for the audience to think of something else besides the devastating effects of the hurricane Wilma, which had hit the area in the recent past.

as a space in which to come together and share values, and these are some of the reasons why I want to start there, on stage, my study of idolatry in the first period after the colonial encounter and answer some of the following questions: How did Spaniards react to the religious and ritual practices of the indigenous peoples in the Indies and especially in New Spain? What was the reaction of the Indians? What are the mechanisms by which Spaniards created *otherness* in New Spain? What were the most immediate antecedents of these actions; that is, what situations and behaviors that had taken place in Spain informed the decisions and actions taken in New Spain, especially in the first years following the arrival of the Spaniards, before the particular situation of the different parts of New Spain started to shift the ideas that the conquerors had brought with them? And finally, how did the Spaniards build an image of Spain as a hegemonic power in the New World invested with both *potestas* and *auctoritas* to dominate the world?

Jumping ahead, I would like to anticipate some of the points that will be part of my conclusion. I will argue that the conquest of America was presented, in its first instances, as a virtual extension of the Reconquista that had taken place in Spain since 711 and during which Spaniards fought to build an empire based, among other things, on the discrimination of others in religious terms. The fight against the heathens (Moors and Jews) provided the necessary experience and mindset to experiment and practice with the repression of the *other*, making of Spain a cultural laboratory that would travel across the Ocean Sea.[4]

Before I go on, let me explain my premises. The reason why I am using theater has to do with the ideological and political function of this genre, used very differently on either side of the Atlantic. This way, in Europe it became a vehicle to show the importance of the prince, serving as a Machiavellian tool for the state in formation; therefore, the dramas, mostly represented in court settings, would be displays of wealth and power, mirrors for the ideal image of the state in the process of becoming, models for both the ruler and the subjects (Greer 1991: 7). Nevertheless, Aracil Varón portrays the dramatic experience in the American colonies as a synthesis or cultural fusion, as a coming together of elements where, accompanying the very incipient European text, there was room for indigenous contributions in terms of dances, costumes, and other, allow me to say, "audiovisual" elements that completed the performances. We have to keep in mind that Spaniards settled in very densely populated areas and came up against very sophisticated societies and political organizations, whereas the English, by contrast, established their settlements in sparsely settled regions, inhabited by small tribal polities. (Kirk and Rivett 2014: 27)

---

4   On this topic, also see Ricard (1986); Garrido Aranda (1980); Aracil Varón (1999); and Lupher (2003).

In this context is where the early missionary drama develops, on the one hand, as direct heir of the medieval sacred theater still full of its character as an act of faith, and on the other, as a catalyzer of a new context never explored before. In this sense it was conceived, both as a didactic vehicle and as an instrument to stimulate piety among the spectators. It was also used as a way to encourage devotion and to affirm the identity of those on stage and those attending the performance as part of the same group: the devout Christians (Surtz 1983: 11). The wish is, therefore, for the play to help to achieve those goals in the creation of a Christian community, now formed by two groups of active participants: the Spaniards, in their different categories (soldiers, friars, landowners, etc.) and the natives, integrated in the social life of the colonies.

But let us go back to the performance of *La conquista de Jerusalén*, according to the identification by Motolinía in his *Historia de los indios de la Nueva España*. It took place in 1539 under the bishopric of Juan de Zumárraga, and I have chosen it because, as the bishop under whose tutelage it first saw the light and its possible author, Motolinía himself, the play is an example of an artifact defined by its transitions, modeled by the different and unique circumstances that come together when you are born in one world and delivered in a completely new one.[5]

Zumárraga himself was also a product of the transition I am referring to. Born in Durango, Biscay (Spain), he entered the Franciscan Order and was made administrator of the monastery of Abrojo, near Valladolid, in 1527. It was there that he met Charles V, who would later recommend him for the title of first bishop-elect of Mexico and protector of the Indians in New Spain. He arrived at his new appointment in 1528, but before he had the chance to work on the new issues that arose in the colonies, Zumárraga had proven himself as an inquisitor in Spain, an experience to which he would refer later on as his first contact with idolatry, a phenomenon that was going to indelibly mark his experience in the New World.

The story of this first encounter with what he called idolatry developed as follows: In 1527 (the year before he arrived in Mexico), in Pamplona, Spain, two girls appeared voluntarily in front of the inquisitors and confessed to have participated

---

5   I will focus extensively on this play in the next chapter. Suffice is to say for now that, like with many other such performances, all we have is the chronicler's description (in this case, Motolinía's), not the surviving text. It was first performed in Tlaxcala in 1539 at the initiative of a group of Indians from that village and as a response to the performance of *La conquista de Rodas*, a drama that a number of Spaniards put on stage. On this play see García Icazbalceta (1971a); Horcasitas (1974: 505–9); Aracil Varón (1999: 449–96).

    Joaquín García Icazbalceta, (August 21, 1824–November 26, 1894) was a Mexican philologist and historian. He edited writings by Mexican writers who preceded him, wrote a biography of Juan de Zumárraga, and translated William H. Prescott's (2001) *Conquest of Mexico* (*Diccionario enciclopédico Espasa* 1978, 803–4).

in several *aquelarres*.[6] What they proposed then was to reveal the names of the witches in charge of these diabolical meetings if they themselves were absolved from any guilt and not made to suffer any punishment. The inquisitors, thinking that the witches in charge of the satanical *rendezvous* would be better preys than the malleable victims that they had before them decided to follow up and soon after found the supposed witches they were looking for and obtained their confession (Sandoval 1955–56: Vol. 81, 250–51).[7] Considering the possible danger that this group could pose to the surrounding community, Charles V commissioned Zumárraga to act as an inquisitor in this case and the friar started his research on the matter. For this job he used the help of Fray Andrés de Olmos, who would later accompany the newly appointed bishop to New Spain and become one of the most renowned missionaries in the first years after the conquest.

The fact that Zumárraga participated in the investigation of the Pamplona witches can be considered under two very different lights. For some, the mere fact that he was ready to lend an ear to this case means that the friar believed in the validity of the charges and was ready to consider the existence and the wrongdoings of the servants of Satan. On the other hand, his research per se does not prove his belief on the matter one way or the other, but rather it proves that he was commissioned by the emperor to carry out an investigation and he put all his effort into it.[8] This idea is stressed by the fact that while I cannot find any evidence of Zumárraga's belief in witches, his writings seem to indicate that he did not believe in their existence. Thus, when discussing the

---

6 *Aquelarre* or *akelarre* is a Basque word that means "meadow of the he-goat." It is also the name of a place in Zugarramurdi, Navarre, Spain, where a famous witch episode took place in 1610 and that was the basis for the greatest auto-da-fé ever celebrated in Spain. The word means "Sabbath" and describes a supposed meeting place of witches with the Devil with the intention of worshipping him. To this secret location, the witches would arrive mounting their flying brooms, and, covered in ointment, they would engage in all kinds of diabolic rites that might include black masses, Devil worshipping, dances, orgies, and/or attacks on the property of close-by neighbors.

7 García Icazbalceta attributes the beginning of this episode to the migration of a French individual by the name of Hendo or Endo, who supposedly was a famous sorcerer and swindler who spread his supposedly diabolical creed among his neighbors in Endaya. He managed to escape unharmed, but his teachings stayed in the community, and, as a result, there were aquelarres performed in the area near Pamplona (García Icazbalceta 1881). Actually, García Icazbalceta talks about this mysterious character as being a "sorcerer" who introduces the community to a number of diabolical behaviors, among them, the participation in aquelarres, or witches' *Sabbath*. I do not believe this to be conceptually possible since sorcerers, by definition, were not servants of the Devil, had not established a pact with him and, therefore, were not invited to these gatherings. To have been present in the aquelarres and teach about them, the mysterious French person must have been touched by the Devil, and, therefore, he would have established a feudal vassalage with the Devil and have been ready to worship him as his master while explicitly renouncing God and the teachings of the Catholic Church.

8 Gerónimo de Mendieta assures us that Zumárraga "hizo aquel oficio con mucha rectitud y madureza" (Mendieta 1973: book V, part I, ch. 27) and does not make any further comments on his actions, which leads me to believe that Zumárraga's instruction of the case was just what would have been expected under the circumstances, and lacked any other element that deserved special mention.

possible ways of disrupting the first commandment, and after having introduced his audience to his definition of idolatry,[9] Zumárraga writes in his *Doctrina breve* (1543):

> E yerran más peligrosamente contra este mandamiento muchos malos cristianos que en ofensa de su santa fe católica *creen en muchas cosas vanas y supersticiosas*, por la Santa Madre Iglesia reprovadas y condenadas, como son los que creen en agueros de muchas maneras, en sueños, en estornudos, en hechizos y encantadores y adevinos, y sortilegos y en otras muchas abusiones. Otros que miran en cantos y graznidos de aves, en encuentro de algunas animalias é criaturas, en partir o comenzar camino o otro viage en martes, o en otras horas y tiempos; en cortar ropa y en cortar cabellos y uñas o otras cosas en tiempos o dias señalados. En coger yervas o frutas, y en otras muchas maneras, como si los unos dias fuesen de Dios y los otros no. En el nacimiento de los hombres, cuanto á los planetas ó los signos, y que los unos han de haber infortunios adversos y otras prósperas fortunas. Traer consigo nóminas, letras o caracteres o señales no aprobadas y sospechosas; hacer hechizos é invocaciones de los demonios, presumiendo saber las cosas pasadas y las por vernir, como profetas; y en otras muchas maneras quitan la honra debida á Dios, cuanto á la *credulidad de cosas malas*, contra la santa fe catholica.[10] (Zumárraga 1928: Folio B V)

Moreover, he goes on, saying that "tambien se reduce a esta especie de idolatria el negocio de las brujas o sorguinas[11] *que dicen que hay* en nuestra tierra, y han sido

---

9   He talked about idolatry as the vain ceremonies that simple people engage in, saying some prayers that seem sacred and good but that are, in reality, bad and serve the Devil and not God ("Las vanas ceremonias que muchas personas simples, por indiscreta devocion hacen, diciendo algunas oraciones que de si parecen santas y buenas; mas dichas en las tales observancias vanas son perversas, y con ellas se sirve no Dios sino el diablo"). (Juan de Zumárraga 1928: Folio D III).

10   My translation: And many bad Christians dangerously err against this commandment and offend their holy faith by believing in many vain and superstitious things, rejected and condemned by the Holy Mother Church like omens performed in multiple ways, through dreams, sneezes, in charms, divinations, and spells and other concoctions. Others look to birds' songs and cawing, in the pairing of some animals and creatures, to trips started on a Tuesday, or at a particular time; to cutting clothing or hair or nails or other things in specific times or days. To harvesting herbs or fruits in certain ways, as is some days were godly and not others. To the birth of men in relation to the planets or horoscopes, and if some would have bad fate or prosperous fortunes. Bringing nonapproved and suspicious papers, letters or characters or signs; performing enchantments and diabolic invocations, pretending to know the past and the future, like the prophets; and in many other ways deny God his well-deserved honor, giving credulity to bad things against the Holy Catholic Faith.

11   Sorginas (*Jorginas*): "Dizen ser nombre vascongado, y que vale tanto como la que haze adormecer o quitar el sentido, cosa que puede acontecer y que con intervención del demonio echen sueño profundo en los que ellas quieren para hazer mejor sus maldades. *Vide verbo hechizera*. Enjoginarse, tiznarse la cara con el hollín de la chimenea; y este término tuvo origen de la opinión del vulgo, que quando se untan las hechizeras y el demonio las lleva por los aires, que salen por el cañón de la chimenea, y assí se tiznan por el hollín" Covarrubias Orozco 1611: 716–17). (My translation: From a Vasque noun. The one who puts you to sleep, who renders you unconscious, which can happen. And with the help of the Devil, they can sleep and do evil deeds. *Vide verbo hechizera*. To have a black face from the soot of the chimney, and it is

condenadas y quemadas"[12] (Zumárraga 1928: Folio C V). Judging from these statements, I am inclined to say that Zumárraga looked upon witches merely as women suffering from hallucinations produced by the Devil and, therefore as if, in their condition as witches, they did not exist at all.[13] Nevertheless, we have to consider that these writings belong to his *Doctrina*, which was written in 1543, sixteen years after the episode of the witches in Pamplona, but it would be very unlikely to think that, if he actually found some evidence of the existence of witches in Spain, he would have made this kind of statements in the New World, especially in the midst of his own fight against Indian idolatry.

What I find very interesting is that Zumárraga refers to witchcraft as a type of idolatry, as we saw above, rather than just as a heretical crime, as it would have been considered at the time in Spain. In this sense, and since his writings about witchcraft were produced after being immersed in his years in Mexico, we can clearly see the influence of this new setting filtering into the experiences that he brought from Spain, since he talks about an instance of Catholic dissent (i.e., heresy and, in this particular case, the practice of vain observances in the form of witchcraft) with the vocabulary of someone used to dealing with pagans and neophytes of different degrees, not with rebellious Catholics.[14] As I discussed in the previous chapter, the term "idolatry" implies the worship of an idol other than God, that is, it is a pagan belief developed by someone far removed from Christianity, but that was clearly not the case when referring to the Pamplona witches. These women were, most likely, very familiar with the Christian creed: they knew of God and of his teachings and, if in this case, they were actually believed to be witches, rather than women under the spell of illusion, they would have had to know of God in order to renounce him and, especially, to offend him more efficiently. (We must not forget that aquelarres and black masses[15] are based

---

popularly believed that when the sorceresses grease themselves and they are flown by the Devil, they leave through the chimney and that is how they are blackened by the soot.)

12 My translation: It is reduced to some sort of idolatry this business of the witches or *xorguina* that are said to exist in our land and that have been condemned and burnt.

13 Zumárraga assures his reader that there are men so lost that God allows them to be lied to by the Devil, so it is God who allows the Devil to act, and not the special abilities of the latter ("Y por esso como ay hombres perdidos permite Dios que los engañe y ciegue el demonio haziendo venir las tales vanidades en efecto aunque no tenga virtud ninguna para ello," Zumárraga 1928: Folio D II).

14 As it was stated in the first chapter, the main difference between pagans and heretics is that the latter had never been baptized and, therefore, had not deviated from the Catholic norm willingly but by ignorance and lack of contact with it, whereas the former were dissenting Christians.

15 Black Mass: This term appears, for the first time, in the nineteenth century to refer to an act of Devil worship. It consists of a countercelebration of a Catholic Mass, a parody of it. It is performed over the body of a naked woman lying on the altar that is used as the basis for a heretical liturgy. Among other elements, there would be inverted crosses; urine, instead of holy water or wine; black candles, and black clothes for the minister. Nevertheless, Rosemary Guiley believes that these rituals belong more to the sphere of the imagination rather than to reality (Guiley 1999: 22–23).

on the rituals of Christianity, only to do the opposite of what was expected to be seen in church.)[16]

Soon after this episode, Zumárraga was recommended by Charles V for the post of first bishop of Mexico. Without having been consecrated and with only the title of bishop-elect and protector of the Indians, he left Spain with the first civil officials, auditors (*oidores*), at the end of August 1528 and reached Mexico on December 6.[17] Thirteen days later, two oidores, Parada and Maldonado, persons with years of experience, died. Their companions, Matienzo and Delgadillo, assumed their authority, which was also shared by Nuño de Guzmán.[18] Their administration (Primera Audiencia) proved to be one of the most disastrous epochs in New Spain and one of great difficulty for Zumárraga.

In the meantime, Cortés had returned to Spain to appeal a case in front of the emperor, and in his absence no limits seem to have been placed on the abuses of the oidores. They impoverished the Indians through taxes, sold them into slavery,

---

16 As I pointed out in the first chapter, the adoption of this formula (idolatry rather than heresy) is also seen in the sermons of St. Vicent Ferrer (1390–1412), who, when preaching for the evangelization of the Moors and Jews in Spain, call them "idolaters," the same term that would be later used to refer to a completely different reality in the New World.

17 *Oidores*: In the context of New Spain, they were judges who worked as representatives of the king and, in his name, heard (the infinitive is *oir*) the different parts that were involved in a trial. For this reason, the act of administering justice was known as *audiencia*. The oidores were, then, the equivalent to the current magistrates. "Antiguamente llamarónse oidores en España los jueces letrados que existían en las chancillerías y que, como delegados del rey, conocían de las alzadas, oyendo á las partes que ante ellos concurrían en demanda de justicia. De ahí que el acto de administrar justicia se llamase audiencia y que este nombre se aplicase después al Tribunal colegiado formado por los oidores. Estos equivalían, por tanto, à los actuales magistrados de la Audiencia" (*Diccionario enciclopédico Espasa* 1978, 39, 884). "Juez de los supremos en las chancillerías oyentes del rey, dichos assí porque oyen las causas y lo que cada una de las partes alega" (Covarrubias 1611: 835).

18 Juan Ortiz de Matienzo was a Spanish colonial judge and a member of the first Real Audiencia in the New World, that of Santo Domingo. From December 9, 1528, until January 9, 1531, he was a member of the First audiencia of Mexico, which was the governing body of New Spain during that period. It consisted of a president and four oidores. The president was Nuño Beltrán de Guzmán, and the oidores were Ortiz de Matienzo, Diego Delgadillo, Diego Maldonado, and Alonso de Parada. As I mentioned above, Maldonado and Parada were sick on their arrival and soon died, so they never participated in the government. The audiencia "was a peculiarly Spanish institution, being a supreme court, council, and executive body in one" and responsible for "easing the old conquistadores out of power, while setting up a permanent civil government in New Spain." It was a court that traveled throughout the colony listening to cases. It represented the crown and answered to the Council of the Indies. It was meant to oversee the administration of the colony, but the Council of the Indies was far away and little involved in the day-to-day life of New Spain, which resulted in increasing opportunities to develop a corruptive system (See Letter to Charles V from Zumárraga, García Icazbalceta 1881: appendix num. 1, 1–42). Under Guzman's leadership, the audiencia proved inadequate as a tool of royal authority. It was corrupt, inefficient and inflicted a lot of injustices on the population, both indigenous and Spanish. This misadministration of the first audiencia continued until the return of Cortés in July 1530, when they even tried to depose him. Shortly thereafter, Nuño de Guzmán was removed from office. The members of the second audiencia arrived and took power in January 1531. They proved to be very different from their predecessors (Simpson 1966: 33–39).

raped Indian women, and so on. Bishop Zumárraga, as protector of the Indians,[19] tried, in vain, to defend them. His position was critical: the Spanish monarchy had not defined either the extent of his jurisdiction nor his duties as protector of the Indians. Moreover, he had not received official consecration as a bishop and was thus at a disadvantage when he attempted to exercise his authority. The Indians appealed to him as protector with all kinds of complaints about the treatment they were getting from some Spaniards, which started a confrontation between the

---

19 On this title, see Chauvet (1949: 283–95). Chauvet looks for the origin of this title in the ecclesiastical law by which a bishop was to be the father and protector of the weak. More accurately, and in the context of Spain, Chauvet finds the title in the kingdom of Peter III of Aragon (1196–1213), from where it would have extended to Castile and, from there, to the Americas. In this new context, it "was a civil institution that had for its object to take under its patronage the natives of Spanish America, defending them against the oppression and the mistreatment of the Spanish colonists and whites in general. Unfortunately, … the Spanish Crown never specified, with the necessary clarity and desired judicial precision, the rights and duties proper to [his] office" (284). In the particular case of Zumárraga, he was appointed to this office by Charles V on January 2, 1528:

> Confiado de vuestra fidelidad e conciencia, buena vida y ejemplo, que en esto guardaréis el servicio de Dios y nuestro y con toda la retitud y buen celo entenderéis que en ello es nuestra merced e voluntad, que cuanto nuestra merced y voluntad fuere, seáis protector e defensor de los indios de la dicha tierra, por la presente vos cometemos y encargamos y mandamos que tengáis mucho cuidado de mirar e visitar los dichos indios e hacer que sea bien tratados e industriados y enseñados en las cosas de nuestra santa fe católica por las personas que los tienen e tovieren a cargo e veáis las leyes e ordenanzas e instrucciones e provisiones que se han fecho o ficieren cerca del buen tratamiento e conversión de los dichos indios. (Carreño 1944: 69–71)
>
> [*My translation: Trusting in your loyalty and conscience and in your good and exemplary life, and in doing so you would understand that it is our wish that you protect and look after the Indians in that land, and make sure that they are visited, and see to it that they be well treated and taught in matters of our holy Catholic faith by those who are or will be in charge of them, and to study the laws and ordinances and instructions and provisions that have been given or shall be given concerning the kind treatment and conversion of said Indians.*]

Therefore, according to Chauvet, Zumárraga "was appointed supreme judge and supreme executer of all the laws and instructions given in favor of the kind treatment and religious instruction of the natives," and not even the rulers themselves were exempted from his jurisdiction. The power struggle with the first audiencia was the next step, since their corrupt ways met the opposition of the protector of the Indians. The audiencia, then, banned direct communication with the Court in Spain, and the bishop felt forced to smuggle a letter to the Spanish authorities telling them of the situation in the colony. Zumárraga was then called to Spain and, although previously he had asked from the king to be relieved of the office of protector and to have Fray Domingo de Betanzos appointed instead (letter dated on August 27, 1529, García Icazbalceta 1881: appendix num. 1, pp. 1–42), this act did not take place until September 29, 1534, when Zumárraga was allowed to step down from the office of protectorship of the Indians (Carreño 1944: 97).

encomenderos[20] and the new bishop (Mendieta 1973:[21] Book V, part I, ch. 27), and the Franciscans, who had labored so hard for the welfare of the Indians, became increasingly frustrated in the face of the excesses of the auditors and the failure of their evangelization campaigns.[22]

Following Pope Alexander VI's bulls on the New World (*Inter caetera* and *Dudum siquidem*),[23] which required Ferdinand and Isabella to take responsibility

20 The *encomienda* was a system that distributed land and labor amongst the conquerors in the Spanish Empire. It rewarded conquerors with the labor of particular groups of Indians. Through this system, the conquered peoples were considered vassals of the Spanish monarch and were managed by the encomendero, who was entrusted with their evangelization.

21 Mendieta, Jerónimo: Spanish missionary; born at Vitoria, Spain, 1525. He died in the City of Mexico in 1604. While still very young, he took the habit of St. Francis at Bilbao and arrived in New Spain in 1554 where, being desirous of helping in the conversion of the Indians, he applied himself with zeal to study the Mexican language. In 1569 Mendieta accompanied Miguel Navarro on his way to the general chapter in France to whom he suggested some changes. In his view the authority of the Viceroy of New Spain should be increased and that of the audiencia diminished and limited exclusively to judicial matters. In the administration of justice, except in criminal cases, he would desire separate tribunals for Spaniards and for Indians, particularly in suits concerning the possession of land. He also thought that Indians should be forced to work, but he pointed out that in some cases the Indians voluntarily entered into contracts to work for hire and that this ought to be wisely encouraged and facilitated. Mendieta's principal work is his *Historia Eclesiastica Indiana*, completed in 1596 (see *Diccionario enciclopédico Espasa* 1978: 34, 602).

22 In fact, the confrontation presented by the Franciscans did not end there. They also objected to the exploitation of the Indians and even their submission to the colonial structure. The friars longed for the creation of a new Christian society, pure and holy, an idealized version of what they imagined the primitive church to have been, where the Indians would be friar-like subjects only dependent on religious men (Mendieta 1973: vol. 261, 90–92). But this new society was very much in conflict with the colonial enterprise and the system that the Crown was to establish in the new lands. Together with their intention of preserving the purity of the indigenous people of New Spain, there was a deliberate attempt to segregate the Indians from any contact with the corruption coming from the Old World, namely, through the encomenderos and other Spaniards. This general opinion about the vices coming to the New World through the Spaniards is established by Cortés himself, who, in a Fourth Letter to the Emperor dated on October 15, 1524, assures that "Si todos los españoles que en estas partes están y a ellas vienen fuesen frailes, o su principal intención fuese la conversión de estas gentes, bien creo yo que su conversación con ellas seria muy provechosa; mas como esto sea al revés, al revés a de ser el efecto que obrare; por que es notorio que la mas de la gente española que acá pasa, son de baja manera, fuertes y viciosos, de diversos vicios y pecados; Y si a estos tales se les diese libre licencia de se andar por los pueblos de indios, antes por nuestros pecados se convertirían ellos a sus vicios que los atraerían a la virtud, y sería mucho inconveniente para su conversión" (Cortés 2004: 264). Because of this, the Franciscans were in favor of excluding the lay Spaniards, as a whole, from the government of the Indians in favor of the mendicant orders. They even got to the point where they would not teach the Indians to speak Castilian as a measure to ensure the maintenance of a certain distance from the "dangerous Spaniards" and the vices coming through them from the Old Continent. But, in the long run, this same distance would be responsible for one of the most worrying issues even in modern Mexico: the marginalization of the Indians and their difficult incorporation to the mainstream while relegated to a position of subalternity and oppression that is still current nowadays (Ricard 1986: 417–18)

23 The bull *Inter Caetera* was issued in June 1493 to stop disputes between Spain and Portugal over territories in the New World and became a major document in the development of subsequent legal doctrines regarding claims of empire in the colonies. The document established a meridian one hundred leagues west of Cape Verde Islands. Lands west of that line should belong to Spain and those on the east to Portugal. Therefore, in the practice, the bull assigned to Castile the exclusive right to acquire territory,

for the evangelization of the Indians, the different religious orders established in Spain shared their efforts in the mission of proselytizing the new territories. In this context, therefore, the question of conversion, and the subsequent fight against idolatry, was not only a matter of belief. Pressed by the pope and his documents, conversion became a question of public policy, a commitment taken by the Spanish authorities to the papacy: if they failed to Christianize the natives, they would be failing the pope and they would be putting in danger the possibility of exercising legitimate political power over the New World (Seed 1993: 629–52).

It was the conquistadores themselves who introduced the new faith. As early as 1519, Bernal Díaz del Castillo, soldier in Cortés's army, narrates the celebration of the first Easter in the New World, very soon after their arrival (XXXVIII–XL). Two chaplains who traveled with the conquistadores to take care of the spiritual needs of the seamen were the first ones who planted this seed in a completely new scenario. From this very moment, it becomes obvious that the future of these men in those newly discovered lands would be in constant dialogue with the spread of Christianity.[24]

Soon after the first expedition, a group of Franciscan missionaries arrived in New Spain. It was 1523 when Juan de Tecto, Juan de Ahora, and Pedro de Gante first set foot in the New World and, although the first two died prematurely, the latter devoted his whole life to the indoctrination of the indigenous population in Christian catechism and dogma. The task, of course, was not an easy one and, in a letter to Phillip II in 1558, Gante laments his slow progress and few results.

Frustrated, Pedro de Gante resorted to a strategy used before, specifically during the Reconquista of Granada, and so he started getting to know the indigenous people and to understand them and the way he should interact with them, until he learned that "toda su adoración dellos á sus dioses era cantar y bailar delante dellos . . . y como yo vi esto y que todos sus cantares eran dedicados á sus dioses, compuse metros muy solemnes sobre la Ley de Dios y de la fe . . . y también díles libreas para pintar en sus mantas para bailar con ellas, porque ansí se usaba entre ellos"[25] (García Icazbalceta 1971b: 2, 223–24). Pedro de Gante therefore, finds a way

---

trade in, or even approach the lands lying west of that meridian (Weckmann 198–215). This division, however, was unequal and possibly heavily influenced by the Spanish monarchs, (Alexander VI was of Spanish origin himself), leaving Portugal almost entirely out of the territories in America. The Treaty of Tordesillas (June 7, 1494) was the follow-up. It moved the north-south line further west, allowing Portuguese claims to Brazil. The papal bull *Dudum Siquidem*, issued by Pope Alexander VI in the fall of 1493, confirmed the bull *Inter Caetera*. Also see Pagden (1982: 29–30).

24 I will return to this topic at the end of this chapter, in the section entitled: "First Impressions of New Spain: A Landscape of Idolatry."

25 My translation: All their worship to their gods was singing and dancing in front of them . . . and since I saw this, and that all their songs were dedicated to their gods, I wrote very solemn rhymes about the law of God and faith . . . and also gave them some symbols to paint on their blankets to dance with them, as they used to.

to connect with the indigenous populations and establishes a precarious contact with them, combining Christian doctrine and symbols with indigenous forms of expression, displaying a very conciliatory tone and an inclusive open mind, rescuing ways of cultural integration that had already been rehearsed in Granada.

Fray Hernando de Talavera (1428–1507), confessor to Queen Isabel of Castile even before she reached the throne, became one of the most influential people in the context of the Reconquista. A man of faith, not comfortable in the public sphere, Talavera used his appointment in 1493 as archbishop of Granada to preach the Christian dogma. Under the very difficult circumstances that he lived in, he tried to spread Christianity and to reach sincere conversions, rather than imposing the new religion for fear of expulsion. In order to do this, Talavera tried to get familiarized with the communities he was trying to convert: their way of life, their traditional songs and dances, and so on, to make the new doctrine as accessible to them as possible. In his attempt to get closer to the non-Christian communities, he learned Arabic and Hebrew and used this knowledge to persuade rather than impose, using a conciliatory tone and showing evidence of an openness to diversity very unusual in his time and context. He also used drama in order to reach the groups he wanted to convert as well as simple language in his sermons, as Marcel Bataillon observes: "Lo que él procura es atraer el pueblo a la Iglesia, concediéndole una participación más amplia en la liturgia: reemplaza los responsos con cánticos piadosos apropiados a las lecciones y consigue de ese modo que los fieles acudan a maitines lo mismo que a misa. Se sirve del teatro religioso para conmover los corazones. No falta quien vea con malos ojos esta invasión de los templos por la lengua vulgar, pero él no hace caso"[26] (Bataillon 1966: 58–59).

Once Talavera attracted the community to church or church events, the next step would be to educate them in the teachings of the Catholic faith in order to achieve a sincere conversion, one based on knowledge of the dogma taught in their native language.

Nevertheless, the hardest moment of all occurred when this individual, fully knowledgeable in the new faith and sincerely converted, tried to enter his new Christian community. At this point, Talavera insisted in eliminating the labels of "new Christian" and to welcome the newly converted with open arms, as they had embraced the waters of the baptism. But this message of inclusion and lack of distinction were completely revolutionary in the Spain that Talavera was living in and constituted a very clear threat to the "old Christians" who refused to admit the

---

26 My translation: What he tries is to attract the community to church, allowing for greater participation in the liturgy; he replaces funeral prayers with pious songs appropriate for the lessons and manages this way to get more people in matins and in Mass. He also uses religious drama to move their hearts. There are people who do not approve of the invasion of vulgar language in church, but he doesn't care.

conversos as equals. This acceptance would have implied admitting that the cleansing waters of baptism were able to erase the difference between the two groups, and, at this point Talavera found the resistance of those who refused to change their own attitude.

At this point Talavera found himself immersed into a new educational enterprise that was twofold: on the one hand, the non-Catholics he was trying to convert and, on the other, the ones who should facilitate the integration of the first ones in an effort toward inclusion never seen before. This is the strategy that Pedro de Gante and later the first twelve Franciscans recovered in the New World, preferring persuasion to force and sincere conversion over imposition.

Needless to say that Talavera's policy was, in nature, of slow application since it was based on individual journeys of learning, acculturation, and integration. For this reason Talavera's sophisticated methods were not recognized by his peers, and, in 1499, when the Court temporarily moved to Granada, he clashed with the inquisitorial ways, prone to the expulsion of those not willing to convert. The Catholic monarchs, eager to supervise the progress achieved by the evangelization campaigns, became disappointed with the situation and decided to leave Cisneros in charge instead. But the archbishop of Toledo had a different idea from that of Talavera, and, in a few years, he destroyed the climate of trust that the friar had created with years of work and mediation between the faiths. For Cisneros, the confrontation with the infidels was inevitable: the negotiation path was definitely broken and the measures taken precipitated a rebellion that took place in Albaicín, Granada, in December 1499. This would just be the first of a number of rebellions that developed in the same area and that would culminate with the rebellion of the Alpujarras in 1568.

However, although Talavera's method did not completely come to fruition in Granada, it became the basis for the first evangelization on the other side of the Atlantic Ocean. But even in this new context, the spreading of the new faith was a task developed by very few, with not much support and with no systematic approach to it, which made the enterprise that much harder (Ricard 1986: 82).

Charles V requested a papal bull from Adrian VI (*Expo nobis*, may 10th, 1522) by which he obtained apostolic authority when spreading the gospel in America, and privileges for those mendicant orders that were carrying it out (Mendieta 1973: 193). This bull was the final push that fray Francisco de los Ángeles, head of the Franciscan order, needed to send the famous twelve.[27]

---

27 The group consisted of Fray Martín de Valencia (their leader), Fray Francisco de Soto, Fray Martín de Coruña (also known as Fray Martín de Jesús), Fray Juan Juárez, Fray Antonio de Ciudad Rodrigo, Fray Toribio de Benavente Motolinía, García de Cisneros, Fray Luis de Fuensalida, Juan de Ribas, Fray Francisco Jiménez, Fray Andrés de Córdoba, and Fray Juan de Palos. Juan de Palos, a lay Franciscan, took the place of Fray Bernardino de la Torre, who did not sail with the group. Fray Andrés de Córdoba was also a lay brother.

The group arrived in San Juan de Ulúa in May 1524 carrying two documents—
"La instrucción" and "La obediencia"—to provide some order to the process they
were about to continue. The first of those texts, written in Spanish (not Latin), in
1523 established the model that the friars were to follow in their mission: to teach
with words, not with the sword, and to model their teachings in their everyday lives,
following the strategy that Talavera already used in Granada: "pues vais a plantar el
Evangelio en los corazones de aquellos infieles, mirad que vuestra vida no se aparte
de é . . . porque el concierto y buen ejemplo que viesen en vuestra vida y conversación sería tanta parte para ayudar a la conversión como las palabras y predicaciones"
(Pérez Luna 2001: 80, 82).[28] We are, therefore, following the same model proposed
by Talavera: conciliatory tone, getting to know the communities before preaching
the Gospel, giving them time to follow the example of others, and so forth. But we
also see an added degree of flexibility since the experience in Spain is to be used only
as a point of reference and not as an absolute dictator of the experience in the New
World (Pérez Luna 2001: 80). Therefore, the plan implemented by the Franciscans
follows Talavera's extremely faithfully, even when it encourages the friars to let the
infidels' way of life dictate the next steps and remain flexible in the missionary work.

The second document that the friars carried with them, "The Obedience,"
reflected the worries of the order and showed the Franciscan commitment to the
salvation of the Indians' souls and, therefore, added extraordinary value to the apostolic mission at hand:

> Por eso, confiando en la bondad divina, para convertir con la palabra y el ejemplo a
> los pueblos que no conocen a nuestro Señor Jesucristo, que están retenidos por la ceg-
> uedad de la idolatría bajo el yugo de la cautividad satánica, y que moran en las Indias
> que comúnmente son llamadas Yucatán o Nueva España o tierra firme, yo, con la
> autoridad de mi oficio, en el nombre del Padre y del Hijo y del Espíritu Santo, os des-
> tino y envío, e igualmente os impongo por el mérito de la santa obediencia, y mando
> que vayáis y produzcáis fruto, y vuestro fruto permanezca.[29] (Pérez Luna 2001: 53)

This is the beginning of the evangelization campaign, led by the Franciscans
with the purpose of obtaining sincere and permanent conversions, urged by the

---

28 My translation: Since you are going to plant the seed of the Gospel in the hearts of the infidels, make sure
   that your lives don't go far from it . . . because the order and good example that they will see in your lives
   and conversation will be as important in helping the conversions as your words and preaching.
29 My translation: Thus, trusting in the divine good will to convert by the word and example, all those
   peoples that don't know Jesus Christ, Our Lord, and that are retained by the blindness of idolatry under
   the yoke of the Satanic captivity and that live in the Indies that are commonly called Yucatán or New
   Spain, or mainland, I, with the authority of my position, in the name of the Father and the Son and the
   Holy Spirit, send you and, by the vow of holy obedience, I command you to go and bear fruit and that
   your fruit remain.

worry of the end of times approaching and the need to save the Indians' souls via conversions.

Soon after, the Franciscans were followed by Dominicans, Augustinians, and Jesuits, establishing areas of influence that were kept perfectly separated from each other. But in spite of the presence of the other missionary orders, the Franciscans distinguished themselves for keeping a particularly zealous sense of their mission in the New World and a tight control over their territories while regarding their role in the conversion of the Indians as a final millennial chapter toward the Christianization of the world. This privileged position, somewhat aided by the fact that the first bishop of Mexico (Fray Juan de Zumárraga) was a Franciscan himself, opened a general rivalry with the Dominicans that resulted in an ongoing confrontation that included, among other issues, a debate over the intellectual capacity of the indigenous population of America and their possibility to be converted to Christianity.

The Franciscans defended the methods they had been using since their arrival, arguing that the Indians were perfectly ready to be converted and that many of them had already been, thanks to the efforts of the first missionaries and, although they had no doubt about the final success of their campaigns, they admitted that the endeavor had been much more difficult than anticipated. For their part, the Dominicans questioned both the capacity of the Indians and the Franciscan methods, accusing the latter of urging the Indians to receive their baptisms without undergoing the comprehensive religious instruction that was required to fully understand the significance and further implications of the sacrament (Georges Baudot 1995: 276–78). Ironically—says Patricia Lopes Don—"to prove their affectionate defense of the Indians (and the rationale for their own mission), the Franciscans gradually began to move in the 1530s toward a much tougher enforcement of religious life in the indigenous communities than they had in the early days" (Lopes 2006: 27–48). As a result, the 1530s saw the establishment of the Apostolic Inquisition for the first time in Mexico City, and, with the encouragement of the Franciscan community, the bishop fray Juan de Zumárraga was named by the archbishop of Seville and general inquisitor, D. Álvaro Manrique, the first Apostolic inquisitor of Mexico City and its bishop. This title would grant him the capacity to create an inquisitorial tribunal of his own, to appoint the necessary officials, to set their salaries, and to assign the most severe punishments to the prosecuted, including death.[30] The first tribunal of the Inquisition was, thereby, established in the New World.

In the first years after the arrival of the Spaniards, the Inquisition was not instituted as such. Similar functions were performed by a number of bishops who

30 The letter by D. Álvaro Manrique appointing Zumárraga as Apostolic inquisitor was written on June 27, 1535, and is reproduced by García Icazbalceta (1947: appendix num. 17, 78–79).

traveled to New Spain from their respective locations in Spain and who were authorized, by the inquisitor general of Spain (Cardinal Ximénez de Cisneros) on July 22, 1517, to carry out all Episcopal functions, including the roles of inquisitorial ecclesiastical judges. The Inquisition was then, episcopal; that is, managed by independent bishops, decentralized, and, as a result, always susceptible to be understood differently in the various bishoprics. To supplement this system, the Franciscan Order appealed to Pope Leo X and Adrian VI who, via the Bulls of 1521 and 1522, respectively, empowered the friars to perform episcopal functions as well wherever the existing priests or bishops could not reach. This fragmentation of authority only helped to increase the chaos and to demonstrate the need for a figure who could centralize the efforts of all those fighting the indigenous idolatry in disperse ways. This figure was going to be Fray Juan de Zumárraga, who assumed the position of first Apostolic inquisitor. By this title there was a recognition of the more consistent work that needed to be done in New Spain and, instead of sending some bishops from Spain to cover those needs, now Zumárraga was, in the first place, bishop (and later archbishop) of Mexico and, eventually, backed up by the inquisitor general of Spain and the Pope.[31]

Zumárraga's downfall as an inquisitor came, nevertheless, because of his Indian policy. On the one hand, there was no consensus about the nature of the Indians themselves, and particularly about whether they were eligible to become Christians in the full extent of the word; but also, even among those who believed in the intellectual capacity of the indigenous population of the New World, there was disagreement about whether the Indians should be judged by the Inquisition and, therefore, be subject to the same levels of adherence to the Catholic creed as was any Spaniard, no matter their relative inexperience in this new form of religious life. Zumárraga obviously did not consider these facts to be enough deterrent and implemented the Indian Inquisition in full force. From this standpoint he wanted to fight idolatry and submit to trial all those pagan behaviors that were putting in danger the success of the evangelization campaigns that had developed since the first arrival of the famous twelve Franciscans, not fearing the last consequences. In the end, the crash with the central administration was tougher than he had expected, and, as a result,

---

31 Nevertheless, he ended up being removed from his job as Apostolic Inquisitor and replaced in 1544 by Tello de Sandoval, the visitor general of Mexico, who assumed those responsibilities over the entire viceroyalty. Sandoval remained in office for only three years, after which the inquisitorial powers reverted back to the different bishops and the Inquisition went back to being episcopal. In 1554, when Alonso de Montúfar became the second archbishop of Mexico, he never received the Apostolic, commission and the Inquisition remained episcopal during his term. Nevertheless it was proven unsatisfactory not only because there were several cases of abuse of power, but also because large numbers of heretics were said to remain among the population. For these reasons, Phillip II established the first tribunal of the Holy Office of the Inquisition of Mexico in 1569, and Dr. Pedro Moya de Contreras was put in charge. A tribunal of the Holy Office was authorized at the same time in Peru. Greenleaf (1961: ch. 1).

he was superseded in his office as inquisitor, largely because he relaxed Don Carlos, the cacique of Texcoco, to the secular arm for burning, a decision that was sharply criticized in Spain.[32]

In the meantime, in Spain, both civil and religious authorities were trying to handle the phenomenon of the incorporation of the New World into their imaginary. Let us not forget, as I have pointed out in the previous chapter, that this incorporation is taking place in a very particular context, one in which Europe presents itself as fragmented, both in terms of religion and of politics, with wars and struggles that dominate a good part of the Old Continent. In this situation, and with the ideal of a Christian union crumbling at its feet, the state stands out as the last chance for coming together, the last possibility for inclusion and for restoring order. But at what price? Was anything allowed in the pursuit of the conservation of this state? Did the end (in the Spanish case, religious, through the incorporation of the "heathen Indians" to Catholicism) justify the means, no questions asked?

The elements found at this crossroads were not particularly new or so different from the ones that had been present all along during the process of the Catholic Reconquista of the Iberian Peninsula against the first *heathens* the Catholic kingdoms came in contact with, that is, Moors and Jews who were also fought on the grounds of their religious difference. I do not mean to say that the two situations (that occurred in Spain with the Moors and Jews, and that developing in the New World around the incorporation of the Indians) were identical or that the confrontations with these two groups of *others* were approached in the same way. I am aware of the great differences in time, geography, circumstances, and features particular to these groups, but I think that it is safe to say that some of the elements and the processes used in the Caribbean first, and later in Mexico and Peru, had already been rehearsed in Spain, and this experience shaped the expectations of the conquistadores as well as those of the authorities who dealt with the formation of hegemony that characterized the Spanish sixteenth century.

Up until the consolidation of the absolutist states, and together with the centralization of power that was characteristic of this new form of government, the conservation and delineation of political boundaries became a goal in itself. It is in this period that the term "state" is first introduced into political discourse, and Machiavelli (1469–1527) used it to refer to a territorial sovereign government in *The Prince*, published in 1532. It is there where he defends an idea of state in which religion becomes just an instrument of the precious stability that is sought after,

---

32 The most serious outcome of an inquisitorial process was the *relaxation to the secular arm*, which implied burning at the stake. This punishment was frequently applied to impenitent heretics and those who had relapsed. It was followed by a public execution. In the final moments, if the condemned repented, he was garroted before his body was given to the flames. If not, he was burned alive.

portraying a head of state who should make efforts to *appear* religious in order to sway the populace, rather than actually having a monarch who placed religion in a prominent position. As an example of this, Machiavelli does not hesitate to refer to Ferdinand of Aragon in the following terms:

> Nothing gives a prince more prestige than undertaking great enterprises and setting a splendid example for his people. In our day we have Ferdinand of Aragon, the present king of Spain. He may be considered a new prince, since from being a weak king he has risen to become, for fame and glory, the first prince of Christendom; and if you consider his actions, you will find all of them very great and some extraordinary. At the beginning of his rule he attacked Granada, and that enterprise was the cornerstone of his reign . . . *Money from the Church and the people enabled him to recruit big armies*, and in the course of this long war to build a military establishment which has since won him much honor. Apart from this, *he made use of the pretext of religion to prepare the way for still greater projects, and adopted a policy of pious cruelty* in expelling the Moors from his kingdom and despoiling them; his conduct here could not have been more despicable nor more unusual. (Machiavelli 1992: 60–61, my emphasis)

Therefore, the ideal prince should endeavor to be seen as compassionate, trustworthy, honest, and religious just because it was imperative that the prince be willing to do anything necessary to maintain power and stability.

Machiavelli strongly asserted that, above all, the prince must be feared rather than loved; thus, he disregards the connection between ethics and politics, a value system that disturbed many, among them Pedro de Ribadeneyra (1526–1611; in *Obras escogidas*), but also Tomás Fernández Medrano (in *República mixta*), Eugenio de Narbona (*Doctrina política civil escrita en aforismos*), Fernando Alvia de Castro (*Verdadera razón de estado*), Lorenzo Ramírez de Prado (*Consejo y consejero de príncipes*), and so forth. Let us concentrate for a moment on the first one, Ribadeneyra, contemporary to the first arrival of the Spaniards in Mexico.

Pedro de Ribadeneyra, a Jesuit, offers in his *Tratado* the way by which a prince can retain control of his realm.[33] In his view, this goal should only be attainable by strictly following the Catholic teachings and in frontal opposition to Machiavelli and his ideas of the politicians. Therefore, he designs a framework in which the reasons of state are not rejected or forgotten but rather subordinated to religion or, in the worst-case scenario, at least respectful of the moral values of the Catholic religion. For him, the dogma he believes in already contains all the elements necessary to keep

---

33 The complete title of his book is *Tratado de la Religión y Virtudes que debe tener el Príncipe Cristiano para gobernar y conservar sus Estados*, and was first published in 1595. For information on Ribadeneyra, see Fernández-Santamaría (1986); and also Peña Echeverría (1998).

and advance the res publica, since God, and not men, puts the king in power and guides his decision along the way. The king then, is the viceroy of God on earth, and so his government should reflect this belief (Fernández-Santamaría 1986: 33). In this spirit, Ribadeneyra does not hesitate to label as "heretics" those who, as Machiavelli and the politicians, do not give religion the place that Ribadeneyra thinks fundamental. Actually, for him they are worse than heretics because if those who deviate from religion still hold it in some recognition, they are perceived as apostates:

> Los herejes, con ser centellas del infierno y enemigos de toda religión, profesan alguna
> religión, y entre los muchos errores que enseñan, mezclan algunas verdades. Los
> políticos y discípulos de Maquiavelo no tienen religión alguna, ni hacen referencia
> que la religión sea falsa o verdadera, sino si es a propósito para su razón de Estado.
> Y, así, los herejes quitan parte de la religión, y los políticos toda la religión. Los herejes
> son enemigos descubiertos de la Iglesia católica, y como de tales nos podemos guar-
> dar; mas los políticos son amigos fingidos y enemigos verdaderos y domésticos, que
> con beso de falsa paz matan como Judas, y vestidos de piel de oveja, despedazan como
> lobos el ganado del Señor, y con nombre y máscara de católicos, arrancan, destruyen y
> arruinan la fe católica.[34] (Ribadeneyra 1927: 455)

In this frame of mind there was no room for the autonomous existence of politics or any kind of independence from religion. As a matter of fact, Ribadeneyra thinks it necessary to even punish those Christian people in power who do not follow this formula:

> Amonestar a los príncipes cristianos y a los consejeros que tienen cabe sí, y a todos los
> otros que se presian de hombres de Estado, que se persuadan que Dios solo funda los
> Estados y los da a quien es servido, y los establece, amplifica y defiende a su voluntad,
> y que la mejor manera de conservarlos es tenerlo grato y propicio, guardando su santa
> ley, obedeciendo sus mandamientos, respetando a su religión y tomando todos los
> medios que a ella nos da o que no repugnan a lo que ella nos enseña, y que ésta es la
> verdadera, cierta y segura razón de Estado, y la de Maquiavelo y de los políticos es
> falsa, incierta y engañosa.[35] (Ribadeneyra 1927: 456)

---

34 My translation: Heretics, as sparks from hell and enemies of all religion, profess some religion and amongst the many mistakes they teach, they mix some truth. Politicians and disciples of Machiavelli have no religion and never address whether religion is true or false if it is not for state reasons. And so, heretics take some from religion, and politics, all. Heretics are declared enemies of the Catholic Church and as such, we need to keep away; but the politicians are fake friends and true homeland enemies who, with a kiss of false peace kill us a Judas, and dressed with lamb skin, and with name and mask of Catholics, rip off, destroy and ruin the Catholic faith.

35 My translation: Reprimand the Christian princes and the counselors that they have nearby and all the statesmen, that they become persuaded that only God founds states and gives them to whom is worthy of them and establishes them and grows them and defends them willingly, and the best way of keep them is to have Him on your side, being grateful and favorable, keeping his holy law, following his command-

It is important to consider this take on the relationship between church and state or, rather, politics and religion in the context of the conquest of the Americas, and for that it is necessary to turn to the Valladolid debate.

This debate took place between 1550 and 1551 and put in question the legality of the conquest and the ulterior justification for it within the dispute concerning the existence of souls in the natives of the so-called New World.

It opposed two main attitudes toward the conquests of the New World. The Dominican friar Bartolomé de Las Casas upheld the humanity of the Amerindians and insisted on their being treated as free men in the natural order, according to Catholic theology. Influenced by the School of Salamanca and the humanist movements, Las Casas insisted that even unknown human people were nevertheless as human as the Europeans themselves, possessed souls, and were capable of attaining salvation; lastly, as true humans and who had not committed any aggression or provocation to justify punishment, they retained the right to remain free men and not be enslaved. Nevertheless, Las Casas recommended the instruction of the natives in the Catholic faith and made of this the main goal regarding the presence of the Spaniards in the Indies.

The opposing position, represented by the Jesuit Juan Ginés de Sepúlveda, was that these newfound peoples were not truly human or, more accurately, that they were natural slaves, appropriately subject to others, as children are to adults and women to men (see Pagden 1982: 33–57). This party speculated that since Christendom had not reached them, it was only because they were not human or possessed no souls, so they could not attain salvation. Therefore, since the Amerindians did not have "souls," they could be reduced to slavery.

These are the basic positions that came up for debate over the (mis)treatment of these natives by the conquistadores and colonists. Moved by doubts, the King of Spain Charles V called a *junta* (jury) of eminent doctors and theologians to hear both sides and to issue a ruling on the controversy. The junta ruled in favor of Las Casas's position and implemented a set of rules called Leyes Nuevas to ensure the proper treatment of the natives, physically and spiritually. Although implementing this position was strenuously opposed and to a large extent sabotaged by the colonists, it also became the official position of both the king of Spain and of the Catholic Church, though it only lasted from 1542 to 1545. However, it did put on the table the issues surrounding the legality of the conquest, and it traced a shift in the justification of the presence of the Spaniards in the Indies: from political and economic terms based on the use of the natural resources (including the natives) to

ments, respecting his religion and using all the resources given by it and that don't defy it, since this is the true and reliable reason of State and that of Machiavelli and of the politicians is false, untrue and deceptive.

a religious goal that involved the preaching of the Gospel in order to work toward the salvation of the Indians.

Further criticism of Machiavelli's position can still be found years later, when Saavedra Fajardo (1584–1648) defended that, in the context of the Catholic Spain, that scheme was not only unacceptable but almost heretical and fought for just the opposite: a state that enabled and helped the citizens to attain the ultimate salvation, a goal that was presented in religious terms.[36] "San Isidoro pronosticó, en su muerte, a la nación española, que si se apartaba de la verdadera religión, sería oprimida; pero que si la observare, vería levantada su grandeza sobre las demás naciones . . . Siendo, pues, el alma de las repúblicas, la religión, procure el príncipe conservalla"[37] (Saavedra Fajardo 1976: 263–64). Cultural and national homogenization figured prominently in the rise of the modern state system but, in the case of Spain, and since the ideas of a nation and nationality were not fully developed yet, the two pivotal points in the consolidation of the state were the church and the king. Both of these (king and church), according to Saavedra Fajardo, needed to cooperate but keeping their spheres of power perfectly independent from each other and keeping religion as the top priority: "Si bien toca a los reyes el mantener en sus reinos la religión, y aumentar su verdadero culto como a vicarios de Dios en lo temporal, para encaminar su gobierno a la mayor gloria suya y bien de sus súbditos, deben advertir que no pueden arbitrar en el culto y accidentes de la religión; porque este cuidado pertenece derechamente a la cabeza espiritual, por la potestad que a ella sola concedió Cristo; y que solamente les toca la execución, custodia y defensa de lo que ordenare y dispusiere"[38] (265–56). But in the end, reality inclined Saavedra Fajardo toward an unavoidable existentialist pessimism: the prince must be warned of the many tricks other rulers can use against him so that he can avoid them while trying to exercise politics based on Christian values. The problem, of course, lies in the fact that Christian virtues do not harmonize easily with political exigencies or with the struggles of building an empire, a process that necessarily implies the defeat and prevalence over others, not always in the most elegant of fashions.

---

36 Nevertheless, Saavedra Fajardo acknowledges the fact that religious homogeneity makes for a more peaceful, durable state (Saavedra Fajardo 1976: 24) but shifts his emphasis toward the prevalence of religious and ethical values over a political stability devoid of morality.

37 My translation: Saint Isidore predicted, on his deathbed, that if the Spanish nation abandoned the true faith it would be oppressed; but if it kept it, it would see his grandeur lifted above all nations . . . Being religion the soul of all republics, the prince should ensure its preservation.

38 My translation: Although kings are responsible for the maintenance and expansion of the true faith as temporary vicars of God, in order to bring their governments to a higher glory for the good of their citizens, they should not mediate in religious matters or anecdotes because these pertain solely to the spiritual leader, for the right given by God, and so he is responsible for the implementation, custody and defense of what is a stake.

Nevertheless, in this fragmented Europe of the Reformation and the Counter-Reformation, the alliances between king and church had to be adjusted and, in the case of Spain it resulted in a tight collaboration between the most powerful Catholic state at the time (Spain) and the most visible Catholic head, the papacy, that gave legitimacy to Spain's imperial enterprises (especially in America, but not only) and placed religion as the main goal, over political or economical interests (Peña Echeverría 1998: xxiii).

In this context we can address the confrontation of modern Spain with the Moors and Jews as a matter of state, that is, as a political decision made by a modern state in the making, one that had outlined a plan for itself and that did not include the *other* within. This state set itself apart from the control of the church of Rome and through the intervention of state (not ecclesiastical) institutions like the Inquisition, created a nation that, following the flag of Christianity, would go on to dominate the world.

Both Moors and Jews, in spite of their differences, shared some basic positioning versus the Catholic Spain that was being developed. Therefore, both were seen as a threat to the nationalistic agenda, either as separate groups or, even worse, if they decided to ally, just as Talavera (1961) stated in his *Católica impugnación*. In this sense the rejection of these *others* had a lot to do with religious differences, but as the evangelization campaigns progressed in Spain it became more obvious that incompatibility of creed was only part of the problem. It also extended to clothing, food, and traditions, and became a disagreement in the way of life, something baptism alone could not solve.

Therefore, in the sixteenth century, both Moors and Jews were together in the shared colonial wound,[39] the common experience of being the *other* in a project that did not include them, of being the outsiders.

Nebrija, author of the first Spanish Grammar published in 1492, talks about this national project in the following terms: an empire needs to partner with a language and that way, in his preface, excludes from that enterprise the cultures that do not

---

39 Ironically enough, before then, the Moors had actually made a colony of Spain, although they did not force the native Spaniards to convert to Islam.

This term, "colonial wound," was coined by Walter Mignolo in the chapter "After" Latin America: The Colonial Wound and the Epistemic Geo-/Political Shift" included in his book *The Idea of Latin America* (Mignolo 2005: 95–148). In it he defines "colonial wound" as "the dominant conception of life in which a growing sector of humanity become commodities (like slaves in the sixteenth and seventeenth centuries) or, in the worst possible conditions, expendable lives. The pain, humiliation, and anger of the continuous reproduction of the colonial wound generate radical political projects, new types of knowledge, and social movements" (Mignolo 2005: 97–98). I use this term in a slightly different way than its author to refer to those communities, in my case, of Jews and Moors in the Spain of the Reconquista, who suffered the alienation of *being* the other in the midst of a project of nation building that did not include them, the *others* of coloniality, the excluded groups that, by virtue of this position, became commodities, just as Mignolo points out.

commune with the same form of expression. This way, Nebrija alienates from the hegemonic project all those groups of people with pretenses in conflict with the Castilians (Jews and Moors) and separates the Spaniards from previous empires (Greek and Roman) in an attempt to learn from the past but also to forge a different and unique future.

The strategy of alienation was fairly straightforward. Both in the case of the Jews and the Moors, it started with increasing limitations and with a drastic reduction of their movements. This measure was taken in all aspects of their lives though it was sporadic at first and very unevenly applied. Nevertheless, it grew to include regulations in terms of what they could wear, what jobs they could do, whom they could relate to, where they could live, and so forth. This situation became increasingly unsustainable, especially when the state in formation was controlling their every move.[40] (The restrictions also applied to the children, who were submitted to a Christian upbringing that clashed with everything they saw at home.)[41]

The next movement was to try to convert all these non-Christians who threatened the national unity that was being rehearsed. But, although the evangelization campaigns were reasonably successful, the Jews and Moors who chose to be baptized were mostly neither believed nor trusted, continuing a climate of suspicion that did not end even after the final expulsion of the two groups. As a result, once it was realized that conversions could not erase cultural differences, the last resort was the expulsions, started in 1492 in the case of the Jews, and in 1609 in the case of the *moriscos*.[42] But this action only came to interrupt a process of assimilation that had been happening in the core of the two minorities who, though they wanted to

---

40 Saint Vincent Ferrer, the Valencian Dominican missionary to whom I referred above, includes some of these prohibitions in his sermons, especially in the one composed to celebrate the festivity of Saint George. There he talks about separating the activities of Jews and Christians ("Veis que San Jorge hizo apartar a los cristianos de los infieles … Los cristianos no deben habitar con ellos ni participar en circunsiones, ni en sus entierros, ni en sus banquetes, ni nutrir a sus hijos ni al contrario, porque los que hacen esas cosas son infieles en la medida en que honran sus ceremonias y sus ritos"; Ferrer 2002: 187), and the sermon planned for one Saturday in Advent when he talked about limiting Jewish access in a wide variety of jobs ("Los infieles deben ser evitados en los oficios, esto es, que no sean jueces, notarios, arrendadores, abogados, cobradores de impuestos, medicos, cirujanos ni boticarios, etc. La razón es que los judíos quieren mayor mal a los cristianos que nosotros al Diablo, como bien sé yo que voy por el mundo predicando" (Ferrer 2002: 537).

41 For more information on the *convivencia* of the three cultures, see also *Los orígenes de la Inquisición en la España del siglo XV* (Netanyahu 1999:115–90); and *Communities of Violence Persecution of Minorities in the Middle Ages* (Nirenberg 1996), among many others.

42 I want to emphasize that the fact that the Spanish Christians had had a history of hatred towards the two minorities (Moors and Jews) does not mean that the movements toward the expulsion of the two were born as the product of an spontaneous collective outburst but rather was the result of a well-thought-out process of manipulation of the bulk of the population in order to achieve some specific goals in the political arena. Thus, there was nothing improvised or surprising about the popular reaction. It was a controlled process with a goal in mind.

maintain their differences with the Christians and with each other, were increasingly becoming more alike.

But even when I have just talked about these two minorities as one, the differences between the two were fundamental. To start with, the bulk of the moriscos never attempted to become one with the rest of the population, to mingle and disappear in a culture that, for them, was totally foreign from so many points of view. Arriving as the invading force and one that dominated much of the Iberian Peninsula for an extended period of time, the Moors never presented themselves in an apologetic fashion and fought their way until the end when they were overthrown militarily. This attitude marked the difference in their trajectory when compared to the future of the Jewish community. As opposed to the Moors, the Jews did try to blend, did try to integrate into a society that rejected them and, in many cases, succeeded in an enterprise that was seen as incredibly dangerous from the center in formation.

Levinson, when referring to most of the essays compiled under the title *Modernity, Culture and the Jew* (1998), observes a distinction between the "unmarked" and the "marked" subject; that is, establishing a binary differentiation that groups all men and cultures in two: us and them, the accepted and the others, no matter what their sign might be or their peculiarities. In the second category, and as the representation par excellence of the "unmarked" subject and culture, we would find the white man who, although he is defined by his whiteness and the implications (historical, cultural, etc.) are portrayed as the universal, he is the one with no mark, the purest expression of mankind and, therefore, this experience of whiteness fails recognition as an indelible mark (Levinson 2005: 245–58).

Yet against this immaculate image of the unstained white man, we would contemplate the others in their plurality and heterogeneity, but grouped as one in their difference with the white model. The problem in this theory arises when we bring this differentiation to the case of the soon-to-be Spain of the fifteenth century, when the relative success of the evangelization campaigns had created a large mass of former Jews who could now blend with the Christians. It is that lack of a mark, once baptism is performed, that became a threat, the lack of recognition, the disappearance of a difference that was very much felt but that had become invisible.

Levinson traces this lack of corporeal, physical distinction to the religious beliefs of each group and, the same way that, based in the *Old Testament*, the Jews were waiting for the coming of the Messiah, for the corporeal manifestation of the Word, in the same way then, the physical bodies of the Jews were waiting for their mark, for the *incarnation* of their difference. The body, understood in this way, is not only physical but a material and cultural space ready to be branded.

Zygmunt Bauman's (1998) essay, in the same collection, aligns itself with Levinson and, as opposed to most of the articles published under the same title, also advocates for the role of the Jew as the "ambivalence incarnate" and thus, with no marks whatsoever, except for this lack thereof. Thus, if the Moor is seen as the *body impossible to assimilate*, the radically different, the strongly marked body, the Jew is presented as the body impossible to recognize, the invisible mark and, therefore, ready to be assimilated.[43] There is not a Jewish mark that represents the Jewish body (exception made about the mark of the circumcision that Bauman does not mention); that is, it is characterized for its lack, a fact that makes the Jew the most *subversive* and dangerous threat of all.

Let us not forget that we have described the white man above as the pure form, the one "unmarked," the universal. But to say that the Jew has no mark would make the distinction of these two groups impossible, and that is where something needed to be done.

Michel Foucault (2003), in some of his essays, refers to state racism and, though his theory is developed around issues concerning the late eighteenth and nineteenth centuries, some of his ideas can help us to understand fifteenth-century Spain.[44] He talks about a modern state that feels entitled to "take life and let live," a state with powers beyond the management of discipline but rather applied to the living man who surrenders his rights to decide on his own body and the destiny of his life. This man, in the case of the Spanish Jew, becomes the subject of a process of *branding* that forces him to assume a mark that is not his own but that will differentiate him from the white man, making him a *homo sacer* of sorts (to use Agamben's term [Agamben 1998]) who only belongs to the system in the fact that he is excluded from it, from the exteriority that, nevertheless, conditions the articulation of the core.[45] So, if the white man has no mark, in contrast, the Jew will be seen as the one

---

43 However, Calderón will make of the upper-class morisco an unmarked body as well, as Greer (2006: 113–30) discusses.

44 On the use of Foucault to discuss medieval to Early Modern racism in the Spanish empire, see Nirenberg's essay in *Rereading the Black Legend* (Greer 2007), where the author discusses the fact that Foucault denies the medieval and Early Modern existence of a radicalized anti-Semitism prior to the seventeenth century.

45 Dopico Black reflects on this issue in relation with Spain and realizes that the elimination of the difference, through baptism, only created a new need for a different way of discriminating, of trying to avoid the *other* to blend with *us* and become the *same*: "If the expulsion and forced conversion program instituted by the Catholic Monarchs was intended to either banish or incorporate (through baptism) the Semitic Other under the banner of a monolithic, Christian Spain, then once that program was successfully negotiated and the Jewish Other had been (at least symbolically) eradicated from the cultural landscape, the need arose for a *new* Other against which the Self could articulate itself. While this vacancy was partly filled by the body of the morisco and, from across the ocean, by the body of an indigenous, American Other that conveniently appeared on the scene at this precise juncture, its pull was so forceful as to elicit the institutionalization of a secondary division within the category (Christian) that previously conferred sameness. The demarcation that emerged—between *cristianos viejos* and *cristianos nuevos*—formed the basis for what would become perhaps *the* central cultural obsession throughout the sixteenth and seventeenth centuries: the preoccupation over *limpieza de sangre*" (Dopico Black 2001:39).

who denies his mark, that is, who insists in not displaying his difference but never as the one who does not possess one. The Jew would, therefore, be the same but not quite, the *other* within and, subsequently, the one most feared.[46]

Moreover, this lack of physical evidence, the lack of a mark or, in other words, this cultural product with no corporeal representation implicitly opened the possibility of hiding in *any* body, making everyone a potential suspect. In this case, with the conversos trying to blend in, the old rules of identification go out the window and the climate of suspicion presides over all interactions.[47] The converso, with no mark of its own, could be anywhere.

This is the situation that propitiates the creation of the Inquisition, not so much in charge of maintaining the purity of the Catholic religion, but rather invested in keeping the boundaries, in drawing a map of the *safe* spaces, and submitting the rest to inquiries based, in many cases, on the illusion of the deviation, on the fear

46 It is, therefore, no coincidence that, as Dopico Black reminds us, Covarrubias introduces in his definition of Jew this fear factor: "Traer judío en el cuerpo, estar con miedo" (To carry the Jew in one's body means to be afraid) (Dopico Black 2001: 41–42).

47 This lack of visible signs makes Covarrubias's definition of the Jew remember with nostalgia those days in which the *other* could be easily identified:

> Judío: En la palabra hebrea tenemos dicho en qué forma aquel pueblo, que Dios escogió para sí, se llamaron hebreos y después israelitas, y finalmente judíos. Oy día lo son los que no creyeron en la venida del Messías Salvador, Christo Jesu, Señor Nuestro, y continúan el professar la ley de Moysén, que era sombra desta verdad. En España han habitado judíos de muchos siglos atrás, hasta que en tiempo de nuestros abuelos, los Reyes Católicos, sin reparar en lo que perdían de sus rentas, los echaron de España; y assí no ay de maravillar sin en la lengua española aya muchos vocablos hebreos, y juntamente arábigos, porque los unos y los otros habitaron gran tiempo en estas tierras mezclados. El rey Recaredo hizo cierta ley en materia tocante a reprimir las insolencias y los embustes de los judíos, y ellos le ofrecieron una gran suma de dineros porque la derogase o mederasse; y ni la codicia, ni la necessidad le pudo cegar para admitirlos. Verás a San Gregorio, *regist.*, lib. 7, epístola 126. En tiempo del rey don Enrique, cerca de los años de mil e treszientos e setenta, en las Cortés que se tuvieron en Toro, se mandó que los judíos que habitavan en el reyno, mezclados con los christianos, *truxessen cierta señal con que fuessen conocidos y diferenciados de los demás. Esos se llamaron judíos de señal.* Y el año de mil quatrocientos y cinco se ordenó y executó que los judíos truxessen por señal un pedaço de paño roxo, en forma redonda, sobre el ombro derecho. Y de aquí entiendo les vino el llamarlos los enalmagrados, porque parecía señal de almagre, qual se pone al ganado para distinguir un hato de otro, y dende a tres años mandaron traer a los moros otra señal de paño açul, en forma de luna menguante con cuernos, que casi hazía también forma redonda, juntando las dos puntas de los cuernos una con otra. (My emphasis. Covarrubias 1611: 719–20)
>
> Jew: ... Jews lived in Spain from many centuries back, until when, in our grandparents' time, the Catholic Monarchs drove them out of Spain, without regard as to what they would lose in taxes ... In the time of King Don Enrique, around the year 1370, in the Courts that were held in Toro, it was ordered that all Jews who lived in the kingdom, mixed with Christians, should wear a certain sign by which they would be known and differentiated from the rest. They were called signed Jews. And in the year 1405, it was ordered and executed that Jews should bear as their sign a piece of red cloth, cut in a circle, over their right shoulder ... and within three years, Moors were ordered to wear another sign made of blue cloth, in the shape of a waning moon with horns." (Portions of the definition translated by Dopico Black 2001: 41–42.)

of it, rather than on actual evidence. Foucault, in his lecture on March 17, 1976, when referring to the discipline of the modern state, says that "the discipline tries to rule a multiplicity of men to the extent that their multiplicity can and must be dissolved into individual bodies that can be kept under surveillance, trained, used, and, if need be, punished. And that the new technology that is being established is addressed to a multiplicity of men, not to the extent that they are nothing more than their individual bodies, but to the extent that they form, on the contrary, a global mass that is affected by overall processes characteristic of birth, death, production, illness, and so on" (Foucault 2003: 242–43). Although Foucault is referring to the changes that he sees happening in a modern state, I think that we can draw a very clear parallel with the situation that gave impulse to the creation of the Inquisition in Spain and the way it operated, in an open attempt to chip away at the phenomenon of the crypto-Judaism one converso at the time, developing a system intended to attack the global threat of the *other* as a strategy of state formation.

In this light, it then made perfect sense that the Tribunal of the Inquisition depended on the state and not on the church. This way, the Inquisition became the only institution with jurisdiction throughout the monarchy, and it consolidated as part of the machine in charge of organizing the center and destroying the ambivalence, as Bauman puts it, as the new order was being constructed:

> Into this Europe of nations, states, and nation-states, only Jews did not fit, having only gypsies for company. Jews were not an ethnic minority in any one of the nation-states, but dispersed all over the place. But neither were they locally residing members of a neighboring nation. They were the epitome of incongruity: a non-national nation, and so cast a shadow on the fundamental principal of modern European order: that nationhood is the essence of human destiny . . . The Jews were the most obvious ground for otherwise disparate class-bound and nation-bound anxieties, the most obvious buckle with which to pin such anxieties, hold them and harness them to state-initiated ideological mobilization, and the most obvious effigy in which to burn them (Bauman 1998: 153–54).

The situation with the indigenous peoples of the Americas started at a different point. Let us not forget the most obvious differences. In the first place, the expulsion of the Indians was not an option, an argument supported, among other, by the following facts: first, they had not invaded anybody's land but rather had been invaded by the newly arrived Spaniards: they were in their territory, and it was the role of the Spaniards to justify their presence there; second, the Indians were desperately needed as workforce, as the hands that would build the empire and, in this sense, the first so-called Indians were not necessarily seen as a threat.[48] Actually, the first Indians whom Columbus encountered were hospitable and friendly, and the admiral wrote with such awe of the friendly innocence and beauty of these Indians that he inadvertently put the first stone in the construction of the myth of the "noble savage," created much later:[49] "Ellos deben ser buenos servidores y de buen ingenio, que veo que muy presto dicen todo lo que les decía, y *creo que ligeramente se harían cristianos; que me pareció que ninguna secta tenían.* Yo, placiendo a Nuestro Señor, llevaré de aquí al tiempo de mi partida seis a V. A. para que deprendan fablar" (Columbus 1986: 62–63, my emphasis).[50]

It is true that Columbus harbored strong prejudices about the peaceful islanders whom he misnamed "Indians": he was prejudiced in their favor. For Columbus, they were "the handsomest men and the most beautiful women" he had ever encountered. He praised their generosity, contrasting their virtues with Spanish vices. He insisted that although they were without religion, they were not idolaters, placing them in an unusual purity that could be taken as a moral example for the Christians who "discovered" them, a blank canvas on which to start all over. For this reason he was confident that their conversion would come through gentle persuasion, through the use of their natural intelligence, and not through force (Jáuregui 2005: 124).

There is no evidence that Columbus thought that Indians were congenitally or biologically inferior to Europeans, but the fact that he denies their own identity counteracts the effect of the bucolic image that he paints: the Indians are not the creatures of Paradise and the New World is not the Garden of Eden, but to the eyes of he who does not look, that is all he can see. The search for identity other than the one that Spaniards constructed for the Indians becomes, then, a battle that they have been fighting for centuries.

Dussel (1992) puts this encounter in terms of "covering over" (*encubrimiento*) of the *other*, rather than discovery (*descubrimiento*), instead of the actual recognition of difference and the incorporation of it into Western civilization on its own terms. Rather, Dussel considers that looking at the inhabitants of the New World was not an exercise in looking outward but inward, that is, looking at the projection of the same in this other person standing there who, unknowingly, was thought of as the mirror of the newcomers (34). In Columbus's *Diary*, presented by Las Casas, the friar quotes the former as saying:

---

48 The Moors were always seen as one, since they had invaded the Iberian Peninsula. The situation of the Jews in Spain went through a lot of ups and downs; Jews sometimes enjoyed a privileged position and sometimes suffered persecution.

49 See Carlos Jáuregui (2005), especially chapter 1, pages 93 and following.

50 They must be good servants and quick-witted, that they quickly repeat we say. I, will take six of them with me so that they learn to talk before my return [my translation].

llegaron a una isleta de los lucayos, que se llamaba en lengua de indios Guanahani. Luego vinieron gente desnuda, y el Almirante salió a tierra en la barca armada . . . Mas me pareció que era gente muy pobre de todo. Ellos andan todos desnudos como su madre los parió, y también las mujeres, aunque no vide más de una farto moza. Y todos los que yo vi eran todos mancebos, que ninguno vide de edad de más de treinta años: muy bien hechos, de muy fermosos cuerpos y muy buenas caras: los cabellos gruesos cuasi como sedas de cola de caballos, e cortos: los cabellos traen por encima de las cejas, salvo unos pocos de tras que traen largos, que jamás cortan. Dellos se pintan de prieto, y ellos son de la color de los canarios, ni negros ni blancos, y dellos se pintan de blanco, y dellos de colorado, y dellos de lo que fallan, y dellos se pintan las caras, y dellos todo el cuerpo, y dellos solos los ojos, y dellos sólo el nariz.[51] (Las Casas 1967: 61–63)

As we see in this paragraph, Columbus does not see the natives but someone similar to the people in the Canary Islands, and whom he describes according to the world he just left and not with the open mind of somebody who is ready to encounter difference. He sees them in economic terms based on Westerner's view of the world, and physically, as a convenient mixture of the types found already.

For Columbus, the new people represent an early stage of Western civilization; they are himself, potential brothers in Christ, only more malleable and open to renewed possibilities; the same, only in a more primitive stage:

Tengo por dicho, serenísimos Príncipes—dice el Almirante—que sabiendo la lengua dispuesta suya personas devotas religiosas, que luego todos se tornarían cristianos; y así espero en Nuestro Señor que Vuestras Altezas se determinarán a ello con mucha diligencia para tornar a la Iglesia tan grandes pueblos, y los convertirán, así como han destruido aquellos que no quisieron confesar el Padre y el Hijo y el Espíritu Santo; y después de sus días, que todos somos mortales, dejarán sus reinos en muy tranquilo estado y limpios de herejía y maldad, y serán bien recebidos delante el Eterno Criador, al cual plega de les dar larga vida y acrecentamiento grande de mayores reinos y

---

51 My translation: They reached a small island of the Lucayan, called in the language of Indians Guanahani. Then they saw naked people, and Admiral came ashore . . . It seemed to me that they were very poor people. They walked naked as when they were born, and the women too, although I only saw one girl. And all I saw were young men, none above thirty years old: very well formed, with handsome bodies and good faces: their hair coarse, almost like the tail of a horse, and short; they wear their hair down over their eyebrows except for a little in the back which they wear long and never cut. Some of them paint themselves with black, and they are of the color of the Canarians, neither black nor white; and some of them paint themselves with white, and some with red, and some of them with whatever they find. And some of them paint their faces, and some the whole body, and some of them only the eyes, and some of them only the nose.

señoríos y voluntad y disposición para acrecentar la santa religión cristiana, así como hasta aquí tienen fecho, amén.[52] (Columbus 1986: 92–93)

But, even with this first experience, and sailing back in his second voyage with the intention of keeping the friendly, even loving, relations with the natives, there is a change of heart in the admiral, produced after he saw what was waiting for him in the settlement of Navidad.[53] So, in the letter that he wrote to the monarchs after his second arrival in the New World, on January 30, 1494, Columbus manifests his worries in the light of the vulnerability of the Spaniards left there.[54] Now he talks about the need of having guards around the garrison, something that would have been unthinkable in the light of the "noble savage" that Columbus presented in the beginning. Therefore, together with this created and idealized version of the inhabitants of the New World, there is a parallel portrait of other tribes that were assigned reputations for brutality and inhumanity provoked when Columbus discovered, horrified, that the sailors he had left behind in his first trip had been killed and possibly eaten by "cannibals."[55]

---

52 My translation: Most Serene Princes—says the Admiral—I believe that once dedicated and religious people knew their language and put it to use, they would all become Christians; and so I hope in Our Lord that Your Highnesses will determine with all speed to bring such great peoples to the Church and convert them, just as you have destroyed those who refused to confess the Father and the Son and the Holy Ghost; and at the end of your days, for we are all mortal, you will leave your kingdoms at ease, free from heresy and evil, and will be well received before the Eternal Creator, whom it may please to grant you long life and great increase of your many kingdoms and possessions, and the will and the inclination to spread the holy Christian religion as you have done so far. Amen.

53 On the night of December 24, 1492, the Santa María, commanded and owned by Juan de la Cosa and carrying aboard the admiral himself, Christopher Columbus, struck a coral reef in Cap-Haïtien Bay. Columbus was forced to take refuge in an indigenous village on Haiti's north shore and later sailed back to Spain aboard the Niña, but this ship did not have sufficient space aboard for the entire crew of the Santa María. Therefore the grounded ship was dismantled, and a fort was constructed ashore and stocked with supplies in order to house thirty-nine men who were to remain behind. Because of the day that it was built, the fort was named La Navidad, (Christmas). Thirty-nine crewmen were left behind in the tiny settlement and told to wait for Columbus's return. When he sailed back eleven months later, Columbus found the fort burned to the ground and the corpses of eleven of his men nearby. None of the thirty-nine was found alive (Fernández-Armesto 1991: 87 and 105 and following).

54 Although Columbus admits that most of the Indians are without malice, he starts being cautious about the potential risk they present: "También era gran inconveniente dexar acá los dolientes en logar abierto e choças, e las provisiones e mantenimientos que están en tierra, que, como quiere que estos indios se ayan mostrado a los descubridores e se muestran cada día muy simple e sin malicia, con todo, porque cada día vienen acá entre nosotros, nos pareció que fuera buen consejo meter a riesgo e a ventura de perderse esta gente e los mantenimientos, lo que un indio con un tizón podría fazer poniendo fuego a las choças, porque de noche e de día siempre van e vienen, e a causa d'ellos tenemos guardas en el campo, mientras que la poblaçión está avierta e sin defensión" ("Memorial a Torres [1494]," in Columbus 1984: 149).

55 "Cannibal" (from Spanish caníbal) is another misnomer (as the term "Indian" that I have been using throughout my book) born in connection with alleged cannibalism among the Caribe people. This term appears for the first time in the Diary on November 23:

"El viento era Lesnordeste y razonable para ir al Sur, sino que era poco; y sobre este cabo encavalga otra tierra o cabo que va también al Leste, a quien aquellos indios que llevaba llamaban Bohío, la cual decían que era muy grande y que había en ella gente que tenía un ojo

Similarly, when Bernal Díaz reflected, many years later, on his arrival to Mexico with the army of Hernán Cortés, he remembers that he and his fellow Spaniards were not shocked to witness slavery, the subjugation of women, or brutal treatment of war captives. But they were appalled by the native cannibalism and human sacrifices.

But to go back to Columbus's letter, sent to the Catholic Monarchs via Antonio Torres (captain of the *Marigalante* and governor of the city called Isabela), this is the document in which Columbus proposes, for the first time, to initiate the slavery of the natives as part of the practices of the new empire and as the tool of the physical and cultural colonization that was on its way. Columbus phrases his proposal in the following way:

> Sus Altesas podrán dar liçençia e permiso a un número de carabelas suficiente que vengan acá cada año, e trayan de los dichos ganados e otros mantenimientos e cosas de poblar el campo e aprovechar la tierra, y esto en precios razonables a sus costas de los que les truxieren, las cuales cosas se les podrían pagar en esclavos d'estos caníbales, gente tan fiera e dispuesta e bien proporcionada e de muy buen entendimiento, los cuales, quitados de aquella inhumanidad creemos que serán mejores que otros ningunos esclavos . . . y d'esto traeréis o enbiaréis respuesta, porque acá se fagan los aparejos que son menester con más confiança, si a Sus Altesas pareciere bien.[56] (Columbus 1984: 154)

---

en la frente, y otros que se llamaban *caníbales*, a quien mostraban tener gran miedo" (103, my emphasis).

Jáuregui points out that the term "cannibal" constitutes a verbal confluence: Columbus originally assumed the natives of Cuba were subjects of the Great Khan and connects the "Caniba" or "Canima" with him ("Kannibals"):

> "Toda la gente que hasta hoy ha hallado diz que tiene grandísimo temor de los Caniba o Canima, y dicen que viven en esta isla de Bohío, la cual debe ser muy grande, según le parece, y cree que van a tomar a aquéllos a sus tierras y casas, como sean muy cobardes y no saber de armas. Y a esta causa le parecía que aquellos indios que traían no suelen poblarse a la costa de la mar, por ser vecinos a esta tierra, los cuales diz que después que le vieron tomar la vuelta de esta tierra no podían hablar temiendo que los habían de comer, y no les podía quitar el temor, y decían que no tenían sino un ojo y la cara de perro, y creía el Almirante que mentían, y sentía el Almirante que debían de ser del señorío del Gran Can, que los captivaban." (November 26, Jáuregui 2005: 107)

Therefore Columbus, thinking he heard Caniba or Canima, he thought that these were the dog-headed men (cane-bal) that everybody feared (see Jáuregui 2005: 68–89).

56 My translation: Your majesties could give me license and approve a good number of caravels that they may come every year and bring cattle and other things to populate the fields and work the land at a reasonable cost, which we could pay with slaves of these cannibals, fierce people, but well built and proportioned and of good understanding who, taken away from that inhumanity, we believe will be better than any other slaves . . . And you should bring or send a response to this so we can easily make the arrangements that are needed, if your majesties consider it appropriate.

Vilches (2004: 214) reminds us that previously, in the "Relación del segundo viaje," Columbus declared that he was "sending a map with the location of gold and spices to minimize the fact that he [had] found nothing of value except the natives and that he [had] instructed Antonio de Torres to sell a cargo of 500 enslaved Indians."

Therefore, far from the first evangelical mission that Columbus talks about repeatedly during his first voyage, the second and following incorporate a clear change of priorities in which the exploitation for commercial purpose have displaced the search for spiritual salvation (his or anybody else's). Therefore, if the Indians first encountered were optimal for receiving the word of God, the new ones, specifically the Caribs, are only presented as a possible labor force on the grounds of their aggressiveness, and Columbus only talks about their baptism as a way of making them better servants, but never equals. Baptism is then perceived as a tool against inhumanity and savagery, a tool to incorporate the *other* into the modern state, the passport for the ultimate salvation. In this setting the comparison between the Indian *other* and the peninsular heathens (Moors and Jews) was at hand:

> Dixo qu' el domingo antes, onze de Noviembre, le había parecido que fuera bien tomar algunas personas de las de aquel río para llevar a los Reyes porque aprendieran nuestra lengua, para saber lo que hay en la tierra y porque volviendo sean lenguas de los cristianos y tomen nuestras costumbres y las cosas de la Fe, "porque yo vi e cognozco"—dice el Almirante—qu' esta gente no tiene secta ninguna ni son idólatras, salvo muy mansos y sin saber qué sea mal ni matar a otros ni prender, y sin armas y tan temerosos que a una persona de los nuestros fuyen ciento de ellos, aunque burlen con ellos, y crédulos y cognocedores que hay Dios en el çielo, e firmes que nosotros habemos venido del cielo, y muy presto a cualquiera oración que nos les digamos que digan y hacen el señal de la cruz. Así que deben Vuestras Altezas determinarse a los hacer cristianos, que creo que si comienzan, en poco tiempo acabará de los haber convertido a nuestra Santa Fe multidumbre de pueblos, y cobrando grandes señoríos y riquezas y todos sus pueblos de la España, porque sin duda es en estas tierras grandísimas sumas de oro, que no sin causa dicen estos indios que yo traigo, que ha en estas islas lugares adonde cavan el oro y lo traen al pescuezo, a las orejas y a los brazos e a las piernas, y son manillas muy gruesas, y también ha piedras y ha perlas preciosas y infinitas especerías.[57] (November 12, 1594)

---

57 My translation: He said that the previous Sunday, 11 November, he thought it was a good idea to capture some of the people from that river and to take them to the monarchs to learn our language, so that we would know what there is in this land and so that on their return they could act as interpreters for the Christians and adopt our customs and faith. For I have seen and recognize—says the Admiral—that these people have no religion, nor are they idolaters, rather they are very gentle and know nothing of evil, nor murder nor theft nor weapons, and so scared that a hundred of them flee from one of our people even though they may only be teasing them. They are trusting and know that there is a God in heaven, and firmly believe that we have come from heaven, and they are ready to repeat any prayer that we say to them and they make the sign of the cross. So Your Highnesses must resolve to make them Christians, for I believe that once you begin you will in a short space you would have converted a multitude of peoples and acquired great kingdoms and riches and all their peoples for Spain. Because without doubt there is in these lands a huge amount of gold, and not without reason do these Indians I bring with me say that there are in these islands places where they dig up gold and wear it at the neck and from the ears and in very thick bracelets on their arms and legs. And there are also pearls and precious stones and infinite spices.

González de Eslava, a Spanish playwright who developed his career in Mexico in the second half of the sixteenth century, points out this parallelism, and in his *Primer Coloquio* introduces the element of race as something that disturbs human nature, a stain in our natural cloth that links the categories of physicality with non-Christianity, as is the case of Indians, Jews and Moors:

LETRADO: Pues dezidme: ¿de qué modo
          Vino Dios a tener lana?

PENITENCIA: Con una inuención galana,
             Haziendo paño de lodo,
             Que es nuestra natura humana.

LETRADO: Admirable fue la traça
          Con que lo traçó el Diuino.

PENITENCIA: De esta tela el mal nos vino,
             Porque en fin cayó la raza
             En este paño tan fino.

LETRADO: *¿Con qué raza se dañó*
          Paño de tanta excelencia?

PENITENCIA: *Con raza de inobediencia,*
             Quando el mando quebrantó
             de la suma Providencia . . .

YGLESIA: Los Iudíos no preciavan
          Este paño que les dieron;
          Vestirse dél no quisieron;
          Porque en tinieblas andavan,
          Nunca le comprendieron.[58] (González de Eslava 1998: vv.
          121–35 and 731–35, my emphasis)

---

58 LAWYER: So tell me, in what way
           Did God have wool?

PENITENCE: With elegant invention
            Making a cloth of mud,
            Which is our human nature.

LAWYER: Admirable was the design
         That the Divine drew.

PENITENCE: We were unlucky with this cloth
            Because in the end race fell
            On this fine garment.

LAWYER: Which race harmed
         This excellent cloth?

⟶ Race, therefore, becomes a mark of Christian disobedience,[59] a step toward heresy

| PENITENCE: | The race of nonobedience
When it broke the authority
Of Holy Providence. |
| CHURCH: | Jews didn't appreciate
The cloth they were given.
They didn't want to wear it;
Because they walked in darkness
They never understood it. |

59 Let us not forget that the first time that the term *raza* appeared in a dictionary (Covarrubias 1611: 896–97), it was referred to something very different from what we understand nowadays and related, in its second definition, to the cloth that González de Eslava also links it to:

La casta de cavallos castizos, a los quales señalan con hierro para que sean conocidos. Raza en el paño, la hilaza que diferencia de los demás hilos de la trama. Parece averse dicho *quasi* reaza, porque *aza* en lengua toscana, vale hilo y la raza en el paño sobrepuesto desigual. Raza, en los linages se toma en la mala parte, como tener alguna raza de moro o judío. (My translation: The race of pure-blood horses, which were marked with irons to be reconized. Texture in the cloth, the string that is different from the others because in the language in Toscany thread is distinguishable over the cloth as different. Race, in regards to lineage, is used negatively, like the race of Moors or Jews.)

Covarrubias defines "linage" (lineage) as "La descendencia de las casas y familias. Díxose *a linea* porque van descendiendo de padres, hijos y nietos, etc. como por línea recta" (Covarrubias 1611: 768). (My translation: Offspring of a family or house. The line that descends from parents to children to grandchildren, etc. like a straight line.)

Later on, in 1734, the *Diccionario de Autoridades* expands on the notion of race though, first, it confirms the definition given by Covarrubias: "Casta o calida del origen o linage. Hablando de los hombres, se toma mui regularmente en mala parte." What comes next is where *Autoridades* really innovates, since it contributes a definition thought out by the Orden de Calatrava, one of the military-religious orders that had been essential in the process of Reconquista. According to Calatrava, then, race was directly related to lineage, understood as a straight line also carrying religion with it:

Ordenamos y mandamo que ninguna persona, de qualquiera calidad y condicion que fuere, sea recibida a la dicha Orden, ni se le dé el Hábito, sino fuere Hijodalgo, al fuero de España, de partes de padre y madre y de avuelos de emtrambas partes, y de legitimo matrimonio nacido, y que no le toque *raza* de Judio, Moro, Herege ni Villano.

[*We order and decree that no person, of whatever quality or condition, be received in the said Order, nor be given its Habit, unless he be of noble descent, according to the law of Spain, on the part of father and mother and grandparents of both, and born of legitimate marriage, and not tainted by the race of Jew, Moor, Heretic, or Lowborn] (Translated in Greer 2007: preface.)*

The second mention of race in *Diccionario de Autoridades* (1964) comes from Father Mariana's *History of Spain* (1699: Book 22, chapter 1): "No de otra manera que los sembrados y animales, la *raza* de los hombres, y casta, con la propiedad del Cielo y de la tierra, sobre todo con el tiempo se muda y se embastarda." (Not differently from sown fields and animals, the race and caste of men, with the influence of the heavens and the earth and above all over time, changes and is bastardized. Translated in *Rereading the Black Legend*, preface.) Finally, I think it necessary to offer the definition that Covarrubias gives of "casta," which he conceives as "Linage noble y castizo, el que es de buena linea y descendencia; no embargante que dezimos es de buena casta, y mala casta" (316). Later on, the *Diccionario de Autoridades* would see it as "Generacion y linage que viene de padres conocidos" and, following the same line opened in the definition of race, *Autoridades* links *casta* with religion: "Y que de su *casta* y sangre nacería el Mesías, y todas las gentes serían benditas por él" (219).

that was full known in the Spain of the Reconquista and that was preached against in the new territories.[60] But before going to Mexico, the Spanish conquistadores would still find two intermediate steps: the war of Granada and the conquest of most of the Canary Islands, events and spaces that would end up becoming a laboratory in which to practice the skills that were later needed in the newly found land: the Indies.

THE FIRST EXPANSIONISTIC EXPERIMENTS

The war of Granada was specially useful as a preparation for what Spaniards would have to face in the near future. Among other things, this war made the inhabitants of Spain get used to living in conflict, and it encouraged them to pursue other endeavors involving military action. It also stimulated mobility among the population; that is, as the expulsion of both Moors and Jews was advancing, there were plenty of areas in the Iberian Peninsula that suffered from great underpopulation, and the need to claim these areas under the flag of Christianity made migration movements easier all over the territory, taking away the fear of leaving your birthplace for the unknown, a factor that would be key when the transatlantic adventures started demanding this kind of mobility. This war also fortified the authority of the monarchy, in this case under the direction of Isabella and Ferdinand, but the effect extended to the institution in general, creating a sense of central power that added cohesion toward the pursuit of a common goal. In this sense this same effort in pulling all the resources available got the nobility, and their assets, involved in a campaign against the "infidel" that would be essential in Granada but also on the other side of the "Ocean Sea," as the Atlantic was known. At the same time this religious component was strong enough to become one of the popes' main points of reference, with repeated bulls released on the matter (since the thirteenth century) and a call to all Christians to lend a hand in a conflict that became the seed for an international collaboration open to all Christendom and that changed the character of the war of Granada. Thus, instead of limiting itself to be an internal, national issue, it developed an almost pan-Christian dimension that would spread like wildfire. But also, together with this papal support came a sense of *doing the right thing*, to be participating in a just war that was needed, urgent, unavoidable, and completely free of questioning. This war, with all these implications, and especially the final victory, would be a source of pride for all Spaniards and for every good Christian, creating, on the one hand, a sense of belonging, of nation building, and on the other, a sense of

---

60 The irony reaches unsuspected height when we consider that González de Eslava, who here writes about the Jewish religion as a stain in nature, was himself suspected to be a converso, as stated by Othón Arróniz Baez in his edition of the *Coloquios* (González de Eslava 1998: 10), and may very well have left Spain in the 1550s, when the persecution became more threatening.

ties within a solid community. Last but not least, what the war of Granada brought to attention was a clear and open confrontation with other cultures, with an *other* that, as well as the Jews, was too close for comfort and that was seen as interfering in the process of conforming a national unity. This open conflict involved a clear disdain and invalidation of other forms of living, of worshipping, and of relating to each other, and it contributed to the idea that pushing aside other cultures was not only acceptable, but rewarded, promoting a dangerous behavior that would bring terrible consequences. Therefore, it was understood that the peoples conquered could be annulled by the conqueror, expelled, or eradicated in what became both territorial and physical colonialism, but also a cultural invasion of the space of the *other*.

Moreover, the arduous process of conquest of the Canary Islands,[61] together with the previous experiences accumulated during the siege and conquest of Granada, would become, for the Spanish sailors and men-at-arms, the practice ground for what was to come in the adventures of the still unknown New World.[62] Therefore, in my opinion, the conquest of the Canary Islands contributed in the following ways: First of all, and emphasizing a fact that had already been present in Granada, the conquest of these islands put in plain view the issue of confrontation with other cultures, here in the plural as it would be found in the Americas, and it deepened the feeling of entitlement that the Spanish conquistadores had adopted when confronting the *other*. Once again, it was acceptable and almost expected to disdain other forms of living, other civilizations, and to exercise a moral and cultural intolerance that had been learned in a Spain obsessed with the limpieza de sangre and the inquisitorial way of belonging. Following this vein, the arrival of the Spaniards

---

61 The Canary Islands have been known since antiquity. They probably established contact with Greeks and Phoenicians, and are already mentioned in Roman texts (by Pliny the Elder). During the Middle Ages, the islands were visited by Arabs for commercial purposes. After that, especially in the fourteenth century, numerous visits were made by sailors originally, mainly, of Portugal and Genoa, but it was not until 1312 that somebody, other than the native population, settled in the islands. This first foreign settler was Lancelotto Malocello, a Genoese navigator whose name inspired that of the island of Lanzarote, where he settled. His source of funding, in part Portuguese, can be taken to mean that, at least in some proportion, the first expedition to colonize the island was Portuguese in origin and not Castilian. At the time of their incorporation into the European imaginary, the Canary Islands were inhabited by a variety of indigenous communities. The real process of conquest of the island started with the expedition of Juan de Béthencourt and Gadifer de la Salle, Norman nobles who, with the approval of Pope Clement VI and under the orders of King Henry III of Castile, sailed to the island of Lanzarote in 1402. Nevertheless and due to the difficulties of the terrain, the completion of the conquest was postponed until 1496, the year when Tenerife surrendered and the Canary Islands got incorporated into the patrimony belonging to the Crown of Castile. The arduous process of conquest, together with the previous experience during the siege and conquest of Granada, would become, for the Spanish sailors and men-at-arms, the practice ground for what was to come in the adventures of the New World.

62 On the Canary Islands working as a antecedent for the conquest of the New World, see Elliott (1964: 58); and Merediz (2004: ch. 2).

meant the eradication, or at least the pushing aside, of the local cultures with no regard for the communities attached to them.

Second, and as a way of filling the vacuum left by what was taken away, the Spaniards started actively trying to spread Christianity, attempting to incorporate the natives into the ways and customs of the newly arrived and were not so worried about the purity or even the understanding of all the intricate details of the faith. In this sense it is important to notice how Spaniards not only colonialized the present and future of the indigenous population, but also their past, and dared create a Christian genealogy by which the presence of the Virgin in a time previous to the conquest is built as a sign of what was to come, that is, as a justification for the military conquest superseded by higher motives, like the conversion of the natives.[63] Also, the supposed presence of this image before the arrival of the Spaniards and their attempts to convert are clearly intended to give an image of "just war" to the whole affair by implying that the military advance had been determined by a divine plan and, therefore, was not to be questioned.

Third, what the contact with the natives in the Canary Islands brings into the European picture is a first look at an *other* different from the ones known so far, that is, a racially different subject, different from the Jews and Moors who had been alienated, and that had to find its place in the old order of things. This *other*, that Columbus thinks of frequently in his contacts with the *American other*, becomes a point of reference by which to judge subsequent experiences and by which to adjust expectations on the other side of the Atlantic.

In any case, with the incorporation of the Canary Islands into the Western World, a new area of influence completes itself; that is, with the Portuguese Azores in the north, the Spanish Canaries in the south, and the coasts of the Iberian Peninsula and Africa in the east, the *Atlantic Mediterranean* is enclosed, according to the term coined by F. Fernández-Armesto (1987: 152). Nevertheless, I would rather refer to this new circle of influence as the "Catholic Atlantic," a creation not only in the geographical and political sense, but also, and more important, in the colonial aspect, an area where the Catholic values are implanted as a portal through which to access the ways of the European societies and cultures. This "inner sea," created by European sailors as a way to mark the limits of the navigation at the time, the horizons of the known world, becomes the first oceanic laboratory in which to exercise the cultural and geographical colonialization that was still in its early stages of development.

This first encounter with a different *other* is described by many (see, for example, López de Gómara's [1991] dedication of his *Historia General de las Indias* to Charles V) as a continuation of the process of conversion already started in Spain and that

---

63 I will return to the discussion of the presence of the Virgin below.

pursued the spread of Christianity to other cultures as a way of incorporating them into the Spanish values and erasing the differences between the two:

> Los sereníssimos prínçipes don Fernando y doña Isabel, con entrañable deseo que han avido e tienen a serviçio de Nuestro Señor, no solamente han querido fazer guerra a los moros enemigos de nuestra sancta fee, mas trabajaron por a ella a convertir los canarios que de tantos siglos acá han estado fuera del conocimiento de Nuestro Señor.[64] Y como ya algunas yslas de Canaria estuviesen conquistadas y las gentes dellas convertidas y quedase la Gran Canaria obstinada en el desconocimiento de Nuestro Señor, determinaron de enviar por governador de las yslas ganadas e por conquistar la Gran Canaria a Pedro de Vera, veynte y cuatro de Jerez, por ser cavallero esforzado e tal qual les paresçía que convenía para tener el cargo que le davan . . . E visto por los canarios el grand daño que recibían, enbiaron a él a le decir que le plugiese de les dar paz e querían ser cristianos, de lo qual pusieron luego en obra bautizándose muchos dellos, y enbiaron al rey y reyna quatro canarios principales para les dar la obediencia, la qual les dieron en Calatayud. (Diego de Valera 1934, chapter XXXXVII)[65]

This fragment of the *Fontes Rerum Canariaum* by Diego de Valera belongs to the accounts of what happened in 1482 and, in my opinion, leaves no room for doubts.[66] It assumes that the desire to convert the remainder of the islands is the motor that moves the expeditions and pushes aside more practical reasons such as economic and political agendas that, though they were definitely at the core of the operation,

---

64 This sentence seems to imply that there had been knowledge of the Catholic religion prior to the arrival of the Spaniards. Some speculation on this sense has been fed by the myths around the legendary figure of Saint Brendan, an Irish monk very famous in the Celtic folklore. According to the legend, he sailed in search of Paradise and arrived to a cluster of unknown islands ("The promised land of the Saints"), for some located in the Caribbean and for most identified with the Canary Islands (*The New Encyclopedia Britannica* 2005: "Brendan, Saint").

65 Diego de Valera (1934: chapter XXXVII). My translation: Their Serene Highness, don Fernando and Dona Isabel, having served God Our Lord with diligence, not only had they fought the Moors, enemies of our faith, but also they worked for it in order to convert the Canarians that had been out of the knowledge of God for so long. And although some of the Canarian islands were already conquered and converted their people, the isle of Grand Canary persevered in their ignorance of God, so they determined to send the governor of the conquered islands and Pedro de Vera, clerk of Xerez, zealous man and fit for the job, to conquer the island . . . As soon as the Canarians saw the great harm they received, they asked for peace and for the Christian faith and many were baptized, and they sent to the king and queen four Canarian chiefs to pay obedience in Calatayud.

66 Diego de Valera (Cuenca, 1412; Puerto de Santa María, Cádiz, 1488), Spanish writer and historian. He lived the life of a knight: he worked for Juan II of Castile, fought in the battles of Toro and Higueruela (1431), and traveled all over Europe serving the kings Charles VIII of France and Albert of Bohème. He was also the Spanish ambassador of Castle in Denmark, England, and France. As a writer, he left among his works, the *Crónica abreviada o Valeriana* (1482); the *Crónica de los Reyes Católicos*, which includes from 1474 until 1488; and the *Fontes Rerum Canariaum*, plus multiple treatises on weapons and letters with advice for different monarchs (*Diccionario de literatura Española* 1972: 911).

are chosen to be left in the dark in benefit of the more altruistic intention. For this same reason, being a war of Catholics against infidels, it is considered to be just and necessary; therefore, the military conquest and the cultural eradication derived from it are seen as justified and so is the presence of the Spanish colonial power as the means necessary in order to get to an ulterior prize: the spread of Christianity. In this sense, beyond the differences among Jews, Moors or Canarians (and later on, Indians), they all constitute the alterity that is assimilated by the actions of the faith, a system of values that is spread to facilitate the incorporation of the *other* into a colonial machinery that is willing to accept anyone, independent of their origin, as long as they behave like the center. From this same point of view, and as we see in the chronicle of Mosén Diego Valera (1934), surrender necessarily had to be accompanied by baptism.

Part of the scheme to facilitate the conversion of the natives of the Canary Islands was slipped into their own past, integrating the Catholic religion that they were trying to resist into their "original" folklore as read by the colonizers. It is at this point that someone notices the appearance of the Virgen de Candelaria, supposedly already in the islands when the Spaniards arrived. The account of this episode is offered by Espinosa in his *Guanches of Tenerife*, where he states that "In this island and among the people I have described, God was served that one of the greatest relics in the world, and the one that has worked most miracles, should appear many years before the light of faith or the news of the evangel reached them . . . a gift so supernatural, a favour so unusual, a benefit so immense, a piece of good fortune so great, as the most holy image of Candelaria [which] appeared on the island" (Espinosa 1907: 45). When I read these lines and think of this episode, I cannot help but to establish a connection with the myth of Viracocha, the Incan god, and, though I am aware of the differences between the two stories, some details in both myths have a very similar echo. In the latter, and while they awaited the second coming of the god Viracocha, the Incans welcomed the Spaniards in a first instance, since they thought they were representing the expected god, and called them by that name, therefore facilitating the initial moments of the Spanish incursion. In a parallel way, the presence beforehand of the Virgen de Candelaria *helps* prepare the arrival of the conquistadores in a myth that a posteriori justifies the noble mission of the Spaniards and emphasizes the equally noble nature of the natives, though, in the case of the Canaries, that did not reduce the strength of the resistance put up by the natives.

In general, the Guanches are said not to have "any law, nor ceremonies, nor god like other nations.[67] Although they knew of God and called Him by various names

---

67 The precolonial population of the Canaries is generically referred to as Guanches, though, strictly speaking, this term is only appropriate for the original inhabitants of Tenerife, since in Gran Canaria

and appellations" (Espinosa 1907: 29); therefore, they were somehow seen as *predisposed* to receive the Catholic religion, prepared beforehand and just waiting for what was about to happen. Just as the Indians would be later seen (at least in Columbus's first voyage), the Guanches "were uncontaminated Gentiles, without rites, sacrificial ceremonies, or worship of fictitious gods, or intercourse with devils like other nations" (Espinosa 1907: 41), a blank slate ready to be civilized.

One aspect calls my attention, and it is the fact that, in Valera's chronicle of the conquest of the Canary Islands, there is no mention of the physicality of the newly found Canarians, and it is Columbus who covers this gap, facilitating only one detail. When he arrives in the Indies and sees the inhabitants for the first time, he compares them with what he already knows and says that they are of the "same skin color as the Canaries, neither black nor white" (October 11), an observation that he repeats in a number of occasions during his first voyage.[68] He attributes this similarity in skin color to the fact that both groups live in the same line, in the same latitude, establishing a correspondence between people's identity and their geography as well as racial differences in terms of climatic circumstances.[69] Also, in the same way that Columbus compares the people's skin color, he establishes a link between the newly found reality and his best point of reference, the last known port that he had seen before he sailed into the unknown: the Canary Islands: "De aquel puerto se parecía un valle grandísimo y todo labrado, que desciende a él del Sueste, todo cercado de montañas altísimas que parece que llegan al cielo, y hermosísimas, llenas de árboles verdes, y sin duda que hay allí montañas más altas que la isla de Tenerife en Canaria, que es tenida por de las más altas que puede hallarse" (December 20).[70]

---

there were Canarii, in La Gomera Gomeros, and so on, displaying an array of cultures that cooperated occasionally but that maintained their independence from each other. Also, these civilizations did not develop in isolation, since there are accounts of contacts with other peoples since antiquity.

68 His first statement dates from Oct. 11: "ellos son de la color de los canarios, ni negros ni blancos." On November 6, he repeats the same information, this time referring to the women in the Canary Islands (Columbus 1986).

69 "Luego que amaneció vinieron a la playa muchos de estos hombres, todos mancebos, como dicho tengo, y todos de buena estatura, gente muy fermosa: los cabellos no crespos, salvo corredios y gruesos, como sedas de caballo, y todos de la frente y cabeza muy ancha más que otra generación que fasta aquí haya visto, y los ojos muy fermosos y no pequeños, y ellos ninguno prieto, salvo de la color de los canarios, ni se debe esperar otra cosa, pues está Lesteoueste con la isla del Hierro, en Canaria, so una línea" (Columbus 1986: Saturday, October 13). (My translation: As soon as it dawned, many of these people came to the beach—all young, as I have said, and all of good stature—very handsome people, with their hair not curly but straight and coarse, like horsehair; and all of them had very wide foreheads and heads, wider than any other people that I have seen so far. Their eyes were very pretty and not small; and none of them are black, but of the color of the Canarians. Nor should anything else be expected since this island is on an east-west line with the island of Hierro in the Canaries.)

70 My translation: From that harbor could be seen a very wide valley, all cultivated, running down to the harbor from the South East, surrounded on all sides by very high mountains which seem to reach to the sky, and very beautiful, covered in green trees. Without doubt there are mountains there which are higher than the island of Tenerife in the Canaries, which is held to be one of the highest to be found.

Finally, I would like to add, in terms of the things the Spaniards tried in the Canary Islands before going to the New World, the consideration that was given to the natives. Espinosa, in referring to the conquest of Tenerife, points out that the Spanish purpose was to give employment to the natives and not to start an empire: "He [Governor of Canaria, Pedro de Vera] prepared his Canarians by telling them that if they fought like men, and were loyal, they would receive great benefits, and the king, their lord, would show them much favour . . . For the object was not to found a colony, but to give employment to the Canarians" (Espinosa 1907: 86).

Therefore, according to this statement, the Canarians could possibly be treated as equals, just like the Spaniards, only if they showed their alliance to the king. But this possibility seems to evaporate extremely soon, and, for the first time, the colonizers practice slavery and commerce of slaves in their new colonies, something that the natives would protest before the authorities.

The Spaniards invited these allies to come on board, sail was made, and a great many were carried off in this way, to be sold as slaves. The Spaniards thought they might thus repair their fortunes, which is against all reason. Some of those who were sold as slaves, being now taken inland, went to the kings to ask for justice and liberty; explaining that, being free in their own country, they had been carried off to where they now were, by treachery, and sold as slaves, being free men, friends, and allies. The kings ordered that they should be set free, and remain free (Espinosa 1907: 97).

But, although it is presented as a daring move, in spite of the complaints by the indigenous people, the key here is to realize a tendency that initiated in the Canaries and that would continue in the New World.

FIRST IMPRESSIONS OF NEW SPAIN: A LANDSCAPE OF IDOLATRY

In this light, the first thing that the Spaniards notice, at least as told by the account of Bernal Díaz del Castillo, is the places of worship that the Mexicas devote to their pagan idols.[71] Immediately after Cortés's men, eager to find their fortune, realize that those little idols made of simple clay are surrounded by offerings of gold, and

---

71 Let us remember that Bernal Díaz del Castillo (1492–1584) wrote his account many years after the actual events took place. He started writing in 1568, almost fifty years later. In my opinion, his account has multiple advantages and disadvantages, among others, the fact that he wrote so many years later plays an important role in relation to memory, either consciously or unconsciously selective. Of course, no recollection is ever perfect and Díaz del Castillo's is not an exception, which is the reason why I choose to contrast it with Cortés's. Díaz's account is also tainted by the fact that he offered his account as an alternative to the story told by the hagiographic biographers of Hernán Cortés (among them Francisco López de Gómara) who were accused of downplaying the role of the hundreds of soldiers and sailors (Díaz among them) who were instrumental in bringing down the Aztec empire.

SHOULD CONSIDER THAT BERNAL
FOLLOWS GÓMARA MORE THAN
MEMORY

suddenly, the mission seems worthy (Díaz del Castillo 1999: 67). Therefore, the
Spaniards who arrive in Mexico take these idols as a sign of the gold that they are
about to encounter, as evidence of its geographical proximity and, in some occasions, as the perfect excuse to ask about the source of that material, that is about
the mines, where they hope to find more of it: "Pues otra cosa preguntaba el
Diego Velázques a aquellos indios, que si había minas de oro en su tierra; y a todos
les respondían que sí y les mostraban el oro en polvo de lo que sacaban en la isla
de Cuba y decían que había mucho en su tierra, y no decían verdad, porque claro
está que en la punta de Cotoche ni en todo Yucatán no es donde hay minas de oro"[72]
(76–77). So, at least in the eyes of Díaz del Castillo, the idea of providing salvation
to the souls of the Indians was not so much a priority (this author does not even
comment on the idolatrous character of the idols he sees), but rather the men in the
expedition seemed more interested in finding the raw material of which those idols
were made. In the same line we can place the Spanish use of the places of worship as
ordinary dormitories as described by Díaz: "También quiero decir cómo yo sembré
unas pepitas de naranjas junto a otras casas de ídolos, y fue desta manera: que como
había muchos mosquitos en aquel río, fuime a dormir a una casa alta de ídolos e
allí a aquella sembré siete u ocho pepitas de naranjas que había traído de Cuba e
nacieron muy bien"[73] (96). In this case we can see that there seems to be no extra
thought given to the fact that those places that they use to sleep in, in order to avoid
the mosquitoes are, in reality, devoted to worship the same idols the Spanish soldiers seem to hate. Therefore, the Spaniards use these buildings according to their
own convenience, the same way that they intend to use the raw material the pagan
idols are made of, with no further worries about the function that either one of
these things perform for the Indians as the very instruments of a devotion that the
Spaniards think of as an abomination.

From this materialistic perspective of the idolatry of the Indians, there is only a
small step to the plundering of those places of prayer, especially when the conquistadores do not obtain the answers they are looking for or when greed gets in the
way of reasoning, as we can see in the case of Alvarado, who has no qualms when it
comes to taking the offerings left for the idols, as Díaz del Castillo describes: "De
las gallinas mandó Pedro de Alvarado que tomasen hasta cuarenta dellas, y también
en una casa de adoratorios de ídolos tenían unos paramentos de mantas viejas e

---

72 My translation: Diego de Velazques asked those Indians repeatedly whether they were goldmines in their
    land; and all of them answered yes and they showed him the powder gold that they got in the isle of
    Cuba and they said that there was a lot in their land, but they were not truthful because it is clear in not
    in the Point of Cotoche nor anywhere in Yucatán are there goldmines.
73 My translation: I also want to say that I planted some orange seeds next to some houses of idols for as
    there were many mosquitos near the river, I went to sleep in a house of idols and there I planted seven or
    eight orange seeds that I had brought from Cuba and they did very well.

unas arquillas donde estaban unas como diademas e ídolos, cuentas e pintajillos de oro bajo, e también se les tomó dos indios e una india; y volvimos al pueblo donde desembarcamos"[74] (Díaz del Castillo 1999: 118). Testimonies like these make Indians appear to be much more spiritual people and certainly much more respectful than the Spaniards, who present a clear portrait of brutality and closed-mindedness, qualities that, ironically, they were trying to attribute to the Indians they had in front of them.

The way that Spaniards used to approach the Indians at first—that is, focused much more on their search for gold than on the spiritual salvation of the "newly-discovered" peoples—took a different turn when the explorers found evidence of a practice completely out of their frame of mind. I am referring to the proofs of the human sacrifices that the Mexicas were performing and that threw Spaniards into a cultural shock that made them take a different course of action. Therefore, the repeated evidence of human sacrifices became a turning point and moved Spaniards closer to the pastoral mission that, traditionally, was thought of as being the main objective of their out-of-boundaries expeditions. But, although this progression appears clear in Díaz del Castillo's account of the Spanish arrival in Mexico, I would like to emphasize the fact that the incorporation of the topic of conversion is still not brought up for the improvement of a culture that performs human sacrifices but, more accurately, as a way to ensure the survival of the conquistadores themselves, who thought they would be much safer in the new lands if the Indians converted. Thus, the final goal is not so much to make perfect Catholics out of the Indians but to make sure that the Spaniards are not themselves sacrificed, as some of the foreign visitors that they saw who never went back home (see Carlos Jáuregui 2005: esp. ch. 1). Therefore, it is only after the Spaniards see what the future can hold if you are a foreigner in the hands of the indigenous populations that we encounter the first evidence of an incipient movement toward the conversion of the Indians to Christianity, but, as I pointed out above, I am inclined to believe that this turn has more to do with assuring their own survival than with spreading the Gospel, since before, as soon as they saw the idols and the places of worship, they did not react as strongly and only paid attention to the material profit that they could obtain from the native idolatry.

It should not come as a surprise that one of the first converts and, therefore, the person used as advertisement of what any Indians could become if only they let themselves be guided by the Spaniards, is la Malinche (and later Cortés's companion,

---

74 My translation: Of the hens, Pedro de Alvarado asked us to take forty of them and also, in a prayer house they had some old blankets and chests where they kept diadems and idols, beads and paintings of gold, and also we took two male Indians and a female; and we went to the village where we unloaded.

Doña Marina), who finds her truth in the new religion and in the cooperation with
the newly arrived:

NOT SO !

+

FAIRY TALE

> [El capitán Cortés y Aguilar] Tuvieron miedo della, que creyeron que los enviaba a
> llamar para matarlos, y lloraban; y como así los vio llorar la doña Marina, los consoló,
> y dijo que no hubiesen miedo, que cuando la traspusieron con los de Xicalango que
> no supieron lo que se hacían, y se lo perdonaba, y les dio muchas joyas de oro y de
> ropa y que se volviesen a su pueblo, y que Dios le había hecho mucha merced en qui-
> tarla de adorar ídolos ahora y ser cristiana, y tener un hijo de su amo y señor Cortés,
> y ser casada con un caballero como era su marido Juan Jaramillo.[75] (Díaz del Castillo
> 1999: 149)

This statement has the clear mission of showing what the true religion consists
of as opposed to the rites that the Indians were practicing, but in my opinion, it
does something else. It has the effect of adding a shade of Christian redemption to
the portrait of Cortés, who, appearing closer than ever to the image of the Savior,
forgives the Indians their ignorance, as Jesus Christ himself when he forgave the
Roman soldiers who stood at the foot of his Cross (Gospel of St. Luke 23:24). As a
reinforcement of this image, Cortés is presented in other instances of Díaz's account
as the just mediator who is ready to intervene in the affairs of the Indians and punish those who offend them, in a gesture halfway between a contemporary comic
book avenger and a merciful savior ready to step up for the sake of his people. Of
course, there is a political side to this gesture, since Cortés needed to do anything
in his power to ensure alliances with some sectors of the Indian population who
ultimately helped him conquer Montezuma. **?**

Nevertheless, these types of qualities attributed to the leaders of the conquistadores add up to configure, in Díaz del Castillo's eyes, a godlike persona, a divine nature
that the Spaniards have no interest in undermining and that the Indians create in
response to a group of people who conduct themselves in a way that, to them, does
not seem natural, but rather heaven-sent, like that sign they received even before
the Spaniards' arrival and that foretold the episodes that were about to happen.[76]

---

75 My translation: They were afraid of her, thinking that she was sent to kill them and they wept; and as
doña Marina saw them crying she consoled them and told them not to be afraid because when they sent
her to Xicalango they did not know what they were doing and she forgave them. And she gave them
many gold jewels and clothing and she told them to go back because God had claimed her away from the
idols and to be a Christian, and to have a son with her lord, Señor Cortés and to be married to a gentle-
man as Juan Jaramillo.

76 "Dijeron los indios mexicanos, que poco tiempo había, antes que viniésemos a Nueva España, que vieron
una señal en el cielo que era como verde y colorado y redonda como una rueda de carreta y que junto
a la señal venía otra raya y camino de hacia donde sale el Sol y se venía a juntar con la raya colorada; y
Montezuma, gran cacique de México, mandó llamar a sus papas y adivinos, para que mirasen aquella cosa
y señal, nunca entre ellos vista ni oída, que tal hubiese, y según pareció, los papas lo comunicaron con

Having a sign from above that anticipates their arrival and extraordinary acts is the only explanation that seems possible for the Mexicas who call them gods: "E viendo cosas tan maravillosas e de tanto peso para ellos, dijeron que no osaran hacer aquellos hombres humanos, sino teules, que así llaman a sus ídolos en que adoraban; e a esta causa desde allí adelante nos llamaron teules, que es, como he dicho, o dioses o demonios" (Díaz del Castillo 1999: 169).[77] The fact that the Indians do not hesitate to call the Spaniards "gods" indicates the ease with which they could attribute divine nature to different things or people, but also, it clearly shows that, according to their spirituality, worshipping a divinity is a matter that plays an important role in their everyday normal activities. Unfortunately for the invaders, this privileged status did not last, and the Indians did not take long to realize that the Spaniards were not as divine as they once thought.[78]

Following in this attempt to separate the true creed of Christianity from the false religion that is practiced by the Indians, Díaz del Castillo includes, in his account, a systematic recollection of all the measures taken by the Spaniards in order to eliminate the Indian paganism, together with the incentives that are offered in return. In this sense, he lives during the destruction of idols and their association with

---

el ídolo Huichilobos, y la respuesta que dio fue que tendrían muchas guerras y pestilencias y que habría sacrificación de sangre humana" (Díaz del Castillo 1999: 367). (My translation: The Indians said that right before we arrived to that land they saw a sign in the sky that was green and red and round like a cartwheel and that next to it there was a line and where the sunrise takes place it joined the red line; and Montezuma, a great chief in Mexico, called for his popes and his fortune tellers for them to look to that thing in the sky, never seen nor heard of before. And the popes consulted with the idol Huichilobos and he answered that they would have many wars and diseases and that human blood would be sacrificed.)

77 My translation: And in seeing so many wonderful things and so important to them they said that those men could not be made human, but teules, as the gods they worshipped; and from then on, they should be called teules, which is, as I said above, gods or demons.

In response to this reaction, on the part of the Indians, the first missionaries who arrived in New Spain—that is, the Franciscans—explicitly address the issue of their nature, and Bernadino de Sahagún does start his *Coloquios*, denying this divine element: "No somos dioses ni emos descendido del cielo, en la tierra somos nacidos y criados, comemos y bebemos y somos passibles y mortales como vosotros; no somos más que mensajeros embiados a esta tierra" (Duverger 1996:63). (My translation: We are not gods, neither have we come from heaven. We were born and raised on earth; we eat and drink and we are mortals like you: we are but messengers sent to this land.) This statement can be found in the opening of the *Coloquios y Doctrina Christiana con que los doze frayles de San Francisco enbiados por el Papa Adriano Sesto y por el Emperador Carlos Quinto convertieron a los indios de la Nueva Espanya en lengua mexicana y espanola*. This text was, as it is said in the title, composed in a bilingual version (Nahuatl and Spanish) by Sahagún in 1564 and reconstructs the first encounter between the pagans and the friars and the subtleties around the acceptance or rejection of Christianity in the New World.

78 "Los adivinos y hechiceros tlaxcaltecas revelan que los extraños visitantes no son teules y aconsejan un ataque por la noche, momento en que éstos son mas vulnerables" (Díaz del Castillo 1999: 195). [My translation: The Tlaxcaltecan fortune-tellers and sorcerers reveal that the strange visitors are not teules, and they recommend an attack at night, when they are the most vulnerable.]

the Devil and symbols related to Hell,[79] and the mandate issued by the Spaniards prohibiting the further practices of human sacrifices and cannibalism. But beyond what is being allowed or not, what Díaz is witnessing is the process of change of hegemony, first presented as a way of improving that society that ate humans but later translated into an open entitlement to manipulate the lives of the Indians as the Spaniards saw fit. The dilemma presented to the Indians is clearly exposed: on the one hand, they are strongly encouraged to abandon the traditions of their ancestors and enter into the Spanish system, accepting Charles V as their king and redeemer. In return, a better life is offered, not only here on earth but also after death. But, more important than that, the conversion of the Indians and their possible incorporation to the Spanish imaginary are shown as the passport that would give them access to marry the conquistadores and, therefore, allowing interracial marriages and the possibility of getting protection from the Spaniards, since they would become part of their families. In sum, what is being sold is the incorporation to the civilizing process that the Spaniards are preaching, a better life or, rather, the colonizers' version of it:

> También dijeron aquellos mismos caciques [tlaxcaltecas] que sabían de aquellos sus antecesores que les había dicho su ídolo en quien ellos tenían mucha devoción, que vendrían hombres de las partes de hacia donde sale el sol y de lejanas tierras a les sojuzgar y señorear; que si somos nosotros, holgarán dello, que pues tan esforzados y buenos somos; y cuando trataron las paces se les acordó desto que les había dicho su ídolo, que por aquella causa nos dan sus hijas, para tener parientes que les defendían de los mexicanos; y cuando acabaron su razonamiento, todos quedamos espantados, y decíamos si por ventura dicen verdad; y luego nuestro capitán Cortés les replicó, y dijo que ciertamente veníamos de hacia donde sale el sol, y que por esta causa nos envió el rey nuestro señor a tenerlos por hermanos, porque tiene noticias dellos, y que plegue a Dios nos dé gracia para que por nuestras manos e intercesión se salven; y dijimos todos: "Amén."[80] (Díaz del Castillo 1999: 214)

---

79 "Un poco más apartado del gran cu estaba una torrecilla que también era casa de ídolos, o puro infierno, porque tenía a la boca de la una puerta una muy espantable boca de las que pintan, que dicen que es como la que están en los infiernos con la boca abierta y grandes colmillos para tragar las ánimas. E asimismo estaban unos bultos de diablos y cuerpos de sierpes junto a la puerta, y tenia un poco apartado un sacrificadero, y todo ello muy ensangrentado y negro de humo y costras de sangre (Díaz del Castillo 1999: 269). My translation: A little further away there was a little tower that was also a house of idols, or pure hell, because it had a very frightening mouth painted at the door, which they say is like the one in Hell, with an open mouth and big fangs to swallow the souls. And there were some figures of devils and serpents next to the door, and a little further, the place of sacrifice, all of it covered in blood and blackened by the smoke and bloody crusts.

80 My translation: Those same caciques said that their ancestors had said that their very revered idol had foretold the arrival of some men far away lands, coming from the gates where the sun comes to govern them and to be their lords; and if we were them, that they were happy since we were good and earnest;

But, since a cultural encounter always affects both sides, Díaz del Castillo does not forget to point out the spread of pagan superstition that is reaching the Spaniards themselves who, in their desperation in the new and adverse circumstances, decide to recruit the services of a necromancer who even has a Devil for his personal use, and who recommends that the Spaniards abandon Mexico if they want to save their lives: "Estaba con nosotros un soldado que se decía Botello, al parecer muy hombre de bien y latino, y había estado en Roma, y decían que era nigromántico, otros decían que tenía 'familiar,' algunos le llamaban astrólogo; y este Botello había dicho cuatro días había que hallaba por sus suertes y astrologías que si aquella noche que venía no salíamos de México, y si más aguardábamos, que ningún soldado podría salir con la vida"[81] (Díaz del Castillo 1999: 308). On his part, Cortés is much more reserved when it comes to describing the paganism of the Indians. His references to their idolatry (committed to paper some fifty years earlier than those of Díaz del Castillo's) are not as frequent or as colorful as the ones found in Díaz del Castillo. His narration (Cortés's) is much more focused on emphasizing his personal contribution to the hegemonic project, as designed by the king of Spain, than in relating to the Indians' way of life and, of course, his role is much bigger in the terrain of the militia than it is in any other arena, especially if we refer to religious affairs.

Nevertheless, and as Columbus did in his first voyages, Cortés feels (or so he says as a possible justification a posteriori) the presence of God with him at every step of the way and attributes to this divine inspiration the successes that he has in battle; that is, he sees God behind every decision he makes and acknowledges this fact on numerous occasions in his writing: "Bien pareció que Dios fue el que por nosotros peleó, pues entre tanta multitud de gente y tan animosa y diestra en el pelear, y con tantos géneros de armas para nos ofender, salimos tan libres"[82] (Cortés 2004: 45). The recurrent presence of Cortés's account of the hand of God in his mission has a number of consequences: First of all, it shows Cortés as a messenger of sorts of the divine, as a person who acts in God's name and who carries through with a mission of divine inspiration, which makes Cortés, as Columbus had been before by his own account, an instrument chosen by God to deliver his effects to the "newly-discovered"

and we confirmed what their idol had said and for that same reason they would give us their daughters, so to have relatives that could defend them from the Mexicas; and when they were finished they asked if they were right and Captain Cortés replied that we indeed came from where the sun rises and that God sent us to be their brothers because He knows of them and it would please Him that for our intercession they would be saved, and we all said "Amen."

81 My translation: There was a soldier by the name of Botello with us, good man and versed in Latin, who had been to Rome and was said to be a necromancer, and others said that he was an astrologer; and that Botello had said four days before that his astrologies said that if we didn't leave Mexico that night that none of the soldiers would ever leave alive.

82 My translation: It seemed to me that God fought for us since against such a multitude and so lively and ready to fight and with so many weapons to attack us, we remained unharmed.

people. But, on the other hand, the fact that God's hand is on Cortés's side during the battles implies that he (God) is, in some way, fighting against the Indians, a paradoxical position to assume if the effect that is considered primary in the whole process of colonization is to pursue the conversion of the pagans.

In this sense, Cortés presents the discovery of the new lands and his arrival there not as a random act but rather as part of a divine plan materialized in the political arena in the global process of the Reconquista, started in Spain centuries ago and that keeps on going on the other side of the Atlantic. Therefore, for Cortés the Indians are nothing but a variety of Moors who dress and live in the Moorish fashion, and the battles that he is involved in are nothing else than a continuation of the war of Granada, albeit on a greater scale since there are more Indians than Moors ever were in Spain:

> los vestidos que traen es como de almaizales muy pintados, y los hombres traen tapadas sus vergüenzas, y encima del cuerpo unas mantas muy delgadas y pintadas a manera de alquizales moriscos, y las mujeres y de la gente común traen unas mantas muy pintadas desde la cintura hasta los pies y otras que les cubren las tetas, y todo lo demás traen descubierto . . . las casas, en las partes que alcanzan piedra son de cal y canto, y los aposentos dellas, pequeños y bajos, muy amoriscados, . . . con éstos tienen sus mezquitas y adoratorios y sus andenes, todo a la redonda muy ancho, y allí tienen sus ídolos que adoran.[83] (Cortés 2004: 25)

Cortés, as he shows throughout his account, is incapable of seeing the *other* that he is facing at the moment, to open his eyes and really study the reality that opened in front of him. As had already happened in the case of Christopher Columbus, for Cortés the new reality is nothing but a continuation of the one left behind, a variation on the things he already knows and some revolutionary discoveries, as the sight of Tenochtitlan. He is unable to remove the filter of his expectations and appreciate the novelty that he has encountered. But, differently from Columbus, who always thought that he was indeed in a part of the world already seen and already discovered by others, Cortés has the certainty that he is in unknown territory (at least, for the Western eyes), and he still is unable to register that fact in the way he looks and in the image he perceives when he does so.

[Handwritten margin note: WHICH IS PRECISELY WHY NOTHING HE SAYS CAN BE TAKEN FOR GRANTED]

---

83 My translation: The garments that they wear are like very colorful *almaizales* and the men are barely covered and on top of their bodies they wore very thin blankets, painted as the Moorish *alquizales*, and the women and the commoners wear some very colorful blankets from the waist to their feet and other ones that cover their breasts and everything else is uncovered . . . the houses, in the parts where the stone reaches, are made of lime and the rooms are small and low, in the Moorish fashion [. . .] and they have mosques and places of worship everything around very wide and that is where they have the idols they worship.

He lingers, nevertheless, in his description of the abominable things that he sees the pagans do, especially in the gruesome details of the human sacrifices and the extracting of the hearts to build their idols:

> los bultos y cuerpos de los ídolos en quien estas gentes creen son de muy mayores estaturas que el cuerpo de un gran hombre. Son hechos de masa de todas las semillas y legumbres que ellos comen, molidas y mezcladas unas con otras, y amásanlas con sangre de corazones de cuerpos humanos, los cuales abren por los pechos, vivos, y les sacan el corazón, y de aquella sangre que sale de él, amasan aquella harina, y así hacen tanta cantidad cuanta basta para facer aquellas estatuas grandes. E también, después de hechas, les ofrescía más corazones, que asimismo les sacrifican, y les untan las caras con la sangre.[84] (Cortés 2004: 81)

Thus, Cortés dwells on the fact that the Indians eat the bodies of the sacrificed victims and, upon viewing these horrible things, he has no doubt that God has guided his mission to those lands in order to end with these savage practices. But, in a curious turn, Cortés seems to present those terrible vices of the Indians as an offense against the king of Spain, rather than to God himself and, that way, he feels compelled to incorporate these peoples into the Spanish imaginary not following a mandate of God but, rather, coming from the king himself. Cortés also appeals to the intervention of a second figure of maximum authority—the pope—since according to his opinion, the vices of the Indians constitute not only an offense to the hegemonic power of Spain but also a sin against the authority of the Church of Rome, especially when there are reasons to believe that those sacrificed are indeed Catholics, as the expedition led by Alvarado seems to confirm.[85] "Podrán Vuestras Majestades, si fueren servidos, hacer por cosa verdadera relación a nuestro muy Santo Padre para que en la conversión desta gente se ponga diligencia y buena orden pues que dello se espera sacar tan gran fruto, y también para que Su Santidad haya por bien y permita que los malos y rebeldes, siendo primero amonestados, puedan ser punidos y castigados como enemigos de nuestra sancta

---

84 My translation: The shapes and the bodies of the idols in which these people believe are bigger than the height of a tall man. They are made of all the seeds and legumes that they eat, ground and mixed together and they knead them with blood of human hearts, which they have taken from the chests while alive and with that blood they knead that dough and they make a very big quantity to build those big statues. And, once done, they offered to them more human hearts, from sacrifices and they lather their faces with blood.

85 "Los de la ciudad, luego que hubieron la victoria, por hacer desmayar al alguacil mayor y Pedro de Alvarado, todos los españoles vivos y muertos que tomaron los llevaron a Tlatelulco, que es el mercado, y en unas torres altas que allí estaban, desnudos los sacrificaron y abrieron por los pechos, y les sacaron los corazones para ofrecer a los ídolos; lo cual los españoles del real de Pedro de Alvarado pudieron ver bien de donde peleaban, y en los cuerpos desnudos y blancos que vieron sacrificar conocieron que eran cristianos" (Cortés 2004: 186).

fe católica"[86] (Cortés 2004: 25). But, in spite of the unequivocal and omnipresent reference to religion all through Cortés's account of his conquest of Mexico,
there is no real emphasis on the pastoral component of his mission and, though
the ingredients that conform to the Catholic creed are mentioned on a couple of
occasions, there is no evidence of a systematic effort for converting the Indians.

NECESSARILY SO, NO?

There is however, an attempt to mention God and the king in equal amounts or,
rather, an attempt to mention God every time that Cortés needs to mention the
king, making the two of them partners in a campaign that has the conversion
to Catholicism as a prerequisite to be a subject of the king. Therefore, vassalage
is presented as a goal for the Indians, and the instruction in the Catholic creed
is shown as a very adequate path to obtain it and to finally aspire to Christian
salvation.

ISN'T THAT ALWAYS THE WAY OF POWER?

In a sense, Cortés puts religion at the service of the project of political hegemony
that brought him to the new lands, and this fact is evident in the substitution of
symbols that takes place all along his journey in Mexico: "Éste es muy hermoso
pueblo; llámase Teutiercas, tiene muy hermosas mezquitas, en especial dos, donde
nos aposentamos y echamos fuera los ídolos, de que ellos no mostraron mucha pena,
porque ya yo les había hablado y dado a entender el yerro en que estaban, y cómo
no había más de un solo Dios creador de todas las cosas, y todo los demás que cerca
de esto se les pudo decir, aunque después al señor principal y a todos juntos les
hable más largo"[87] (Cortés 2004: 295). In this case the change of hegemony is very
obvious: the idols are substituted, not even by the Catholic symbols, but by the
conquistadores themselves who have come to place themselves as the new point of
reference: the change is no longer religious, but political. But, in spite of this lack
of insistence on the creed and the total absence of a proper campaign of conversion,
at least in these first years that Cortés writes about, the conquistadores witness a
number of sudden conversions and instances in which the Indians themselves ask
for the tutelage of the Spaniards in order to avoid their own authorities:

> Fue de mí muy bien recibido, y porque cuando llegó era hora de misa, hice que se
> dijese cantada y con mucha solemnidad . . . y por ellos le fue hecho un sermón con la
> lengua, en manera que muy bien lo pudo entender, acerca de las cosas de nuestra fe,
> y dándole a entender por muchas razones cómo no había más de un solo Dios, y en

---

86 My translation: Maybe your majesties could appeal to the Holy Father to accelerate the conversion of this
   people since this task is expected to bear good fruit and also so the rebels can be punished and as enemies
   of our Catholic faith.

87 My translation: This is my beautiful village. It is called Teutiercas and has beautiful mosques and two in
   particular where we settled and threw away the idols and they did not show much sorrow for I had already
   talked to them about the mistake they had made and that there was only one God, creator of all things and
   everything else I could say about this, although later, their lord would talk to them at length.

yerro de su secta, y según mostró y dijo, satisfízose mucho, y dijo que él quería luego destruir sus ídolos y creer en aquel Dios que nosotros le decíamos, y que quisiera mucho saber la manera que debía de tener de servirle y honrarle, y que si yo quisiese ir a su pueblo, vería cómo en mi presencia los quemaba, y quería que le dejase en su pueblo aquella cruz que le decía que yo dejaba en todos los pueblos por donde yo había pasado.[88] (Cortés 2004: 304)

As we can see, if Díaz's account told about the efforts of the Spanish troops to find the idols and the temples as a way to get to the offerings in gold that the Indians regularly gave to their divinities, in Cortés's story there is no place whatsoever for this search for the precious metal. In his case the very sporadic attempts to find the idols were motivated by his obedience to the king first, and to the Pope and God, in a second instance.

Both Spaniards are horrified by the human sacrifices that they witness or hear of and spend a great deal of their chronicles trying to convey the horror they felt, but, if Díaz presents his expedition as the door to salvation, and Cortés as the figure of the redeemer, the latter chooses to present Charles V as the main protagonist in leading the Indians in the *right* direction, apparently swallowing his ambition and ~~CONTEXT?~~ proud ways and attributing this deed to the emperor rather than to himself. But what Cortés lacks and where Díaz fills in the gap, is in his observance of the pagan traditions of the Indians that, for the leader of the expedition, are seen as old realities with a new face and that Díaz recognizes as a different manifestation of false religion and, as such, presents in much more detail.   ~~TOO MUCH CREDIT TO BERNAL~~

Nevertheless, both authors coincide in pointing out some of the elements that the conquest of Mexico had in common with the more familiar efforts undertaken during the Spanish Reconquista. That way they would have no problem in describing the *other* in religious terms, rather than focusing on his physique or on any other attributes; they establish the necessity of converting the Indians, not only as a precautionary measure taken for their own survival but also for the wellbeing of the colonial enterprise; and they take for granted that the mechanisms of building an empire necessarily include a number of steps in which the extirpation of other people's paganism and the acceptance of baptism are just the first prerequisites. Therefore, both authors and, in general, the Spaniards who witness the development of the territorial expansion, expect a subsequent spiritual expansion

---

88 My translation: It was very welcome and when the time of the Mass arrived, I made it be sung and very solemn . . . they had a sermon in their language, so that they could very easily understand matters of our faith like that there is only one God and the mistake of their religion; and he was very happy and said that he wanted to destroy his idols and believe in our God from then on and serve Him and honor Him and if I wanted to go to his village, I could see how he burnt them in my presence, and he wanted in his village that cross that I left everywhere where I had been.

as well, following the same pattern that had already been rehearsed in the Spanish Reconquista and that placed America as one of the last legs of the crusade of sorts that had been fought back at home.[89] López de Gómara, fully aware of this double process, gives echo to this parallelism, and in his dedication of his *Historia General de las Indias* to Charles V states that "Comenzaron las conquistas de los indios acabada la de los moros; por que siempre guerreasen españoles contra infieles" (the conquests of the Indians began when that of the Moors was finished, so that Spaniards might always war against infidels" (López de Gómara 1991: 8). Thus, the natives of the New World are portrayed as the alter ego of the heathens found in the Old World (Moors and Jews) while the Spaniards choose to project themselves as the last crusaders.

But, what did the new bishop, the Franciscan Juan de Zumárraga, find upon his arrival in Mexico? How did he deal with idolatry, especially that of the Indians? How successful was he? These are some of the questions that I will address in the next chapter.

UNWIELDLY

DEMANDING FOR ITS

WIDE SWINGS FROM ONE

SIDE OF THE ATLANTIC TO THE

OTHER Y ONE TIME PERIOD

TO ANOTHER

CALLS FOR A CERTAIN DEGREE

OF KNOWLEDGE ON THE ISSUES

DISCUSSED

INTERESTING: THE MANY PARALLELS

W/ THE CONQUEST OF THE CANARY ISLANDS

TOO MEANDERING

ACCOUNT OF THE CONQUEST LACKS PROPER

---

89 This notion of crusade is reinforced by an apparent need on Queen Isabella's part to count on the pope's approval. In fact, most of her important enterprises had its own corresponding papal bull, approving and guiding the fight against the infidel, especially in the war of Granada in which she was personally very involved as we can see in F. Pulgar's account (Pulgar 1943: Vol. II.)

CONTEXT AND NECESSARY QUALIFICATIONS

3

Idolatry in New Spain

Zumárraga's Bishopric (1528–1548)

As soon as fray Juan de Zumárraga arrived in Mexico, he declared that he was faced with a dissolute land, a territory of pagans with no knowledge of divine justice and no fear of God, a land possessed by idolatry and described by Motolinía as an equivalent of hell:[1]

> A ellos [a los Indios] les era gran fastidio oir la palabra de Dios, y no querían en otra cosa sino en darse á vicios y pecados dándose á sacrificios y fiestas, comiendo y bebiendo, y embeodándose en ellas, y *dando de comer á los idolos* de su propia sangre, la cual sacaban de sus propias orejas, lengua y brazos, y de otras partes del cuerpo, como adelante diré. *Era esta tierra un traslado del infierno*; ver los moradores de ella de noche dar voces, unos llamando al demonio, otros borrachos, otros cantando y bailando: traían atabales, bocinas, cornetas y caracoles grandes, en especial en las fiestas de sus demonios ... Era cosa de gran lástima ver los hombres criados á la imagen de Dios vueltos peores que brutos animales; y lo que peor era, que no quedaban en aquel solo pecado, mas cometían otros muchos, y se herían y descalabraban unos á otros, y acontecia matarse, aunque fuesen muy amigos y propincuos parientes.[2] (Motolinía, *Historia de los Indios de Nueva España*, in García Icazbalceta 1971a: 22–23)

[handwritten margin note: HYPERBOLE, NO?]

---

1 "Tierra muy disoluta en costumbres, sin temor de la justicia divina." My translation: dissolute land in traditions, with no fear of divine justice. (Mendieta 1973: Book V, part I, ch. 27)
2 My translation: To them [the Indians] it was very bothersome to hear about the word of God and they didn't want to know about anything else except engaging in vices and sins, sacrifices and festivities,

DOI: 10.5876/9781607328018.c003

In spite of Cortés's and his men's opposition to these practices, their efforts proved mostly insufficient in fighting human sacrifices and other aspects of indigenous religious expression. Actually, the pagan temples were in full operation at least until 1525, the year in which Motolinía records this activity.[3] In the meantime, the Franciscans continued to hold large baptismal events[4] ("no centenares, sino millares de indios" [not hundreds, but thousands of Indians], Motolinía, *Historia de los Indios de Nueva España*, in García Icazbalceta 1971a: 95) with very little religious instruction, urged by their millennial panic and the need to convert as many as possible before the end of times. But as other missionary orders began to arrive, the Franciscans' detractors focused on the permanence of pagan behaviors and questioned the validity of the given sacrament.

This situation, that is, the administration of massive baptisms, had its parallel in the aftermath of the Battle of Pavia (1525), when Charles V, after defeating Francis I of France and having taken him prisoner, offered to God a massive baptism of Moors as a sign of gratitude:

---

eating and drinking, getting drunk and feeding the idols drinks of their own blood that they took out of their own ears, tongue and arms and from other parts of their body, as I will say later. This land was a copy of hell; to see the natives scream at night, some calling the devil some drunk, others singing and dancing: they carried kettledrums, horns, bugles and big snails, especially in the festivities of their demons . . . It was a pity to see men, created in the image of God, become worse than animals, and the worst is that was not their only sin, but they committed many others, and they hurt themselves and injured their heads and sometimes killed each other even their best friends and relatives.

3   "En todos los templos de los ídolos, si no era en algunos derribados y quemados de México, en los de la tierra, y aun en el mismo México eran servidos y honrados los demonios. Ocupados los Españoles en edificar á México y en hacer casas y moradas para sí, contentábanse con que no hubiese delante de ellos sacrificios de homicidio público, que á escondidas y á la redonda de México no faltaban; y de esta manera se estaba la idolatría en paz, y las casas de los demonios servidas y guardadas con sus ceremonias. En esta sazón era ido el gobernador Don Hernando Cortés á las Hibueras, y vista la ofensa que á Dios se hacia, no faltó quien se lo escribió, para que mandase cesar los sacrificios al demonio, porque mientras esto no se quitase, aprovecharía poco la predicación, y el trabajo de los frailes seria en balde; en lo cual proveyó bien cumplidamente. Mas como cada uno tenia su cuidado, como dicho es, aunque lo habia mandado, estábase la idolatría tan entera como de antes; hasta [que] el primero dia de año 1525." My translation: In all the temples of the idols, except in some ruined and burnt in Mexico, in those on the mainland, and in Mexico proper, demons were served and worshipped. Since the Spaniards were busy building houses for themselves, they were happy if there were no sacrifices in front of them, so in private, there were many; and this way, the idolatry was left alone, and the houses of the demons were taken care of and the ceremonies kept taking place. Governor Hernán Cortés was gone to Hibueras, but seeing the offenses to God, someone wrote to him, so that he ordered the cessation of all sacrifices to the Devil, because while this was not exterminated, preaching would be of no use and the work of the friars would be for nothing; and he did so. But, despite being ordered, since each person takes care of their own business, the idolatry kept intact until the first day of 1525. (Treatise I, chapter III. García Icazbalceta 1971a: 25–26). Also see Motolinía (1996: 155–56).

4   Among all friars fray Toribio Motolinía stands out, of whom Mendieta says that he baptized more than 400,000 Indians all by himself (Mendieta 1973: Book V, part I, ch. 22).

Decía el Emperador que, pues Nuestro Señor en aquel año le había dado victoria y sabía preso al rey de Francia, no sabía otro mayor servicio que le hacer si no era mandar que todos los infieles de sus reinos se bautizasen. Cuando se hacían estas provisiones, pusiéronle muchos temores los del Consejo de Aragón . . . Respondió el Emperador: . . . Venga lo que viniere y suceda lo que sucediere, que yo estoy determinado que, pues Dios trajo al rey de Francia mi enemigo a mis manos, he de traer yo los moros sus enemigos a la fe; porque no puedo yo dar gracias cumplidas a Dios con alguna cosa, por tantos y grandes beneficios como he recibido de su mano, como es en limpiar de infieles y herejes todos mis reinos.[5] (Sandoval 1955–56: 81, 122).

In the case of Mexico, where the battle of Pavia was remembered under the title of the drama *La conquista de Rodas* (1539), the obvious resistance of the Indians was generally blamed on the baptism practices that the Franciscans offered, sometimes massively, in the course of theatrical representations. That is the case surrounding the performance of *La conquista de Jerusalén* (in García Icazbalceta 1971a), a play that saw the light in Tlaxcala. It was at the end of this performance, among other occasions, that the Franciscans administered massive baptisms, an initiative that brought reactions and criticism from many. Even the bishop Zumárraga had to admit that the Indian idolatry was a much tougher enemy than he had expected as he wrote, in the company of the bishops of Oaxaca and Guatemala, to the General Council on November 30, 1537: "Los naturales áun usan sus ritos gentílicos, especialmente en las supersticiones é idolatrías é sacrificios, aunque no públicamente como solian, mas de noche van á sus adoratorios, *cues* y templos, que áun del todo no están derrocados, y dentro del centro de ellos tienen sus ídolos en la misma veneracion que solian, y se cree que pocos de los mayores han dejado sus sectas y afección del todo, ni dejan de tener sus idolos escondidos, aunque los amonestamos muchas veces y los amenazamos"[6] (García Icazbalceta 1881: appendix, 21, 91). For this reason, the bishops asked the council permission to destroy the places of worship and burn the idols in order to make them fulfill the first commandment in the terms that

---

5   My translation: The Emperor said that, since Our Lord had given him the victory that year and he had captured the King of France, that he knew of no better way to honor him than to order that all the infidels in his kingdom were baptized. When this was ordered, there were many objections from the Council of Aragon . . . to which the Emperor answered: . . . Whatever happens and whatever comes I am determined because, since God brought the King of France, my enemy, to my hands, I have to bring to his the Moors, the enemies of the faith; because I can give thanks to God for the many gifts I have received from Him by cleaning my lands of infidels and heretics.

6   My translation: The naturals still use their ceremonies, especially in the superstitions, idolatries and sacrifices, although not in public as they used to, but at night they go to their places of worship, cues and temples, that are still not totally destroyed, and inside, they had the same reverence they used to have toward their idols, and it is believed than among the elders, very few had abandoned their sects, or their hidden idols, no matter how much we punish and threaten them.

Zumárraga established in his *Doctrina Breve* (1543):[7] "El primero: es creer que es un solo Dios y no muchos como creyan los gentiles, paganos y otras diversas naciones que creyan y adoravan los ydolos de oro y plata y de otros metales y de piedra y de madera. Otros adoravan los planetas del cielo como eran el sol, la luna y los otros planetas. Mas es necessario creer que este Dios eterno immortal: infinito y uno en esencia que es trino en personas"[8] (Zumárraga 1928: Folio A III). The answer from Spain is not known in its entirety, but the fragments that we know of show the open disposition of the emperor to fight Indian idolatry, to have the idols burnt, their temples destroyed, and the stones reused to build Catholic churches and, in the worst of cases, he allows the unruly to be sent to Spain.[9] Even before the complaint from the Mexican bishops had been completed, the answer from Pope Paul III had already been prepared in the form of a bull named *Altitudo divini consilii*, dated on January 1, 1537, a document that did not reach Mexico until the next year. In it, and addressing the issue of the possible invalidity of the baptism given without all the ceremonies and/or necessary instruction, the pope tries to comfort the criticized Franciscan friars saying that they did not sin and acted appropriately according to the rough circumstances in which they have to perform their duty, in lands so far away from Rome. But, with the same gesture, Paul III gives some advice about how

---

7   "Suplicamos á V. M. que sea servido de mandar aplicar y hacer limosna á las iglesias de aquellas tierras y posesiones de sus templos é adoratorios que solían poseer los papas é ministros de ellos, con la piedra de ellos para edificar iglesias, y nos dé facultad para que se lo hagamos derrocar de todo punto, y les quememos y destruyamos sus ídolos que dentro tienen, pues por el primer mandamiento somos obligados todos á destruir la idolatría; y la latria ó religión cristiana no se podrá plantear en estos sin desarraigarles y apartarles sus ritos." My translation: We implore to your majesty that you ask for alms in the churches there, and let us use their possessions in their temples and places of worship where they used to have their popes and ministers and their stones to build churches and that we are allowed to burn and destroy the idols that are kept inside, for by the first commandment we are urged to destroy all idolatry; and the worship of Christian religion will not be successful if we don't; take them away from their rites and uproot them. (García Icazbalceta 1881: appendix 21, 91). Notice that the bishops refer, in this document, to the heads of the indigenous religions as *papas*, just as the bishops call their maximum authority, although in the plural, acknowledging the heterogeneity of the religions practiced by the Indians. With this label, the same bishops that write to their authorities arguing for the destruction of these native religions, ironically, give to them the same status as theirs, explicitly assuming that they share elements and are organized in the same way. Of course, by the same token, it shows the way that these bishops were looking at these native practices, not with open eyes to something potentially different but with recognition of the same elements that they were already familiar with. Greenleaf refers to this label in the following terms: "The Spaniards frequently used the word *papa* (derived from the Aztec *papatli*) as a general term for the native priests. Consequently, the missionary clergy could not use the Latin *papa* (Pope) in religious instruction of the Indians; *Pontifice* (Pontiff) was always used instead (1961: 49).

8   My translation: The first: is believe that there is only one God and not many as the gentiles, pagans and other nations believed, that they worshipped idols made of gold and silver and other metals and of stone and wood. Others worshipped the planets in the sky such as the sun and the moon and the other planets. But it is necessary to believe that this God is eternal and immortal: infinite and one in essence but three in person.

9   This letter is dated on August 23, 1538 (García Icazbalceta 1881: appendix 21, 102).

to avoid this controversy in the future by respecting a number of requisites regarding the elements and the circumstances in which the sacrament should be administered.[10] Nevertheless, in 1539 and barely two months after receiving the reaction from Rome, the Franciscan friars organized the celebration of Corpus Christi in Tlaxcala and included the performance (and subsequent massive baptism) of *La conquista de Jerusalén*, which Othón Arróniz reads as a "deliberate act in support of the sacrament as it was administered by the Franciscans" (82) and, therefore, as a challenge from the Order to the most visible authorities of the time: the Church of Rome and the colonial power of Spain who put in question the line of action taken by the Franciscans and their progress in the New World.

Other difficulties arose apropos of another sacrament: marriage. In their pagan tradition, the Indians were used to having many wives and concubines (living in polygamy was the norm), and when they were converted the question arose about which ones were wives and which concubines. Bishop Zumárraga took part in all these discussions until the case was submitted to the Holy See and Paul III, in the aforementioned bull, decreed that the converted Indians should keep the first woman they had taken as their only wife and, in the case that they were not sure which one that was, they should just choose one and leave the rest. Nevertheless, and before the papal intervention, the Franciscan friars tried to channel this debate and chose, as the most widespread vehicle they could think of, a theatrical representation. This election is particularly remarkable since by the time this play first saw the light—1533—drama was not that developed, not even in Spain (we are still far away from the great splendor of the Golden Age and, although there were very important names on the stage at that point—such as Juan del Encina, Gil Vicente, and Bartolomé de Torres Naharro—theatrical performances had not become so popular yet). In any case, the first friars who arrived in New Spain thought it to be a vehicle with great potential in order to address the masses, a spectacle that could carry their doctrine to the hundred of idolaters who populated the new lands and, just as the baptism via aspersion allowed them to convert thousands in one day, the first Franciscans hoped that theatrical performances would spread their message and permeate the idolatrous conscious of the masses.[11] Their intent was to make the Indians live a righteous life and especially to follow the seventh sacrament (marriage) in a timely fashion since the end of the world—and, subsequently, the day of the Final Judgment—was approaching, according to the millenarist ideas that

---

10 Mendieta offers the full version of this bull in Latin and with an explanation in Spanish following the original document (Mendieta 1973: Book III, chapter 37).

11 Let us not forget that, together with this developing Spanish drama that the friars brought, they found a rich tradition of prehispanic theatrical representations of different kinds all over New Spain (see María Beatriz Aracil Varón 1999, esp. ch. 2).

shaped the Franciscans' campaign.[12] Thus, the name of the first play performed in the New World: *Ejemplo del Juicio Final*, first seen in Mexico in 1533, barely a decade after the first arrival of the missionaries.

The play was written by Friar Andrés de Olmos and does actually still exist and can be read in a bilingual version (original Nahuatl and Spanish) in Fernando Horcasitas's book *El Teatro náhuatl: Épocas novohispana y moderna* (Horcasitas 1974: 561–93). Its author, Friar Andrés de Olmos, was a Franciscan friend of Zumárraga's who had embarked on the American adventure at the same time the bishop did, getting to their destination in New Spain in 1528. Together, they had just participated as inquisitors in the trial against the witches of Biscay, an episode to which I referred in the previous chapter, and that played a part in the way they faced the events that were taking place in New Spain.

The drama I am referring to is based on the prophet Hosea's portrait of the relationship between marriage and idolatry, which I will describe briefly. Hosea refers to Israel's relationship with God in the same terms that a husband and a wife relate to each other: he denounces the idolatry of the chosen people, mostly their worship of Baal, and portrays it as abandonment of God, unfaithfulness, and breakage of a bond as deep and as personal as marriage itself. According to him, and as exemplified in his own life,[13] idolatry is portrayed as adultery toward God,[14] as cheating in the relationship with the sacred and, as such, punishable with the hardest of

---

12 "Vivid vuestra vidas rectamente en cuanto al séptimo sacramento, porque ya viene el día del juicio. ¡Ha llegado! ¡Ya está aquí!" My translation: Live proper lives according to the seventh commandment because the Final Judgememt is near! It's here! (Horcasitas 1974: 509)

13 God asks Hosea to marry a prostitute and have children with her. They have three children who are named by God with names representative of the bad relationship that had been established between God and Israel due to the idolatrous ways of the latter. God later asks Hosea to take another wife, most likely his first wife, who had been unfaithful to Hosea but whom he still loves. Hosea obeys and that way symbolizes God's love for his people, since he is able to go back to the unfaithful and forgive even when the Israelites had given themselves to other gods and pagan worships.

14 This same *motif* is presented in *Revelation*, chapter 17, where the "great harlot" is portrayed as the source of both corruption and idolatrous ways. It is also present in Covarrubias's definition of adulterate, which he describes as

> Adulterar. Es tener ayuntamiento carnal con persona que es casada, o siendo ambos los que se juntan casados, y haziendo traycíon a sus consortes. Adulterio, el tal ayuntamiento ilícito; adulteium quasi ad alterum. Adulterino, el hijo concebido desta cópula. Transfiérese a otras cosas, quando son sacadas de su propio ser y las falsifican y contrahazen. En la Sagrada Escritura, adulterar, vale idolatrar. (Covarrubias Orozco 1911: 45)

> To commit adultery. Is to have carnal relations with a person who is married or, both the parties who have intercourse being married, and betraying their consorts. Adultery, such illicit coupling, adulterium, as if ad (toward) alterum (the other). Illegitimate child, the child conceived from this joining. It is transferred to other things, when they are taken out of their proper context and are falsified and counterfeited. In Holy Scripture, adultery means idolatry. (Translation by Dopico Black 2001: 28)

measures.[15] Therefore, if a woman can be stoned if she is an adulterer, in the same way, a person who turns his back to God should encounter the coldest wrath of the legal system, which in the inquisitorial mindset equaled uncontested physical death because, as opposed to what Hosea shows to us in the *Bible*, God can forgive but the Inquisition does not.[16]

The God portrayed in the *Ejemplo del juicio final* shares in this inquisitorial attitude and, instead of forgiving, appears as the harsh judge who has no patience for sinners. He does offer advice, in Nahuatl, on how to behave through the characters of Confesión and La Santa Iglesia; he shows the uncontrollable passage of Time; but in the end, there is no escape for those who sin over and over (up to four hundred times) and Lucía, made to become the representation of the pagan Mexican peoples, condemns herself for eternity ("Tal vez debería haber escuchado, creído en lo que me dijeron mi padre, mi madre y todos mis parientes que me aconsejaron a que cambiara de vida, pero yo menospreciaba el bendito, el santo sacramento del matrimonio! Ya pasó, ahora soy cuatrocientas veces infeliz!")[17] (Horcasitas 1974: 577)

Doomsday finally arrives and, as expected, the good people are sent to the right hand of God while the sinners are given to the evil spirits. This is when Lucía reappears and the ultimate lesson of the *exemplum* is displayed with all its consequences:

JESUCRISTO: Ven tú, viva. ¿Acaso cumpliste con mis diez mandamientos divinos? ¿Acaso amaste a tu prójimo y a tu padre y a tu madre?

LUCÍA: Seguramente. Primero te amé a ti, Dios mío, Señor mío, y luego a mi padre y madre.

JESUCRISTO: Si es cierto que soy tu Dios y que me has amado primero, y luego a tu padre y a tu madre *¿guardaste mi mandamiento y el mandamiento de mi amada y gloriosa madre en cuanto al séptimo sacramento sagrado, el bendito matrimonio?* ¿Viviste con castidad en la tierra? ¿La manifestaste?

---

15 "My people ask counsel at their stocks, and their staff declareth unto them: for the spirit of whoredoms hath caused them to err, and they have gone a whoring from under their God. They sacrifice upon the tops of the mountains, and burn incense upon the hills, under oaks and poplars and elms, because the shadow thereof is good: therefore your daughters shall commit whoredom, and your spouses shall commit adultery. I will not punish your daughters when they commit whoredom or your spouses when they commit adultery" (Hosea 4: 12–4).

16 Of course, as it is widely known, much earlier than Torquemada, the Romans adopted this policy wholeheartedly and submitted the Catholics to all kinds of physical punishments as followers of a God different than theirs; but they were not the first and, certainly, not the only ones.

17 My translation: Maybe I should have listened to and believed in what my mother and my father and all my relatives told me, advising me to change my life, but I undervalued the divine and sacred sacrament of marriage. It's done, now I am four hundred times miserable!

LUCÍA: No, no te he servido, ni reconocí a tu amada madre. Pero
                  perdóname, Dios mío, Señor mío.

JESUCRISTO: En la tierra tu corazón jamás se dirigía a nosotros. Sólo te
                  la pasabas jugando. Vete. Que se cumpla. Tal vez recuerdes
                  tu vida viciosa para que sufras trabajos. Así es que ya no
                  espere nada tu corazón del cielo. *Te has vuelto desgraciada
                  porque nunca quisiste casarte en la tierra.* Te has ganado
                  la casa infernal que será tu tormento. Vete a ver a los que
                  serviste, pues yo no te conozco.[18] (Horcasitas 1974: 587, my
                  emphasis)

And with instructions to be taken to the devils, Lucía abandons the stage to leave
space for the final punishments to occur. We will have the opportunity to see her
once more, as she is flogged in front of the audience and thrown into the gates of
Hell. At that point a real priest (not an actor) would address the spectators with the
following message: "¡Oh amados hijos míos, oh cristianos, oh criaturas de Dios!
Y habés visto esta cosa terrible, espantosa. Y todo es verdad, pues está escrito en
los libros sagrados. ¡Sabed, despertad, mirad en vuestro propio espejo! Para que lo
que sucedió [en la comedia[19]] no os vaya a pasar. Esta lección, este ejemplo, no lo
da Dios"[20] (Horcasitas 1974: 591). This is, therefore, the lesson that the friars hoped
to teach the Indians who saw the play and the behavior they wanted to impose on

---

18 My translation of the last exchange: Jesus Christ: On earth, your heat was never devoted to us. It
    constantly played. Go. Let it be done. Maybe you will remember your licentious life when you suffer. So
    you heat your expect nothing from heaven. You have become miserable because you never wanted to get
    married on earth. You have earned the infernal house that will become your torment. Go and see whom
    you served since I don't know you.

19 This is a very early, seemingly anachronistic use of the term *comedia*, if taken in Castilian. Perhaps this
    could be explained by the fact that the copy from which Fernando Horcasitas quotes is dated in 1678
    (Horcasitas 566), which is a later translation (after Lope de Vega) of a Nahuatl word. Nevertheless and
    although the *Ejemplo del juicio final* was probably first performed between 1531 and 1533 and, therefore,
    it is still a long distance away from Lope's *Arte Nuevo de Hacer Comedias* (1609), it already presents
    some complexities that indicate the way *comedias*, in Spain, were leading in a movement away from the
    Aristotelian unities. This play is born in a completely different set of rules: written in Nahuatl and under
    the influence of the prehispanic literature. Nevertheless, there are some aspects that we can relate with.
    For instance, there is a clear violation of the unity of time, since the action develops along several days
    leading up to Doomsday. Also, there is a break of the unity of place, since the action, divided in three
    stages, is said to move from Earth to either Heaven or Hell. The theme, however, is just one and it is
    based on the Gospel (Luke 21: 25–33; and Matthew 25: 31–46), reviving a topic that had been very popu-
    lar in Medieval Spain, one that encouraged Christians to have their souls ready for the imminent arrival
    of Doomsday and in order to guarantee their place in Heaven.

20 My translation: Oh my beloved children, oh Christians, oh children of God! And so you have seen this
    terrible, horrible thing. And it's all true because it's written in the sacred books. Wake up and look into
    your own mirror! So what happened [in the *comedia*] does not happen to you. God gives us this lesson,
    this example.

the newly converted Christians. Drama became, then, one more instrument in the spiritual conquest that the Europeans used to their advantage.

Together with this, Bishop Zumárraga fought for the opening of some schools in which to teach Indian children of noble families (like the one in Tlatelolco) and ordered a series of *visitas*, or inspection visits, into the villages and towns of the Mexico Valley to check on the daily lives of the indigenous people and enforce Christian living among the newly baptized. These various mechanisms of repression (imposition of monogamous marriage and Christian schooling,[21] control visits, and regulation of life through the administration of sacraments) are just the preparatory steps leading to the full implementation of the Inquisition, an institution that, although it was first claimed to be needed to control the immigration of European Catholics guilty of misconduct—especially previous Jews and Moors, or New Christians to the New World—was later regarded by the first bishop as a necessity for monitoring the Indians, as well as the settler community (Greenleaf 1961: 7). Nevertheless, together with the element of control that is derived from schooling the children of the Indian *caciques*, there is another dimension to this in the merging of cultures and opening of all kinds of possibilities for the encounter of two cultures that, in the setting of the Colegio de Tlatelolco, seemed to reach new heights.[22] Of course, the fact that one of the most renowned students at this center, Don Carlos of Texcoco, was burnt at the stake under charges of heresy did not help the future development of the institution, but it is undeniable that bishop Zumárraga did all in his power to do what he thought was in the best interest of the Indians and their future, including creating new hospitals and importing the first printing press to New Spain, together with books that he printed for the Indian religious instruction (Greenleaf 1961: 36).

The schooling of Indians became intricately related to the issue of their priesthood, whether that education should be given to them and what they would do with it. In general terms, the Franciscans thought that though the Indians were

---

21 These measures echo the ones that had been proposed by Hernando de Talavera in Granada apropos the integration of the moriscos. I will return to this point later in the chapter.

22 The request for this school is contained in the letter that the bishop Zumárraga writes to Juan de Sámano, secretary of the king, on December 20, 1537: "Y entre todo lo que á S.M. escribimos, la cosa en que mi pensamiento más se ocupa y mi voluntad más se inclina y pelean con mis pocas fuerzas, es que en esta ciudad y en cada obispado haya un colegio de indios muchachos, que aprendan gramática á lo menos, y un monasterio grande en que quepan mucho número de niñas hijas de indios, tomadas á sus padres desde seis ó siete años abajo, para que sean criadas, doctrinadas é industriadas en el dicho monasterio cerrado, porque es así la condicion y costumbres de los indios, que tienen comunmente todos los principales á sus mujeres é hijas en estrecho cerramiento, y así las darían de mejor gana que las dan" (García Icazbalceta 1881: appendix 22, 106). The document by which the school of Tlatelolco is authorized is recorded in García Icazbalceta 1881: appendix 21, 102. On the contrary, the monastery for the formation of Indian girls was not authorized "porque estando en el principio de la conquista, no era tiempo oportuno de concederse el real permiso" (García Icazbalceta 1881: appendix 21,102).

intellectually capable of becoming good Catholics and even priests, they lacked the right disposition to be ordained; that is, they did not think that the Indians could lead the church.[23] On the other hand, the Dominicans, with the exception of Las Casas and his followers, reached the same conclusion: "The Indians could not command the respect of the people and they would be liable to error because they were not firmly rooted in the faith. Indeed, many Dominicans felt that the Indians lacked the basic intelligence needed to understand the things of the faith because of their ignorance of Spanish, and that even if they had a command of the language, they would still be inadequately endowed because mere language could not properly transmit the dogma" (Greenleaf 1961: 29).[24] This controversy about the rationale of the Indians was continued both in Mexico and in Spain, and it reached unprecedented heights in the debate that took place in Valladolid in 1550 and where Las Casas and Ginés de Sepúlveda discussed this matter to its fullest. Unfortunately, in the years preceding this controversy, the accusation against the cacique Don Carlos did not help the situation, and it almost seemed to prove that nothing right could come from the instruction of the Indians, which might explain why this *proceso* was treated so harshly.

---

23 Zumárraga himself accounted for his change of heart about the school in a letter addressed to Charles V on 17 April 1540. In that document the bishop admitted that he did not know for how long the school of Santiago de Tlatelolco was going to last, since the Indians were more prone to marriage than to continence and, therefore, were not good candidates for priesthood, the goal of their education. ("El colegio de Santiago [á cargo de frailes] no sabemos lo que durará, porque los estudiantes indios, los mejores gramáticos, *tendunt ad nupcias potius quam ad continentiam.*" García Icazbalceta 1881: appendix 27, 137.)

24 "Los indios no deben estudiar, porque ningún fruto se espera de sus estudio, lo primero porque no son para predicar en largos tiempos porque para predicar se requiere que el predicador tenga autoridad en el pueblo y ñesta no la hay en estos naturales porque verdaderamente son viciosos, más que los populares, éstos que estudian, e son personas de ninguna gravedad si se diferencian de la gente común en el hábito, no en conversación porque de la misma manera se tratan en esto que los hombres bajos de el pueblo. Lo segundo porque no es gente segura de quien se debe confiar la predicación del evangelio, por ser nuevos en la fe e no la tener bien arraigada, lo cual sería causa que dijesen algunos errores, como sabemos por experiencia haberlos dicho algunos, lo tercero, porque no tienen habilidad para entender cierta y rectamente las cosas de la fe ni las razones de ellas, ni su lenguaje es tal ni tan copioso, que se pueda por él explicar sin grandes impropiedades que fácilmente puedan llevar a grandes errores. De aquí se sigue que no deben ser ordenados porque en ninguna reputación serían tenidos, más que si no lo fuesen porque aun el Sacramento de la Eucaristía no se les administra por muchos motivos que personas muy doctas e religiosas para ello tienen, así por ser nuevos en la fe, como por no entender bien qué cosa será e cómo se deba recibir tan alto sacramento, porque todas las cosas se ordenan a algún fin. Quitadas estas razones porque ellos debían estudiar, como cosa muy necesaria queda, que se les debe quitar el estudio. En Santo Domingo de México, cinco de Mayo de 1544. Firmado: Fray Diego de la Cruz, Provincial, Fray Domingo de Betanzos." (Cuevas 1921: 389–90). Also see Aracil Varón (107). About the reasons given not to educate the Indians, see "El orden que los religiosos tienen en enseñar á los indios la doctrina, y otra cosa de policía cristiana," a document offered by García Icazbalceta 1971a: 62–64.

DON CARLOS'S CASE: ZUMÁRRAGA'S TRIAL BY FIRE

Once Fray Juan de Zumárraga gained jurisdiction as Apostolic Inquisitor (June 27, 1535), he used his authority to hold numerous trials for religious crimes against a number of Indians living in and around the Mexico Valley. This initiative started a new trend since, both before and after this brief campaign (1536 to 1543), the trials of Indians for paganism or idolatry were either absent or few and generally lacked the support of the crown of Spain. As I mentioned above, this effort by the Spanish authorities was not only unprecedented but also the most decisive initiative in the application of the institution to the indigenous population in New Spain and the reason why Indians were submitted to all kinds of punitive actions from trials to prison, from flogging to banishment and, in the case of one indigenous leader, Don Carlos of Texcoco, the stake.

The case of Don Carlos brought to Mexico the unprecedented measure of punishing idolatry with death and, therefore, addressing a religious, spiritual crime in a physical manner rather than opting for a response equally spiritual or religious, such as excommunication. Of course, this shift to physical punishments had long been used in Spain by the Inquisition and written about as early as in *Deuteronomy*, where death and destruction are prescribed as the answers to idolatry.[25]

In his attempt to get control over the idolatrous ways of the Indians, Bishop Zumárraga decided to have some *Ordenanzas* (ordinances) publicly proclaimed three times a year, with instructions for the new society the Spaniards were trying to establish in an attempt to make the Indians police themselves.

The *Ordenanzas* mostly consisted of the following. It was a document that urged the Indians to believe in God and in Him only, abandoning all other worship and sacrifices. If anyone was caught performing pagan acts, he would be punished with public flogging (one hundred lashes) and his hair would be cut off, a sign of loss of status in the community. The second time he would be submitted to trial. If someone did not want to be a Christian, he would be whipped and if declared against the Christian religion, he would be *severely punished.*

---

25 "If thou shalt hear say in one of thy cities, which the Lord thy God hath given thee to dwell there, saying, certain men, the children of Belial, are gone out from among you, and have withdrawn the inhabitants of their city, saying, Let us go and serve other gods, which ye have not known; Then shalt thou inquire, and make search, and ask diligently; and, behold, if it be truth, and the thing certain, that such abomination is wrought among you; *Thou shalt surely smite the inhabitants of that city with the edge of the sword, destroying it utterly,* and all that is therein, and the cattle thereof, with the edge of the sword. And thou shalt gather all the spoil of it into the midst of the street thereof, and shalt burn with fire the city, and all the spoil thereof every whit, for the Lord thy God: and it shall be a heap for ever; it shall not be built again" (*Deuteronomy* 13: 13–16, my emphasis)

The first time the *Ordenanzas* were made known (on June 10, 1539) proved to be the most effective, and twelve days later Francisco, an Indian from the village of Chiconautla, presented charges against Don Carlos, the cacique of Texcoco.[26]

Don Carlos was part of a circle of privileged families before the conquest, and after it he remained in an advantageous position, being brought up in the house of Cortés and educated at the Colegio de Santa Cruz de Tlatelolco. He had been baptized by the Franciscans around 1524 and, when his brother died seven years later, he took over the caciqueship of Texcoco. It seemed that his life was fairly easy until he was accused before the Holy Office as a dogmatizer against the Catholic faith.

As I have mentioned above, the Indian Francisco said that in the first days of June, and because of the intense drought that devastated the village of Chiconautla, the Father Provincial had encouraged the Indians to pray and make processions to plead for the much needed rain. Don Carlos's sister was married to the cacique of that village and, when Don Carlos decided to visit her, he arrived in the middle of the supplications. In the *proceso*, Francisco declared that Don Carlos ridiculed the whole process and the teaching of the friars who, the cacique considered, were deceiving the indigenous people. Also, and always in Francisco's words, Don Carlos was accused of saying that the Christian doctrine was nothing and that the instruction given to the *principales* in the schools was a joke (González Obregón 1910: 40).[27]

Upon the defense of the doctrine made by Don Alonso, cacique of Chiconautla and Don Carlos's brother-in-law, the latter insisted in his attacks and responded that both that cacique and his sons should be killed because they were too knowledgeable in God's affairs (too much for being Indians, that is). After these accusations, Don Carlos was immediately apprehended and put in jail. His house was inspected and his possessions were being confiscated when the inquisitors found a painting of the Devil, as seen by Spanish eyes, that the Indians used to celebrate, two altars and a number of stone idols.

During the trial, more accusations came up, and so bishop Zumárraga and Bernardino Sahagún, among others, heard the following charges: Cristóbal, an Indian from Chiconautla said that he overheard Don Carlos saying to Francisco not to fight the indigenous' traditions and to live like their ancestors had. Also, Don Carlos observed that each of the three orders of friars (Franciscans, Dominicans, and Augustinians) had their own clothing and way of doing things: they preached differently and behaved differently, which is why Don Carlos could not understand why, if they were allowed to maintain their differences, the Indians had to reduce themselves to one single pattern. He offered the alternative to go back to

---

26 The complete document can be read in appendix A in Carreño (1944: 60, 130–35).
27 The whole trial can be found in González Obregón (1910).

the teaching of the ancestors in a turn very similar to the Peruvian Taki Onquoy,[28] but that shift looked extraordinarily dangerous and certainly too close to a frontal attack on the Spanish rule in Mexico as well as the Spanish Church and their representatives:[29]

> ¿Quién son estos que nos deshacen y perturban é viven sobre nosotros y los thenemos á cuestas y nos sojuzgan? Oíd acá, aquí estoy yo y allí está el señor de México, Yoanizi, y allí está mi sobrino Tezapili, señor de Tacaba, y allí está Tlcahuepantli, señor de Tula, que todos somos iguales y conformes, y no se ha de igualar nadie con nosotros, que esta es nuestra tierra y nuestra hacienda y nuestra alhaja y posesión, y el señorío es nuestro y á nosotros pertenece; é si alguno quiere facer ó decir cosa, reiámonos dello, ¡oh hermanos que estoy muy enojado é sentido! Y algunas veces nos hablamos yo é mis sobrinos los señores; ¿quién viene aquí a mandarnos y apreendernos y á sojuzgarnos? Que no es nuestro pariente ni nuestra sangre, y también se nos iguala.[30] (González Obregón 1910: 43)

HEARSAY

This text shows the rage and the indignation of the Indians, as they were deprived of their own land and way of life. On top of this, Don Carlos's son, a boy of about eleven or twelve years old, declared that he had not been taught the Christian

---

28 The *Taki Onqoy* (or *Taqui Onqoy*) was a movement that developed in the decade of the 1560s and the beginning of the 1570s. This movement, whose name literally means "dancing sickness" or the "disease of the dance," constituted the first organized attempt of Native American resistance. It preached the total rejection of Spanish religion and customs, and, instead, it proposed their coming back to the teaching of their predecessors, to the worship of the Sun, their *huacas* (sacred entities or places), and their *mallquis* (the mummified remains of their ancestors). The leaders of the Taki Onqoy, the most important being Tupac Amaru, claimed that they were messengers from the native gods and preached that a pan-Andean alliance of native gods and peoples would come together to destroy the Christians.

29 "Mira que los frayles y clérigos cada uno tiene su manera de penitencia; mira que los frayles de San Francisco tienen una manera de doctrina, y una manera de vida, y una manera de vestido, y una manera de oración; y los de Sant Agustín tienen otra manera y; y los de Santo Domingo tienen de otra . . . Y así mismo era entre los que guardaban á los dioses nuestros, que los de México tenían una manera de vestido, y una manera de orar, é ofrecer y ayunar, y en otros pueblos de otra . . . sigamos aquello que tenían y seguían nuestros antepasados y de la manera que ellos vivieron, vivamos" (González Obregón 1910: 41). "Mira hermano que te lo prohíbo, y te lo vedo, y te lo reprehendo y riño; porque eres mi sobrino, que no lo hagas lo que te dicen el Visorrey y el Obispo ni el Provincial, ni cures de nombrarlos que también me crié en la iglesia y casa de Dios como tú, pero no vivo ni hago como tú . . . ¿Por ventura los xpianos no tiene muchas mujeres y se emborrachan sin que les puedan impedir los padres religiosos? Pues qué esto que á nosotros nos hacen hacer los padres, que no es nuestro oficio ni es nuestra ley impedir á nadie lo que quisiere facer: dejémoslo y echémoslo por las espaldas lo que nos dicen" (González Obregón 1910: 42).

30 My translation: Who are these that destroy us and upset us and live above us and who we have to put up with and who judge us? Listen: here I am and there the Lord of Mexico, Yoanizi, and here is my nephew Tezapili, ruler of Tacaba, and there is Tlcahuepantli, lord of Tula, and we are all the same and in agreement that nobody compares to us, that this is our land and estate and our jewel and our possession and the ownership is ours and it belongs to us; and if someone wants to do or say a thing, we should laugh at them, oh brothers how mad I am and upset! And sometimes I talk to my nephews, the lords: who comes here to order us and seize us and dominate us? It is neither our relative nor our blood but wants to be equal.

doctrine because his father told him not to go to church, so he did not know the basic prayers or the Sign of the Cross (González Obregón 1910: 37). Finally, the cacique was accused of taking his niece as a concubine and having a daughter with her, while he defended this lifestyle as something normal among Indians.

Facing all these charges, Don Carlos's future was very much compromised. In his defense, his wife said that she had not seen him worship any idols or doing sacrifices to them and the little statues found in their house were suspected to have belonged to somebody else and she had forgotten in their hiding place.[31]

Both Don Carlos and his niece admitted to the charges of concubinage and to having a daughter together but he always denied any other accusation, especially in dealing with idolatry. Also, although he admitted his adultery, he denied that he had encouraged others to return to concubinage or that he had praised the way of life that the Indians had before the conquest. He even professed loyalty to the church and the Spanish state, but it seemed that his gesture had no effect. In the end, the Inquisition presented two charges against Don Carlos: heretical dogmatizing and idolatry and, although he was exonerated of the latter, he was convicted of the former.[32]

Don Carlos made one more attempt to save his life and reported that he was being caught as a victim in a plot developed by his enemies in order to get his position as cacique. This accusation, although it would have not been totally out of the question (it was common in a colonial country for subalterns to use the mechanisms of the colonizers as a way to solve their internal affairs), could never be proven and was finally disregarded.

It has been said that Bishop Zumárraga dealt with the trial too quickly, too harshly, or maybe both; that he had not quite weighed the consequences of his decision, and that he already had an agenda against the caciques and their effect in

---

31 Greenleaf adds that Don Carlos's house had belonged to his deceased uncle and that the place had been a shrine and a temple in the period before the conquest. The idols had been hidden inside the walls in the first years after the arrival of the Spaniards, and neither Don Carlos nor his wife knew anything about them (Greenleaf 1961: 71)

32 "El dicho Don Carlos, con diabólico pensamiento ha impedido y perturbado que no se predique ni enseñe la doctrina xpiana, desciendo y afirmando que toda ella es burla, y que lo que los frayles predicaban no era nada; y persuadiendo que ninguno fuese á la iglesia á oir la palabra de Dios ni nadie pusiera su corazón en la palabra de Dios . . . y que era pecado hacer creer á los indios esta ley de Dios y doctrina xpiana, porque su padre y agüelo habían sido muy grandes profetas; y que habían dicho que la ley que ellos guardaban era la buena y que sus dioses eran los verdaderos; dogmatizando públicamente y como hereje, queriendo introducir la seta de sus pecados y volver á la vida perversa y herética que antes que fuese cristianos solian thener . . . porque paresc el dicho Don Carlos quererlos domatizar, volver y restituir á las idolatrías y sacrificios antiguos, herejías y errores suso dichos . . . Don Carlos ha cometido allende de las penas en derecho establecidas contra los semejantes domatizadores, grandes y muy gravisimos y atroces delitos, por los cuales debe ser castigado y ponido, grave y atroz y públicamente condenándole como á hereje domatizante, relaxándole si necesario fuere al brazo seglar, haciendo en su persona é bienes todos los autos" (González Obregón 1910: 64–65).

the general population.[33] But the reality is that the bishop did not decide himself about Don Carlos's future, but rather he passed the decision along to others while he remained in the margin.[34] Moreover, when the bishop had to sign Don Carlos's document for him to be relaxed to the secular arm, he suggested that the cacique be treated mildly ("beninamente") with a sentence more focused on his possessions than on himself. Nevertheless, once outside of the ecclesiastical jurisdiction, Zumárraga could not interfere, it was out of his hands, and Don Carlos was taken in procession, wearing his *sambenito*, directly to the stake. There, and once the accusations against him were publicly read, Don Carlos took this opportunity to address the Indian spectators in their language and exhort them to take him as an example of what not to do, saying that they should abandon their vices and idolatries and turn to God through conversion. With this gesture, Don Carlos not only pleased the authorities, both religious and civil, but also supported the old Spanish belief by which if the leader of the Indians joined them, his people would follow, combining that way in one figure the political and the spiritual values of a group. Therefore, if Christ had a double nature (human and divine), and so did the king of Spain, "the Catholic Monarch" who combined in himself the divine grace (after having been chosen by the finger of God) and the state powers, so did the Spaniards assume about the indigenous leaders, which explains the importance that the former put in converting the latter and the repercussions that the Spaniards expected to be derived from this act.

POINT OF SECTION
UNCLEAR

---

33 In 1536 Zumárraga complained about the vices of the caciques and their refusal to follow the Christian doctrine: "En descargo de mi conciencia, hay gran necesidad que se hagan casas, y en cada cabecera y pueblos principales, donde se críen e doctrinen las niñas y sean escapadas del aldilubio maldito de los caciques; y que es necesario que S.M. dé poder a quien le pareciere para tomarles las hijas de cinco años arriba, y que esto es necesario y lo tengo muy sabido, ni veo mejor remedio sino han de ahorcar los más de los caciques, que hoy en día lo hacen peor en secreto que antes que oyesen la fe católica y evangelio." My translation: To clean my conscience, there is a great need to build houses in each main village so that girls can be raised and taught the doctrine and be safe from the influence of the caciques; and it is necessary that your majesty allows that the girls under five years old be taken; and this is very necessary because I don't see any other measure but to hang the caciques because they act a lot worse now in secret that before they knew about the Catholic faith and the Gospel. (Cuevas 1975: 57).

34 "E después de lo suso dicho, en diez é ocho días del mes de Noviembre del dicho año, su Señoría Reverendísima dixo: que para que mejor esta casa se vea y determine mandaba e mandó que este proceso se lleve al Ilustrísimo Señor Don Antonio de Mendoza, Visorrey de esta Nueva Spaña, é a los Señores Oidores estando en su acuerdo, para que por ellos visto é platicado con otras personas de ciencia é conciencia, dén su parecer y se determine lo que convenga en el caso, para lo cual señaló el Jueves primero que viene, que es día de acuerdo." My translation: And after what I said, on this 18th day of November of the said year, his Excellency said: that for the better instruction of this case, that it should be taken to his Excellency Señor Don Antonio de Mendoza, viceroy of New Spain, and to the oidores, so that after their agreement and conversation with other men of science and conscience, they determine a verdict appropriate for this case, by next Thursday, which is they day of agreement (González Obregón 1910: 81).

LAS CONQUISTAS OVER MEXICO

This expectation was made very clearly in the drama *La conquista de Jerusalén*, the play to which I referred above and that was performed in Tlaxcala in 1539. This play only exists in the chronicles of the period (the text itself has been lost), in the remembrance of those who witnessed it, in particular, Toribio Motolinía, one of the first Franciscan friars, who happened to see its performance in Tlaxcala on Corpus Day, 1539.

The play was conceived as the indigenous equivalent of *La conquista de Rodas* (1539), a theatrical representation of the battle of Pavia that was performed by Spanish actors to celebrate their victory.[35] With this in mind, the site of Rodas is chosen as a way of creating links with the situation that Mexico was experiencing at the time. Therefore, Rodas was not only a place that was taken from the "infidels" (in this case, the Turks), but also it was an island, just like Mexico-Tenochtitlan, surrounded by water everywhere, and where the infidels also had to be conquered. In these circumstances the performance of the siege of Rodas and the omnipresence of ships were used to give a sense of the power that was consolidating in the hands of the Viceroy Mendoza in New Spain and, thus, to show the indigenous population the might of the invaders and what they hoped would happen.

The role of Tlaxcala in the process of conquest and assimilation of their peoples deserves a special mention. When Cortés arrived in 1521, the Tlaxcalan warriors fought him for several days before deciding to ally with him and the other native allies to overthrow Tenochtitlan. The Tlaxcalan, therefore, had an interest, born from their own local disputes and their rivalry with the Mexicas, to promote themselves as the sole or primary allies of the Spaniards in their attempt to conquer Tenochtitlan in order to secure their status in the emerging political order (Ruiz Medrano and Kellog 2010: 22).

The Tlaxcaltecans wanted to protect themselves from being granted as an *encomienda*, and they quickly recognized that they needed to petition the Crown to secure a royal promise prohibiting the granting of themselves or their subjects to a third party as an encomienda, but more than that, they wanted the rights and privileges awarded to Spanish conquistadores. Their petition was twofold: on the one hand, they wanted to remain free vassals of the Crown, but, on the other, they wanted to retain perpetual status as *señores naturales* (natural lords) with jurisdiction over their respective subjects and lands. Charles V and his courtiers clearly knew about the courage and hospitality of the Tlaxcalans. They had also proven themselves to be faithful Christians when they welcomed the twelve Franciscans

---

35 My analysis of this play is based on Horcasitas's study of the same (499–504). In it, and since we do not have the text of the play, he compiles references to it from different chronicles, such as Motolinía's (1996), Díaz del Castillo's (1999), and Las Casas's (1967), among others.

in 1524, and the nobles were immediately baptized, followed by the rest of their people. Therefore, when in 1526 two Mexica lords held court with Charles V and received an encomienda grant, the Tlaxcaltecans were soon to follow, achieving this privilege in 1529 (Ruiz Medrano and Kellog 2010: 24). These civilized Indians who visited the court to ask for privileges challenged the Spaniards, who continued to believe that native people conformed to the Aristotelian concept of natural slaves and were incapable of self-rule. They demonstrated that native people could rationally manage their own affairs. With this grant, the Tlaxcalans became free vassals of the Crown: a self-governing political community directly under the Crown. The Tlaxcalan nobles were to remain the first instances in legal cases, to administer the region on behalf of the Crown, to collect tribute for the Crown, and to evangelize the natives of Tlaxcala from then on.

According to Motolinía, the people from Tlaxcala wanted to see this performance before coming up with their own ("los Tlaxcaltecas quisieron primero ver lo que los Españoles y los Mexicanos hacian, y visto que hicieron y representaron la conquista de Rodas, ellos determinaron de representar la conquista de Jerusalem, el cual pronostico cumpla Dios en los proximos dias"[36] (Motolinía, Treatise I, chapter XV, in García Icazbalceta 1971a 87). Therefore, we are witnessing a product of exceptional complexity, a hybrid product: European in the concept and the direction, but with native adaptation and montage. This is the genesis of *La conquista de Jerusalén*, part of the Spanish hegemonic enterprise but populated by natives who add their own local rivalries and flavor to it. Presented this way, the play served the interests of both communities at the same time: on the one hand, it was used as a vehicle of Christian doctrine (an antecedent of the *acto sacramental*); but, on the other, it allows Tlaxcaltecans to show their support to the Spanish army against the Turks on stage, and against the Mexicas off stage, an interesting way to intervene in local politics using evangelization drama.

For the performance of *La conquista de Jerusalén*, the center of Tlaxcala was completely transformed with the addition of towers, fortresses, and areas specifically conceived to house the two armies that were about to confront each other.[37] The first ones to come on stage were the Spanish men-at-arms, followed by Germans and Italians, although the Indian representation of the different European nationalities was not achieved very accurately since they lacked models. The representation of New Spain came on stage next and, in particular, the viceroy Mendoza and

---

36 My translation: Tlaxcaltecans first wanted to see what the Spaniards and the Mexicans had done, and once they saw that they represented *La conquista de Rodas*, they determined to perform *La conquista de Jerusalén*, and may God fulfill the prediction.

37 For studies of this play, see García Icazbalceta (1896), Ricard (1986), Horcasitas (1974), and Aracil Varón (1999).

the people of Tlaxcala, Mexico, Huasteca, Mixteca, Cempoala, and Acolhuacan, accompanied by a group of actors representing people from Peru, Santo Domingo, and Cuba.[38]

The action starts with the Spanish army attacking and the Moors defending Jerusalem, trying to counteract the Christian forces. One revealing aspect found in this performance is that the Moorish captain was represented by an Indian dressed as Cortés, which is undoubtedly one of the most obvious examples of the indigenous hand being involved in the composition of the play.[39] "Luego salieron al campo á dar la batalla el ejército de los Españoles, los cuales en buena órden se fueron derecho á Jerusalem, como el Soldan los vió venir, que era el marques del Valle Don Hernando Cortés, mandó salir su gente al campo para dar la batalla"[40] (Motolinía, Treatise I, chapter XV, in García Icazbalceta 1971a: 89). Therefore, in a subversive twist, the Indians make Cortés, the man who had taken charge of the conquest of their territory, the face of the colonizer, portray the greatest enemy possible, a Moorish captain, within the new Christian setting into which they had been forced, and, by the same token, they made him the target of all attacks. As could be expected, the Moors are defeated. Cortés's military defeat (acting as the Moor captain) has traditionally been taken as proof of the Indians' resentment against the conqueror. Nevertheless, a close reading of the political situation at the time suggests that his defeat on stage reflects something different: a slow shift in the balance of power by which the central administration was gaining more and more influence, shadowing the individual actions of the conquistadores. Therefore, seen in this light, Cortés's defeat in the hands of Charles V and the viceroy on New Spain became not a gesture against the former but rather an act of adhesion of the Tlaxaltecans to the Spanish Crown.

As the play goes on, the Indian soldiers take their turn in defeating the Moors and helping the Spaniards, but the latter get help from troops coming from Galilee, Judea, Samaria, Damascus, and Syria. This time the Moors win the battle, and Don Antonio de Mendoza, captain of the Spaniards, writes to the emperor, Charles V, to let him know about the course of events. Following this defeat, the soldiers from the islands (Santo Domingo, Cuba, etc.) fail in their endeavor, and the Moors

---

38 As it was the case with *La conquista de Rodas*, my analysis of this play is mostly based on Horcasitas's (1974: 505–9) study. In it, and since we do not have the text of the play, he compiles references to it from different chronicles, mainly from Motolinía's.

39 García Icazbalceta explicitly writes that it should not be understood that Cortés himself was part of the representation, but rather an Indian actor dressed as the conqueror and pretending to be the Moorish captain (García Icazbalceta 1971a: 89).

40 My translation: The army of the Spaniards left for the battlefield, and they went directly toward Jerusalem, when the Soldan, which was the Marquis of the Valley Don Hernando Cortés, saw them, and ordered his people to get out to battle them.

succeed again. Therefore, the defeat is seen as the result of the islanders' weak religious conviction, a weapon against the infidels mentioned at the same level as any other defensive mechanism.

The emperor, accompanied by the kings of France and Hungary, travels to the battleground, wishing to keep a close eye on the confrontation, arriving just in time to witness another defeat of his troops.

By this time we can imagine that almost every Indian in Tlaxcala would be participating in the performance, representing one of the many armies involved but, what is more interesting, from the point of view of the empire in formation, is that the Indians themselves would want to be part of the Christian troops, as soldiers of Christ. So, in a way, the opportunity to participate in the performance gives the Indians an opportunity to assert their condition as Christians (even on stage, in the role they play), but, on the other hand, it also opens the possibility to use the stage as a place to include new perspectives from the point of view of the ones defeated by the Christians.

Upon this new turn of events in the play, Charles V writes to the pope in search of spiritual help, to which the pope responds assuring that the grace of God would become present in the battle, as he asks for a general prayer to the Corpus Christi (since the play was performed to celebrate the festivities of Corpus Christi).

At this point in the play, important parallels can be drawn with the actual situation in Europe where Pope Paul III was trying to form the Holy League (consisting of the Papal States, Spain, Venice, Naples, and Sicily) against the corsair Barbarossa and the Ottoman empire. This initiative, formulated in terms of a crusade by Charles V, was short-lived, and the Christian Alliance was easily defeated. Nevertheless, in spite of the defeat of the European attempt, *La conquista de Jerusalén* presents on stage a similar alliance of Christians: Tlaxaltecans, Spaniards, the pope, and the emperor.

At that moment in the play—that is, once Christianity has joined in prayer for the same purpose—an angel appears in order to tell the soldiers that God has heard them; that they had been put to a test; and that, once cleared, they would receive the help of Saint James, patron saint of Spain and the portrait of the valiant soldier against the infidels. Immediately after, the mighty presence of the Apostle makes the Moors quiver, and they run for refuge, hiding in Jerusalem. Then, the Tlaxcaltecans, seeing that the Christian forces had not conquered the city, try once more and, in their new defeat, pray again. It would then be the turn for St. Hipólito's appearance, which would lead the Indian army side-by-side with the Spanish army led by St. James. Together, they fight the Moors, who realize that they stand no chance of victory. Suddenly, the archangel St. Michael appears to the infidels and talks to them about redemption and the possibility of joining the army of God through baptism, which they do after having asked Charles V for peace and forgiveness. The latter arrives at the gates of Jerusalem and, after conquering the city, offers baptism to those defeated. In the end a real priest goes on stage and christens the Moors, or rather, the Indian actors ("los cuales fueron actualmente bautizados") who are performing these roles, in a massive administration of the sacrament that concludes the Corpus Christi festivities.

MOORS AND CHRISTIANS IN NEW SPAIN

La conquista de Jerusalén, following the tradition of portraying the past in the hope of what the future would bring—that is, the spiritual conquest of New Spain—is based on the battles between Christians and Moors and aims to teach a number of simple aspects of the doctrine to all the possible idolaters who, like the Moors portrayed on stage or the late cacique Don Carlos, challenged the presence of God (and that of the Spaniards in Mexico). Therefore, God's spiritual superiority finds its echo on the battleground (as it did in La conquista de Rodas), where the miraculous appearances of St. James and St. Hipólito do not leave any room for further speculation—God supports his people in a way that the pagan idols do not, and on his side is where victory lies:

> Dios ha oído vuestra oración, y le ha placido mucho vuestra determinación que tenéis de morir por su honra y servicio . . . y para mas seguridad os enviará Dios á vuestro patrón el Apóstol Santiago . . . En esto entró Santiago en un caballo blanco como la nieve y él mismo vestido como le suelen pintar. Y como entró en el real de los Españoles, todos le siguieron y fueron contra los Moros que estaban delante de Jerusalén, los cuales fingiendo gran miedo dieron a huir . . . A la hora entró San Hipólito encima de un caballo morcillo, y esforzó y animó a los Nahuales, y fuése con ellos a Jerusalem.[41] (Motolinía, *Historia*, Treatise I, Chapter XV, in García Icazbalceta 1971a: 93–94)

From this statement, we must understand that the intent was for the indigenous spectators to realize that fighting against the Christian God was a lost cause: "El Soldan que estaba en la ciudad habló á todos sus Moros diciendo: 'Grande es la bondad y misericordia de Dios, pues así nos ha querido alumbrar estando en tan gran ceguedad de pecados; ya es llegado el tiempo en que conozcamos nuestro error;

---

41 My translation: God has heard your prayers, and he was pleased by your willingness to die in his honor . . . and to be sure He will send your patron saint James . . . and in saying this, St. James appeared on a horse white as snow and dressed as he is usually portrayed. And as he entered into the Spanish quarters, everybody followed him and went against the Moors that were in front of Jerusalem, and pretending to be afraid, started to run . . . At that time St. Hippolytus came in on a black horse and encouraged the natives and went with them to Jerusalem.

hasta aquí pensábamos que peleábamos con hombres, y ahora vemos que peleamos con Dios y con sus santos y ángeles: ¿quién les podrá resistir?"[42] (Motolinía, *Historia*, Treatise I, Chapter XV, in García Icazbalceta 1971a: 95). Also, with the same action, the spectators received news of the merciful nature of this superior being open to reconciliation through baptism. It is at this point that the parallelisms are more obvious since the author of the text hopes that, by showing the conversion of the Moors on stage, the Indians would want to react in an identical fashion. The play, thus, is situated in an eternal present, not related to any historical fact, to be able to establish strong connections with the situation in Mexico.

The text expects a clear identification between infidels (Moors and Indians) and a subsequent spiritual conquest of Mexico as the one over Jerusalem is portrayed. It also establishes the power of the Christian God over that of the Mexicas, unable to defend his worshippers from the European invaders. But if we read carefully, we can see that the entrance of St. Hippolytus does point beyond the spiritual, and it touches on the military aspects of the physical conquest of Mexico: "Aunque sois tiernos en la fe os ha querido Dios probar, y quiso que fuésedes vencidos para que conozcais que sin su ayuda valéis poco; pero ya que os habeis humillado, Dios ha oído vuestra oracion, y luego vendrá en vuestra favor el abogado y patron de la Nueva España San Hipólito, en cuyo dia los Españoles con vosotros los Tlaxcaltecas ganastes á Mexico"[43] (Motolinía, *Historia*, Treatise I, Chaper XV, in García Icazbalceta 1971a: 94). This way, although the play starts from a situation that seems alien both to the setting and to the people who are involved in it, both as actors and spectators, the action moves from the general to the particular details of the conquest of Mexico and directly refers to the collaboration between the Tlaxcaltecans and the Spaniards, which finally assured the victory over Montezuma. This way, the conquest of the New World is presented within the spirit of the crusade initiated against the Moors, and emphasizing the presence of the Christian God in the new hegemonic enterprise with native intervention.

This same topos had already been successfully used by Fray Hernando de Talavera, who, apropos of the conquest of Granada by the Catholic Monarchs, makes of that city a New Jerusalem and incorporates the presence of God in the fight for the victory of the Christians and against the Saracens.

---

42 My translation: The Soldan, who was in the city, talked to his Moors saying: "Great is the goodness and the mercy of God because he has illuminated us in the blindness of our sins; but it is time that we recognize our mistake; until now we thought we were fighting men and now we see that we are fighting God and his saints and his angels. Who could fight back?

43 My translation: Although you are still new to the faith, God had put you to the test, and he wanted to see you defeated so that you know that, without his help, you are not worth it: but since you have humiliated, God has heard your prayers and he will send St. Hippolytus, patron saint of New Spain, in your aid because on his day, the Spaniards and the Tlaxcaltecans conquered Mexico.

As we saw before, Fray Hernando de Talavera (1428–1507), confessor to Queen Isabella during the siege of Granada, was put in charge of writing the celebratory mass for the final victory in the war over the Moors. This work, entitled *Oficio de la toma de Granada*, had two main purposes: on the one hand, to exalt the talents of the Catholic Monarchs who had made the victory possible and, on the other hand, to mark a definite intention to separate *them* from *us*, to establish a distance between the winners, in this case, the army touched by the Christian God, and the other ones that, in this case, refers to the Moors in Granada. The case of *La conquista de Jerusalén* (the play performed in Tlaxcala), however, addressed the pagan Indians. In any case, both play on the same assumption: "If God be for us, who can be against us?" (*Romans* 8:31).

In his *Oficio de la toma de Granada* (probably first performed in 1493 or 1494; Talavera 2003: 48),[44] Talavera, later named first archbishop of the city, established a parallelism between the Jews, generally known as the people chosen by God,[45] and the Spanish Christians in their role as the newly elected, and opens, in his first lecture, with innumerable praises to God for his help. Following this exultation and just before raising the figures of the monarchs to the level of biblical heroes, Talavera posits the diabolic nature of the Moors, whose sin he portrays as not only rejecting the Catholic creed but as giving themselves to the Devil and establishing his evil reign in the land of Spain:

> Después de mucho tiempo en que España estuvo
> Dominada por la fiera crueldad de los árabes
> Por fin quiere el Señor que esta crueldad
> Pierda completamente su poder.
> Y allí brille la fe católica
> Y el Pueblo apostólico se alegre con Dios,
> Donde el engaño diabólico, en tanto grado,
> Reinó tanto tiempo.[46] (Talavera 2003: 91).

Due to this presence of evil in the core of what the Catholic Monarchs thought was called to become the Christian center of the world, there was a sense of added importance and relevance. This way, the entrance in Granada was not seen as one more victory, but rather, it was presented by the propaganda around the Reconquista all throughout the Middle Ages as the act of reclaiming the promised

---

44 The entire mass can be read in Talavera (2003)

45 For the complete decree of expulsion, see Appendix B.

46 My translation: After Spain being / dominated by the fierce cruelty of the Moors / for a long time, / finally God wants that this cruelty / loose its power completely / and the Catholic faith shine / and that the apostolic people of God be happy / where the diabolic ruse / reigned for so long.

IDOLATRY IN NEW SPAIN

land, as the final comeback, as victory at last.[47] This is the reason why the *Oficio* by fray Hernando de Talavera was held to be a relevant piece of writing, why it was to be repeated every year to commemorate this date (January 2), and why the comparison with the conquest of Jerusalem could not be avoided.[48] In fact, Talavera himself is aware of this phenomenon and, though he does not specifically mention the promised city, he does refer to it in subtle ways, making of his beloved Granada the New Jerusalem:[49] "De nuestro Rey serenísimo y preclaro. Que como otro Josué, batallando las batallas del Señor, en breve tiempo, es decir, en diez faustos y felices años, *toda la tierra de promisión, esto es, todo el Reino de Granada, que de ninguna manera es diferente de toda aquella tierra famosísima*, recuperó esforzadamente desde la ciudad de Gaucín hasta la ciudad de Granada, con un trabajo incansable y con un continuado batallar . . . El mismo Dios inmortal fue delante de él e hizo que se le humillasen los varones gloriosos de la tierra"[50] (Talavera 2003: 93, my emphasis). This idea of comparing Granada with the New Jerusalem fits perfectly with Talavera's overall master plan: to create a reformed church that would become the foundations for a Christian state, a true city of God where the political system was

---

47 Kamen points out that the war in Granada was presented more as territorial struggles than a religious one and increasingly void of idealism:

> Military idealism continued to be fed by chivalric novels, notably the Amadís de Gaula (1508), but beneath the superficial gloss of chivalry there burned an ideological intolerance typified by the great conquests of Cardinal Cisneros in Africa (Mers-el-Kebir 1505 and Oran 1509), and Hernán Cortés in Tenochtitlán (1521). It is also significant that the new rulers of Spain were willing to pursue an intolerant policy regardless of its economic consequences. In regard to both the Jews and the Mudejars, Isabella was warned that pressure would produce economic disruption, but she was steeled in her resolve by Cisneros and the rigorists. Ferdinand, responding to protests by Barcelona, maintained that spiritual ideals were more important than material considerations about economy. A "crusading" spirit thus replaced the spirit of *convivencia*, and religious exclusivism began to triumph." (Kamen 1985: 3–4)

48 Ronald Surtz, in *The Birth of a Theater*, points out that "Allegorical representation of the Mass was still in vogue when the Spanish vernacular theater was born in the late fifteenth century. Indeed, several commentators of the generation of Encina and Fernández utilize this method of interpreting church ritual as role-playing" (Surtz 1979: 39), and he includes Hernando de Talavera as an example. Not only had Talavera written on the matter, in his *Tractado de lo que significan las cerimonias de la misa*, but his own Mass that he wrote became ritualistic in its being performed every year. Also, he made use of the allegorical aspect in his parallelism with New Jerusalem.

49 Columbus also longed for the conquest of Jerusalem, which he directly connected to the wealth coming from the New World. "The letter that Columbus wrote to Ferdinand and Isabella from Portugal on March 4, 1493 completes these actions with plans to re-conquer the Holy Land. Columbus promises that after seven years he will be able to pay for an army of "five thousand cavalry and fifty thousand foot soldiers for the war and conquest of Jerusalem." (Vilches 2004: 204)

50 My translation: From our serene and illustrious king. Like another Joshua, fighting God's battles, in a short time, that is, in ten lucky and happy years, all this promised land, that is, the kingdom of Granada, that in nothing differs from that other famous land, was recovered from the city of Gaucin to the city of Granada, with tireless work and with constant battling . . . The same immortal God was with them and made the most glorious men on Earth humiliate in front of him.

based on Christian values and where religion was at the top of the list, a system very much in harmony with that promoted by Pedro de Ribadeneyra (and later Saavedra Fajardo) and opposite to Machiavelli's, joining the new idea of Franciscan society in New Spain in a perfect unison.[51]

This conception of world politics, especially in the circumstances in which Spain was living, could only come from a person in a unique situation such as Talavera. Very familiar with the Judaic tradition and belonging to a family of converts, he was a true believer in Catholicism (as I mentioned above, he became archbishop of Granada from 1493 to 1507) and used this conviction in his mission to try to spread his faith to Jews and Moors in Granada. But his frequent contacts with the *infidels,* plus his family's Jewish past, made him a target for the Inquisition, even when he spent most of his life trying to produce conversions. In the light of his problems with the *Santo Oficio,* it does not appear that Talavera's attempts to convert the *other* respond to a way of saving face for inquisitorial purposes. I would argue that this second generation was more zealous in their newly acquired religion than the Old Christians themselves and used every opportunity to voice their agendas, attacking the nonconvinced conversos and, of course, the ones who had resisted the oppression of evangelization. But these same New Christians, in spite of their conviction, were about to face the worst attacks, the most violent hatred and persecutions. This is the case of Fernando de Talavera, who, although he tried to spread Catholicism through his works, still had to face the accusations of the Inquisition.

His most famous work, *Católica Impugnación* (1480–87) presents the debate between a sincerely converted Jew and a *judaizante,* that is, a convinced new Catholic versus a Jew pretending not to be one. The text is written in response to a lost letter, in which the latter states the possibility of combining the two faiths, living as a Christian but keeping the Judaic traditions alive, and the answer by Talavera becomes a defense of the purity of Catholicism against a proposed plan that the author thought of as a heresy.

Talavera was very aware of the common factors between the Moors and Jews that inhabited the peninsula and of the threat their alliance would represent. Together with the Moors, the Jews are then presented by Talavera as the *other* of the Christian kingdoms, the *other* of the modern state in formation, the *other* of modernity. They (Moors and Jews) were united by their position relative to the more and more dominant power of the Christians and, therefore, by the wound of their exclusion, by the experience of being progressively isolated, confined. They formed a population that, though different in many aspects (both constituted translinguistic communities,

---

51 About the debate between Pedro de Ribadeneyra, Saavedra Fajardo, and Machiavelli, see previous chapter.

with different religions and traditions), they did have a common background of life experiences, of resistance, and a shared suffering of *ninguneo* in a society that defined itself by their exclusion.[52]

But, unlike the Moors, the converted Jews were considered a reality too close for comfort. They came from the same Judeo-Christian tradition and, once the religious difference was erased, there were no other marks with which to distinguish them, racial or otherwise, as was the case with the Moors.[53] This is where Talavera's book finds its place.[54]

As opposed to the general opinion that saw the conversos as belonging to a different race or lineage, the *other* that the Christians did not want to assimilate, Talavera starts his Católica Impugnación with a gesture of self-reflection and criticizes the Catholic themselves, not willing to accept the newly converted. But if he asks for honor and human treatment for those converted, he also demands death for those "que seyendo bautizados y teniendo nombre y aún algunas obras o muestras de cristianos, se halla que guardan cerimonias y ritos de moros o de judíos; y esos tales, es verdad, que en algunos casos deben morir como largamente lo dispone el derecho canónico y también el derecho civil"[55] (Talavera 1961: 83).

The main point of debate between the converso and the judaizante is the issue around the images that the first group justifies and the second criticizes. The judaizante's attacks concentrate on the use of images as idols and thereby regarding the Christians as idolaters in the same way that the reformers were doing at the European level.[56] So, the images of saints and virgins are called idols and said to constitute a well-oiled machine kept by the Catholic Church with the sole purpose of making money.

It is also argued that the Christians worship these representations rather than God himself, as well as the remains of the dead, made into relics and worshipped for the well-being and enjoyment of the living clerics. Talavera's defense of the images is based on two points. First of all, it admits the abuse that could happen around the use of the images and, though Fray Fernando de Talavera is perfectly aware of this fact, he considers that the benefits are still worthy: "Así que no permanecieron las

---

52 The anti-Jewish, anti-Moor propaganda even put the two groups together, blaming the first ones for facilitating the invasion of the latter in 711. Haim Beinart (2002: 21).

53 Dopico Black analyzes this threat of the Other too close for comfort or, to use her words, "closest to home," to refer to the threat posed by the wife, and, from there, she opens her analysis to include the Semitic Other. See especially chapter 1. (Dopico Black 2001)

54 See chapter 2 above.

55 My translation: for those that, having been baptized and having name and deeds of Christians, keep Moorish or Jewish ceremonies or rites; and those, in some cases, must die as it is stated in the canon law and in the civil law.

56 See chapter 1 about the attacks of the reformers—especially Luther, Zwingli, and Calvin—towards the Spanish Catholicism and its relationship with the evangelization in the American colonies.

imágenes de los santos en el pueblo cristiano, porque son provechosas a las bolsas de los eclesiásticos, mas porque, como muchas veces ya es dicho, son provechosas para despertar la fé y provocar a mayor devoción al pueblo cristiano"[57] (Talavera 1961: 201). According to the friar, the cult of images is a reasonable practice and a very useful one in order to worship God (Talavera 1961: 137). Of course he is quick to point out that it is not the images that are worshipped for themselves but for what they represent, for being a useful instrument to facilitate the communication between the believers and the divinity. For this reason he rejects the label of "idolaters" that supposedly the first unknown author assigned to Catholics in what Talavera sees as a terrible misunderstanding of a faith that the first author does not fully comprehend.[58] Therefore, Talavera does agree with the first author in his definition of idolatry and accepts the fact that the mere worship of the images needs to be called idolatry, but he assures the reader that misuse is not happening among Catholics (Talavera 1961: 186).[59]

The other argument that Talavera uses in his defense of the Christian ways is a decisive attack on the Jews themselves. He starts by drawing a clear difference between the Jews and the Christians and, in this dynamic based on *them* versus *us,* he places the Holy family. In his analysis, Talavera admits that the Virgin Mary was a Jew but says that Jesus Christ was not, not even a converted one:

---

57 My translation: So the images of saints did not stay amongst the Catholic people because they are beneficial to the pockets of the clergy, but because, as is said many times, they are good for awakening the faith and cause more devotion to Christians.

58 The same argument is made by Saint Vincent Ferrer, in his sermons to the Jews, especially in the one composed for the last Saturday of Advent, that the adoration is not to the stone or the gold that makes the images, or to the image itself, but to what it represents (Ferrer 2002: 574).

59 As I mentioned above, Vicent Ferrer also used this formula (idolatry rather than heresy) in his sermons when preaching for the evangelization of the Moors and Jews in Spain (1390–1412). By using it, he was aiming at two objectives: first, he was undermining other religions and denying them the status that he was ready to confer only to Christianity; and second, he was establishing a link between these other religions and the Christian Devil, accusing both Moors and Jews throughout his sermons of practicing not only a different religion but also one that was deeply rooted in its relationship with the Devil: "Quien tiene una falsa creencia en Dios hace y adora ídolos y por eso los judíos y sarracenos, que no creen que Dios uno es Padre, Hijo y Espíritu Santo sino sólo Dios uno, se hace un ídolo y dios nuevo, que no es Padre ni Hijo ni Espíritu Santo, y por eso adoran un ídolo al hacerse un dios que no es Padre" (Ferrer 2002: 104). "Y así vosotros, judíos, al creer que el único Dios no es padre etc. adoráis un ídolo, haciéndoos un dios para vosotros, pues no hay en el mundo un dios que no sea padre, etc. Y vosotros, judíos, no creáis en la Trinidad como los rústicos, esto es, que el Padre es una persona como Pedro y el Hijo como Juan, etc., porque no lo entendéis bien, sino que tenéis el ejemplo en un solo sol, que genera los rayos, y así el Hijo, y el calor procede de ambos . . . Y por eso, judíos, sois idólatras adorando un dios que no es padre, etc. Y por eso dice Dios: *Quitaré los ídolos,* etc. Y así tenéis este poder de bautismo, cómo limpia el alma puramente por el poder de la Trinidad, no sólo del agua" (Ferrer 2002: 760–61). "Y así por las conclusiones, todos los judíos e infieles están endemoniados y son habitación del demonio, pero bautizados tienen el Espíritu Santo" (Ferrer 2002: 659).

Tambien se podria decir que Jesucristo nuestro Señor no fué judío ni gentil, ni de otro linaje humano, según las carne [*sic*], porque el linaje comúnmente se trae del padre y Jesucristo no le tuvo cuanto a la humanidad, mas fué concebido del Espíritu Santo; así que, cuanto a la humanidad, se podría llamar hijo de Dios y divino, más que humano y más que gentil, ni judío; ... Iten, dice que Jesucristo fué el primero convertido, en lo cual habla muy impropiamente, porque conversión presupone aversión y Jesucristo nunca fué averso, en poco ni en mucho de la voluntad de su Santo Padre.[60] (Talavera 1961: 85)

Talavera, therefore, considers Jesus Christ to be universal, divine, and thus, without a nation or a religion but a place for everyone to learn from. Talavera wants to make a very important point in his argument. First, Jesus Christ was not a Jew; and second, he was not the first Jew converted into Catholicism because he was never opposed to the latter (Talavera 1961: 85). In his view, to convert one needs to have previously opposed a creed and, thus, Talavera rejects this idea in the case of Christ and considers that, in general, for all Jews, Judaism is a good, imperfect departing point from which to aspire to the ultimate goal: to become a Christian.

With this logic, Talavera puts himself in a very contradictory position: on the one side, Judaism is something that should be abandoned; but also, he considers it a good point of departure to achieve Christianity, a place worthy of the Virgin herself. This attitude contrasts with Talavera's wish for death for those who still insist on the Law of Moses and makes the difference between Judaism and Christianity just a matter of being consistent with the times, a matter of keeping up-to-date, in a twist that makes religion (independent of its sign) look like a stage in the process of perfecting humanity, a way of progress.

But let us not be fooled. Talavera does not spare any energy when attacking the Jews. We have already seen that the friar thinks that those infidels who have heard of Christianity and have not converted are in mortal sin and, therefore, deserve nothing but death, but he does not stop there. In his opinion the reason why Jews have no images is due to their intrinsic propensity to evil, a fact that makes them closer to idolatry; therefore, images only become an unnecessary temptation (Talavera 1961: 157). Based on this natural propensity for false worship, Talavera takes the opportunity to offer his own definitions, and he states that there is heresy when there are people who believe in the combination of Christianism and Judaism, that

---

60 My translation: You could also say that Jesus Christ our Lord was not a Jew or a gentile, and not any other human lineage according to the flesh because the lineage normally comes from the father and Jesus Christ did not have a human one, but rather he was conceived by the Holy Spirit; and so in terms of humanity, we could call him Son of God and divine more than human and more gentile and not a Jew ... They say that Jesus Christ was the first one converted, which is very inappropriate, because conversion presupposes aversion, and Jesus Christ was never contrary to the will of his Holy Father.

is, becoming a sham Christian who practices the Law of Moses at home, a ruse that should be punished by death.

Following this thought, Talavera can understand the lack of the *correct* faith by those who have never been in contact with the Gospels, but not those who, being familiar with their contents, choose otherwise.

In the spirit of Alfonso X (to which I will refer below), and later continued in the New World, Talavera advocates conversion through words and not swords, making of the *Bible* and the example his main allies, and attributing his progress to heaven ("no por sus fuerzas, ni por su espada, sino del cielo." Talavera 2003: 95), making use of a *motif* that would be capital in the development of the American colonies from Columbus to Las Casas.

Going back to New Spain, we can see a similar confrontation between Judaism and Christianity presented by González de Eslava (1998), who disguises it as a family feud. In his *Coloquio Octavo*, González de Eslava presents the Old Law (here standing as the Old Testament and, therefore, as the representation of the Jews) claiming her rights to an inheritance. The Old Law admits that she has been punished by the Inquisition in her past but argues that that should not be a reason to be excluded from God's will, since she is also His daughter. At that point, an Angel appears and negates her premise because she does not believe in the New Law (i.e., she is not a Christian). For the Old Law, her family ties have clearly been established since Christ descends from the same line as David; therefore, she says that if the Christians have the right to the inheritance, so much more should the Jews, since their relationship is older, but the Angel keeps denying her rights because of the Jews' ungratefulness. Finally, the last will of Jesus Christ is read, and the exclusion of the Jews is confirmed, although conversion is possible and baptism, always an option:[61]

> Y si a mi gracia boluiere,
> Ara la erencia se admite,
>   Si bautizarse permite;
>   Y si aquesto no hiziere,
> Que la erencia se le quite.[62] (González de Eslava 1998: 374)

In both settings (i.e., during the Spanish *Reconquista* and also in the conquest of the New World, in particular as shown in *La conquista de Jerusalén*, Tlaxcala, 1539),

---

61 Saint Vincent Ferrer included in his sermons the order in which these baptisms should occur: first, the children; second, the adults and the Jews; third, the Saracens; then, the Turks; and finally, the rest of the infidels and pagans (Ferrer 2002: 103).

62 My translation: And if my grace came back / and heritage were admitted / and baptism were allowed / and if this were not done / then heritage should be denied.

the conversion of the infidels implied a political submission and an acceptance of the vassalage to the king of Spain, in an extension of the feudal system that was also a backdrop in the New World: "Entonces respondió su capitan general, que era el adelantado Don Pedro de Alvarado, y todos con él dijeron, 'que se querian poner en manos del Emperador, y que luego el Soldan tratase de manera que les otorgase las vidas, pues los reyes de España eran clementes y piadosos, y que se querian bautizar'"[63] (Motolinía, *Historia de los Indios de Nueva España*, in García Icazbalceta 1971a: 95). Although in the play the pope himself appears in order to perform the baptisms, this happens after the Indians are well aware of the hierarchy displayed before them and by which the Spanish friars had been sent by the pope to the New World with the mission to convert the conquered under the auspices of the emperor, who would recognize the indigenous peoples as his vassals for the salvation of their souls. In this scheme the conversion of the natives is seen as a prerequisite for them to become part of the Christian political order to, later on, aspire to the eternal kingdom. In this sense Soldán, the Moor, surrenders to the emperor in his title of captain of "God's army on Earth"[64] and to the pope, whose presence supports Charles V's double nature as chief of state but also as Christian king. It is this tight collaboration between church and state that Ribadeneyra and Saavedra Fajardo would write about and by which, opposite to what Machiavelli had sustained, the state was to become the vehicle to enable the ultimate salvation that was, undoubtedly, described in religious terms. Therefore, it is expected that just the converted ones would be allowed to become part of the new Catholic state in formation and, by the same token, baptism became the necessary passport to be welcome in it.

BAPTISM: PASSPORT INTO THE NEW POLITICAL ORDER

This issue of inclusiveness-exclusiveness had already been raised when medieval Spain dealt with the population of Jews and Moors who lived in the peninsula. Already in the *Partidas* (1256–65) compiled by Alfonso X, the Learned or the Wise (king of Galicia, Castile, and León from 1252 to 1284), there were strict laws about the coexistence of the Christians with the *others*. To start with, and in keeping with the intricate relationship between religion and politics, religious matters are

---

63 My translation: Then the general captain, who was the governor Don Pedro de Alvarado, answered and with him, all said: "that they wanted to put themselves in the Emperor's hands and that the Soldan should negotiate that their lives be spared, since the Spanish monarchs were merciful and pious and that they wanted to be baptized."

64 "Como Dios del cielo me haya alumbrado, conozco que tú solo eres capitan de sus ejércitos: yo conozco que todo el mundo debe obedecer á Dios, y á tí que eres su capitan en la tierra" (García Icazbalceta 1971a: 95).

INTERESTING MEDIEVAL
CONNECTION

regulated in terms of legal policies, and both Moors and Jews are legally separated as different groups for religious reasons. Nevertheless the coexistence, as a principle, is not challenged (actually, the definition of Jews found in volume VII is "people who, although they do not believe in the religion of Our Lord Jesus Christ, yet, the great Christian sovereigns have always permitted them to live among us" [Alfonso X 2001: 1433]); only the terms in which it is to occur are subject to study by Alfonso X and the team of intellectuals that surrounded him. For this reason these minorities are given laws of *convivencia*, laws that are not necessarily only religious but that extend to other aspects of life, including politics, culture, and so on. In any case, it is obvious that the minorities are allowed to stay, but only if they agree to remain in the periphery of the system, on the outskirts of the Christian society, in the borders and, therefore, helping, in their exteriority, to conform the core of the state that was built on the premises of establishing the margins.[65]

From then on, and because of the bull of 1250, the Jews would not be allowed to share life with Christians, nor meals, houses, or even the same doctors. Even though the Spanish Jews participated fully in the life of the cities, they owned properties, filled public offices, and had influence in the life of the kingdoms, their prosperity together with their difference (religious and otherwise) made them the perfect target for hatred and discrimination. Therefore, in a relatively short period of time, the situation of the minorities in Spain went from being tolerated and their possessions defended (under Alfonso X) to become the target of prosecution from a sector of the Spanish society, an attitude that would lead, for example, to the massacre that

---

65 In the seventh volume of the *Partidas*, we find regulations that are mostly intended not to disturb the life of the Christians. Jews are warned not to try to convert any Christians to the Law of Moses, not to build any more synagogues, and not to marry or sleep with Christians, but the most strict law is, no doubt, the last one (number 11): "Many crimes and outrageous things occur between Christians and Jews because they live together in cities, and dress alike; and in order to avoid the offenses and evils which take place for this reason, We deem it proper, and we order that all Jews, male and female, living in our dominions shall bear some distinguishing mark upon their heads so that people may plainly recognize a Jew, or a Jewess; and any Jew who does not bear such a mark, shall pay for each time he is found without it ten maravedis of gold; and if he has not the means to do this he shall receive ten lashes for his offense" (1437). For their part, the Moors, whose religion was said to be "an insult to God" and their race "barbarous," were to be regulated as follows: "We decree that Moors shall live among Christians in the same way that we mentioned in the preceding Title that Jews do, by observing their own law and not insulting ours. Moors, however, shall not have mosques in Christian towns, or make their sacrifices publicly in the presence of men (1438). This attitude was maintained all during the thirteenth century during which the Christian kings were, in general, favorable to the Jews installed in the peninsula, but the pressure of the church was strong enough to provoke, in the 1230s, the foundation of the Tribunal of the Inquisition in the kingdom of Aragon, governed at the time by James I. In the meantime, Ferdinand III (who permanently united the kingdoms of León and Castile) put Jews in a situation in which they had never been in Spain and, for the first time after the Council of Letrán, they were forced to wear a yellow badge on their clothing in order to keep them from associating with Christians (though it was said that the initiative was implemented for their own safety). This gesture, not so far from the identical measure taken by the Nazi Germans, was the beginning of a cultivated hatred that would explode in 1391.

the Jews suffered in 1391 and to the expulsion (together with that of the Moors) as the modern state became more consolidated (Netanyahu 1999: 118–90).

Ferrán Martínez, archdeacon of Écija (Seville) and highly anti-Semitic, contributed enormously to this environment of hatred. He must have put all his hopes in Henry II, since the king's racial agenda was not a secret.[66] It looked as if, for the first time, there was some movement toward the final extermination of Jews or at least their total expulsion from Spain, and that connected with some sectors of the population of fourteeenth-century Spain. In contrast with Peter I, his predecessor, who had ordered his Christian subjects not to harm the Jews and to preserve the synagogues, his successor appealed to a multitude tired of seeing the prosperity of the Jews, even in the middle of the limitations to which they were submitted. But this same group became greatly aggravated when Henry II, once on the throne, relaxed his anti-Jewish measures and established a dialogue with the hated community.

Martínez was not ready to let this disappointment ruin his hopes and, from his pulpit in Seville, he started to stir the passions of the people and to create an environment where any opposition to the Jews was welcomed. Of course, at that time this sort of attitude was not new, since the Jews had already been expelled from France (1182), Naples (1288), England (1290), and parts of Germany, and Martínez used these facts to support his own agenda. He tried to get a village to expel the Jewish population, convinced that if one started, the rest would follow. For this difficult task he picked Alcalá de Guadaira, in the province of Seville. Unfortunately for him, his attempt did not work, but he did not abandon his xenophobic project and thought of ways to attack the Jewish population that were, up to that point, unprecedented.[67]

The king had no other choice but to intervene, and he not only ordered Martínez not to intervene in any issues that had to do with the Jewish population, but also, he expressed his astonishment because none of the measures taken before had been enough to stop the Andalusian priest.[68] The king even goes on to defend the

---

66 Henry II (born Enrique de Trastámara, January 13, 1334, Sevilla; died May 29, 1379, Santo Domingo de la Calzada) stood out for his use of anti-Semitism as a political tool in Spain. This led to a threat to the convivencia and a period of riots and pogroms that could be seen as sowing the seeds of the persecution of the Jews by the Spanish Inquisition, beginning a hundred years later.

67 Netanyahu attributes to this same Ferrán Martínez one of the most interesting reasons for promoting the conversion of the Moors living in the peninsula: since the Jews were not allowed to have Christian slaves, they had turned to the Moorish population for this service. So Martínez thought that the best way to harm the Jews would be to convert the Muslims, that is, not for the sake of their own salvation but rather to inconvenience the Jews, lead them to bankruptcy, and, hopefully, out of the country. This is to say that all conversions campaigns did not have only religious goals in mind (Netanyahu 1999: 119).

68 In his letter dated August 25, 1378, the king orders: "que non ossadeses nin vos entremetiessedes de judgar pleyto que tañiese á judío en qualquier manera . . . É Nos fasemos nos maravillado en vos entremeter é librar pleyto sobre nuestro deffendimiento, é otrosy de passer degrados é movimientos en ffechos de los dhos. judíos, sin nos lo passer saber; é que mandásemos Nos lo que nuestra merçet fuesse, sabiendo que

Spanish Jews as his property and, therefore, classifies Martínez's invectives as a direct attack on the monarch's possessions, since it was by the royal grace that the Jews were allowed in those territories.[69] This gesture echoes back to the attitude that Alfonso X had already infused in his *Partidas*, a document that, though it segregated the Jews and the Moors, also defended their physical integrity, their possessions, and, above all, the stability of coexistence.[70]

But the process was too advanced and did not stop upon the intervention of the king. Ferrán Martínez persevered and advocated the destruction of synagogues, which he identified as temples of idolatry, initiating a pattern that would be continued in Mexico by the bishop Zumárraga and that proposed the use of spare materials in the construction of Christian churches.[71]

The tipping point in Seville came in the form of an arrest ordered by Juan Alfonso de Guzmán, Count of Niebla and governor of the city, and his relative, the *alguacil mayor*, Alvar Pérez de Guzmán. On March 15, 1391, they decided to have two of the mob leaders arrested and publicly whipped. The fanatical mob, furious, murdered and robbed several Jews. The authorities tried to stop the riot, but it was too late. Ferrán Martínez had reached the point where he wanted to be, and he was

---

los judíos son de nuestra cámara é todos sus fechos requieren á nuestro mandado é á la nuestra merçet, é otro alguno non ha nin debe aver logar nin poder á faser ningunos mouimientos en fecho de los dhos. judíos, sin nuestro çierto mandado" (Amador de los Ríos 1875–76: 581–82).

69 In his letter of August 25, 1383, the king tells Ferran Martínez "que el Aljama de los judíos de la muy noble ciudad de Sevilla se nos enbiaron querellar muy fuertemente disiendo que vos que andades de cada dia pedriacando contra ellos muchas malas cosas ... otrosy que fasedes tornar xpstianos, sus moros que tienen por cativos, encubiertamente é sin derecho, non les guardando en esta rason los previllejos que tienen de los Reyes, onde Nos venimos. Somos mucho maravillado de vos de quándo fustes tan privado nro., por que sopiésedes nuestra entynçion é de la Reyna, é por qué fagades tales cosas como estas ... que sy buen cristiano queredes ser, que lo seades en vuestra casa: mas que non andedes corriendo con *nros judíos* desta guisa, por quel Aljama desa Ciudad sea destroyda por vuestra ocasión é pierdan lo suyo" (Amador de los Ríos 1875–76: 585, my emphasis).

70 In reference to the Moors, *Partidas VII* states that "although the moors do not acknowledge a good religion, so long as they live among Christians with their assurance of security, their property shall not be stolen from them or taken by force (1438; Alfonso X. 2001).

71 The letter in which Ferrán Martínez advocates the destruction of synagogues was signed on 8 December, 1390 and says the following: "Yo, Ferrand Martinez, Arçediano de Écija, é provisor que só por el Dean é Cabildo de la Iglesia de Sevilla, vacante la Sede, mando á vos los clérigos é sacristanes de Santolalla de la Sierra só pena de excomunión que vista esta mi albalá, ffasta tres oras deroquedes la casa Sinagoga, en que los enemigos de Dios é de la Iglesia, que se llaman Judíos, de ese dho. lugar ffasen *su idolatria*; é los libros é cosas que ÿ óbviese, que me los enviedes para que yo faga dellos lo que fuere debido; é la teja, é madera, é lámparas que sean para la obra de nra. Iglesia" (Amador de los Ríos 1875–76: 613, my emphasis). Zumarraga had proposed the same use for the materials taken from the destruction of houses of idols in his letter of November 30, 1537, cosigned with the bishops of Oaxaca and Guatemala: "Suplicamos á V.M. que sea servido de mandar aplicar y hacer limosnas á las iglesias de aquellas tierras y posesiones de sus templos é adoratorios que solian poseer los papas é ministros de ellos, con la piedra de ellos para edificar iglesias, y nos dé la facultad para que se los hagamos derrocar de todo punto, y les quememos y destruyamos sus ídolos que dentro tienen, pues por el primer mandamiento somos obligados todos á destruir la idolatría" (García Icazbalceta 1881: Appendix 21, 91).

not about to stop. In a matter of days, on June 6, the mob attacked the Judería in Seville. Thousands were assassinated, while an equal number of men and children were enslaved. The rest submitted to baptism as the only means of escaping death, putting a halt to a fanatic mob that, in reality, wanted the Jews either dead or gone, not Christianized (Netanyahu 1999: 127).[72]

This violent outbreak was heard as far as Rome and made Pope Benedict XIII compose a bull about the Spanish Jews. In this document, dated in 1415, the pope basically reiterated the laws outlined in Alfonso X's *Partidas* and prohibited the teaching of the Law of Moses, and the construction and improvement of synagogues. He banned the Jews from public office and instituted punishments for those who attacked Christian dogmas. But two points of his bull would have special transcendence not only in Spain but also later on in the New World. First of all, he seemed aware that it was not enough to try to convert the Jews but also the new Christians had to be monitored closely, as bishop Zumárraga realized when he ordered the constant *visitas* to all points of the Mexico Valley; and, second, he advocated a conversion based on kind words ("con dulzura") rather than on force, a conversion by persuasion and not by prosecution.[73] That way, the pope authorizes a society in which the Jews are included but not as citizens with full rights, rather as marginal characters, tolerated but not wished for.

The same reaction and attitude toward the *other* reached the lands of the New World and became particularly obvious when the Inquisition condemned the cacique Don Carlos to burn at the stake. In that situation, Charles V, fearing the rebellion of the mass and the threat that the mob would have in his plans for colonial domination, wasted no time in reprimanding bishop Zumárraga and decide to take away his inquisitorial powers at once (Greenleaf 1961: 14–15).[74] The interesting thing is that, in spite of the differences in years and geography, both the Andalusian priest (Ferrán Martínez) and Zumárraga (the first bishop in Mexico) followed the same

---

72 Although I have referred to the mob as fanatical, there was nothing unplanned in the anti-Semitic attack that developed in perfect progression from South to North, leaving large revenues in Christian hands. From Seville it spread to Córdoba, Jaén, Aragon, Mallorca, and finally Valencia, where an outbreak took place on July 9, 1391. Barcelona was next, followed by Gerona and Lérida. But, in spite of the massive impact that these revolts had on the Jewish population, that was not the end of their worries. Rather, it was just the birth of a whole new class of people: the *conversos*, or new Christians who would, eventually, become the main victims of a legendary institution: the infamous Spanish Inquisition.

73 "Conviene tambien á la religion y mansedumbre cristiana prestar de buen agrado el humano auxilio á los judíos contra las injustas persecuciones... *Con más dulzura que aspereza* deben, por tanto, ser tratados, porque la inhumana crueldad no repela y lance en su ruina á los que debiera llamar acaso al recto camino la benignidad cristiana" (Amador de los Ríos 1975–76: 651–52, my emphasis).

74 By the early 1540s, a consensus developed in councils of the Spanish government that the use of the Inquisition to induce religious orthodoxy among the new converts was inappropriate and possibly dangerous for the security of the colony. The Indian Inquisition ended when the Council of the Indies revoked the bishop's inquisitional powers in 1543.

[handwritten annotations: "SHOWS THAT HISTORY RHYMES BUT THAT DOES NOT PROVE"]

methods: Both of them opted for suggesting the destruction of temples of idolatry and both used the ruins of pagan worship to launch the expansion of the Catholic faith in their territories. But both of them took their initiatives too far (though in different ways) and, in response, they both received complaints from their supervisors, the pope and the king, respectively, in a tight collaboration between church and state. What is even more fascinating is that not only the attitude in the reprimands that these two religious men received was identical, as we could see in the documents from both Pope Benedict XIII and the emperor, but also the wording from these two authorities seems to match and, if the pope asks for "sweet" conversions in 1415, so does Charles V in 1543 in his letter to Zumárraga, portraying the *Reconquista* as a clear antecedent of the conquest of America and establishing the emperor's awareness of this parallelism.[75]

[handwritten annotation: "CAUSALITY"]

ZUMÁRRAGA'S CAMPAIGN: MORE CASES

As I have mentioned before, in the case of Zumárraga, the case of the cacique and its possible consequences ended de facto the Indian Inquisition in 1543 to the point that, even years later when Philip II formally established a Holy Office in New Spain in 1571, he specifically left the indigenous population outside the jurisdiction of the new tribunal, a decision that most historians have attributed to the failure of the earlier Indian Inquisition.

Nevertheless, in the years that the Indian Inquisition worked under the supervision of the bishop, many cases contributed to shape his policy toward the indigenous population. In general terms, the cases of Indians who were tried for idolatrous crimes are not very abundant. These cases are concentrated around 1539 and 1540, and, therefore, the peak of the campaign against idolatry coincided with Don Carlos's case and the ones that were brought up immediately thereafter. For the most part, the Indians accused of idolatry do not occupy a special position in their social circles; that is, most of them were not caciques, though as the number of cases multiplied, the number of caciques tried also increased in a proportional fashion.

The list of Indians that were accused of practicing idolatry in the city of Mexico during the bishopric of Zumarraga reads as follows:

---

75 "Item, que por razon de enseñar la doctrina cristiana no se encepen ni impresionen ni azoten los indios naturales, mayormente los que ya son hombres, en los monasterios ni en otras iglesias, ni haya cepos ni cárceles ni otras prisiones para ellos . . . porque haciendo lo contrario no se usurpe la juredicion real ni la ordinaria episcopal, ni se les haga *amargo*, grave y pesado el yugo *dulce* y carga leve de la ley de Dios y doctrina cristiana, de manera que en lugar de amarlo, lo aborrezcan estos naturales y tomen resabios con ello, como cosa que les dañe y sientan por dañosa" (García Icazbalceta 1881: Appendix 26, 122).

TABLE 3.1. Indians accused of idolatry (1536–1540)

Year	Volume	Document	Description
1536	37	1	Case against Tacatle and Tacuxtetl, Indians baptized under the names of Alonso and Antonio respectively, from Tenacopan (Tanacopan). Charges: Idolatry and making sacrifices according to their old customs.
			Judge: Fr. Juan de Zumárraga. Notary: Martín de Campos. Translators: Diego Díaz, priest, and Agustín de Rodas. Mexico.
1536–57	38	4	Case against Martin Ucelo (Ocelotl), Indian from Texcoco. Charges: Idolatry and sorcerer.
			Inquisitor: Fr. Juan Zumárraga. Fiscal: Dr. Rafael de Cervantes. Secretary: Martin de Campos. Mexico.
1537	38.1	7	Case against Mixcoatl and Papalotl, Indians and Martin Ucelo's brothers. Charges: Idolatry and sorceres.
			Judge: Fr. Juan de Zumárraga. Secretary: Alonso Mateos. Mexico.
1538	40	2	Case against Diego Tacateca, Indian, governor of Tlapanaloa. Charge: Idolatry.
			Judge: Bernardo de Yola, Notary: Cristóbal Sosa, Mexico.
1538	37	2	Case against some Indians of Atzcapozalco. Charge: Idolatry.
			Judge: Fr. Juan de Zumárraga. Secretary: Miguel López. Translator: Alonso Mateos. Mexico.
1539	37	3	Case against Miguel, Indian of Mexico. Accused of hiding idols from the *Templo Mayor*.
			Judge: Fr. Juan de Zumárraga. Secretary: Miguel López. Translator: Alonso de Santiago. Mexico.
1539	42	18	Case against Don Baltazar, Indian cacique from Culoacan. Charges: Idolatry and hiding idols.
			Judge: Fr. Juan de Zumárraga. Secretary: Alonso Mateos. Mexico.
1539	2	10	Case against Don Carlos, Indian cacique of Texcoco. Charge: Idolatry.
			Judge: Fr. Juan de Zumárraga. Secretary: Miguel López. Prosecutor: Cristóbal de Caniego. Mexico.
1539	30	9	Case against Cristóbal and Catalina, his wife, and against Martín, Cristóbal's brother, all of them Indians from Ocuituco. Charges: Idolatry and hiding idols.
			Judge: Fr. Juan de Zumárraga. Visitador: Juan González, translator. Notary: Hortuño de Ibarra. Translator: Alonso Mateos. Mexico.

continued on next page

TABLE 3.1.—*continued*

Year	Volume	Document	Description
1539–40	40	8	Case against Don Juan, cacique of Matlatlán. Charges: Idolatry and living with a woman without marrying her.
			Judge: Fr Andrés de Olmos. The case is preceeded by a letter from the judge to Fr. Juan de Zumárraga, bishop of Mexico and inquisitor. Mexico.
1539–40	37	4. BIS	Case against Alonso Tilanci, Indian from Izucar. Charge: Idolatry.
			Judge: Fr. Juan de Zumárraga. Secretary: Miguel de Legaspi. Prosecutor: Cristóbal de Canejo. Mexico.
1540	40	7	Accusation against Don Juan, Indian cacique of Iguala. Charges: Idolatry and living with a woman without marrying her. Mexico.
1540	1	6	Fragment of a case against some Indians from Oquila (Ocuila) Charge: Idolatry.
1540	212	7	Case against Pedro, Indian and cacique of Totolapa, and against Antonio, his brother. Charges: Both of them were accused of living with a woman without being married. That woman had been living with their father. Also, they were accused of idolatry and hiding idols.
			Judge: Fr. Juan de Zumárraga Defensor: Vicencio Riverol. Prosecutor: Cristóbal de Caniego. Mexico.

Most of the Indians that were brought before the Holy Office were accused of hiding idols and/or performing pagan ceremonies, such as praying to Tlaloc for rain, in private (in the 1530s the pagan ceremonies were celebrated much more in the open but, as time progressed, they moved to private spaces). In these cases, and since the Indians charged had already been baptized (otherwise they would not have been under the jurisdiction of the Inquisition),[76] they were accused of relapsing into paganism (dogmatizing), and for the most part, they were given a generic punishment shared by many.

Normally, the sentence consisted of the following: if it was a first crime, the bishop was merciful and would only warn them so that they would not relapse a second time. But if the Indians were actually convicted as idolaters, the situation was very different. Generally, after their trials they were made to mount on donkeys, bound hand and foot, stripped to the waist, and taken through the streets of Mexico City and Tlatelolco with a town crier who shouted their crimes for everybody to

---

76 In the case against Tlilanci, an Indian from the village of Izucar, his lawyer proved that all the offenses he was accused of had happened before he had been baptized, and the charges were immediately dismissed and he was freed (Case started on September 13, 1539. AGN, Inquisición, Volume 37, exp. 4bis).

hear. Once they reached their destination (normally the markets of Tlatelolco or the one in Mexico downtown), they were shorn of their hair and their idols burnt. After that, often they had to serve some time in prison or in a monastery, where they would be taught the Christian dogma and how not to relapse again.[77] In some cases, however, the convicted idolaters were made to go to church, preferably on a special day of celebration so that there would be a lot of people there, and were forced to stand during Mass carrying a large candle in their hands and their *corozas* on their heads. After Mass, and before the congregation, they would abjure their sins. Afterward, there would be public flogging, their hair would be shorn, and their idols burnt. In all cases the convicted criminals had to pay for the expenses of their cases, and their property was confiscated.

There was a different type of criminal, however, who, far from using idolatry to his own benefit, used it as a way of striking back against the colonizers, that is, as a rebellious act against the Spaniards, their evangelization campaign, and their domination in the New World. Among these we can mention the cases against Ocelotl and another one about two sorcerers who pretended to be related to him.[78] In the later case, Mixcoatl, who identified himself as a god, constantly preached against the Spanish friars and their campaigns, encouraging other Indians to fight baptism and to refuse to learn the Catholic religion. Papalotl, his partner, was only accused of serving Mixcoatl. In the end both of them asked for clemency, and though they received the standard punishment (confiscation of properties, a donkey ride across town with a town crier, jail, and abjuration), their lives were spared as long as they did not relapse again.

For his part, Ocelotl was accused of sorcery and of having contact with the Devil, but, as if these charges were not enough, he was also charged with having started riots and rebellions in the different villages where he practiced his dark arts and with encouraging others to become involved in pagan sacrifices and sexual immoralities. Probably these actions were considered much more threatening than his ceremonies or his predictions about the future, since they addressed the core itself of the imperial enterprise that was developing in New Spain, and they were probably the reason why he met the frontal opposition of the Spanish authorities. Actually, "the Franciscans friars Pedro de Gante and Antonio de Ciudad Real believed that he was jeopardizing the missionary movement and they recommended that he be banished from New Spain" (Greenleaf 1961: 53). This punishment, which was much

---

77 See, for example, the case against Tacatetle and Tanixtetl (case started on June 28, 1536. AGN, Inquisición, Volume 37, exp. 1) or the one against Mixcoatl and Papalotl (cases started on July 10, 1537. AGN, Inquisición, Volume 38, part 1, exp. 7).

78 The first case corresponds to AGN, Inquisición, Volume 37, exp. 4 and was started on November 21, 1536. The second case was first presented in front of the Holy Office on July 10, 1537, and can be read in AGN, Inquisición, Volume 38, part 1, exp. 7.

harsher than any other administered to an Indian idolater (with the exception, of course, of that of Don Carlos), never achieved the results intended, and, though Ocelotl was condemned to be banished to Seville, where he was to spend the rest of his life in jail, he was reported to be performing his rites in the same area of Mexico where he was arrested the first time.[79]

In this same line, there are a number of cases in which the convicted are caciques and are, above all, accused of setting a bad example for their communities. In this subgroup we find not only the case of Don Carlos, to which I referred above, but also those of Don Juan, cacique de Iguala, and that of the cacique de Matlatlán, both tried in 1539–40. In these two cases the charges are similar, the main ones being having multiple concubines and hiding idols, but in the two there are additional offenses such as not going to Mass and encouraging others to do the same; not baptizing their children; not teaching the Christian prayers and stopping those who tried to do so, and opposing the friars in anything they said. However, the outcomes were different. Don Juan received clemency from the inquisitors, but the cacique of Matlatlán (accused of the same faults) was not so lucky, and he paid for his disobedience with his hair and one hundred lashes. On top of that, he was also submitted to Christian education monitored by the same friars he fiercely opposed.[80] His mistake? One very common from then on: letting himself go with the flow, not changing his old habits, not adapting to his new position of subalternity, and not accepting the new vassalage, charges that, in the end make him a passive-aggressive rebel, the ultimate symbol of native resistance.

AFTER ZUMÁRRAGA

As I mentioned before, right after the commotion that was caused by the execution of Don Carlos Chichimecatecuhtli, cacique of Texcoco, Zumárraga lost his title as apostolic inquisitor and so his jurisdiction over the religious crimes of the Indians in the city of Mexico. Overall, under his leadership, the Inquisition tried around twenty Indians and instated the main lines of action that would be followed by his immediate successor, Tello de Sandoval (Greenleaf 1961: 15).

Zumárraga, during his term as inquisitor and as bishop, showed great concern about the development of dogmatizers, that is, Indians who, after being baptized, seemed not to be able to remain within the orthodoxy of the Catholic Church and,

---

79 Patricia Lopes Don (2006) has studied this case in detail in her article "Franciscans, Indian Sorcerers, and the Inquisition in New Spain, 1536–1543."

80 The case against the cacique of Matlatlán can be found in AGN, Inquisición, Volume 40, exp. 8. The one against Don Juan, cacique of Iguala, was started on July 16, 1540, and is documented in AGN, Inquisición, Volume 40, exp. 7.

rather than following the precepts taught by the missionaries or priests from Spain, fell back into the habit of their old religion. Of course these occurrences were not always the result of weaknesses or inability to follow the precepts on the part of the neophytes, but, in many cases, they were the deliberate action of individuals who wanted to challenge the Spanish domination or who had converted just to save face and, therefore, with no intention of keeping their promises. Both scenarios pushed Zumárraga to resort to two measures: first, he established that everybody who sinned according to the Catholic norm would be punished publicly for their own shame and to show the rest of the members in the community the consequences of their actions; and second, these offenders would not be returned to their villages of origin but, rather, and because of the danger they posed of spreading their subversive beliefs, they would be exiled or secluded in schools, jails, monasteries, or convents. Although these measures were not always effective, the intention was, clearly, to separate the bad seed from the rest, and, therefore, it created a system in which it was understood that the sacrifice of the black sheep was done for the good of the community. So, one by one, every Indian could be spared, even the most important ones, but the community had to keep its integrity, remain cohesive, intact.

Zumárraga's successor, Tello de Sandoval, also concentrated on punishing natives who had reverted to paganism, but his main focus was somewhere else. By the time he arrived in New Spain, Las Casas had been successful in creating a new awareness for the well-being of the native Indians that did not exist before. He managed to get from the Junta of Valladolid (1541–42) the approbation of the celebrated "Nuevas Leyes," and with them he established a new, but brief, relationship among the main characters involved in the developing colony. The "New Laws" prohibited the enslavement of the Indians and went as far as to take away those Indians whose owners had mistreated them. Francisco Tello de Sandoval was commissioned to carry out these new laws and, with this purpose, reached Mexico on March 8, 1544.

As his predecessor, Tello de Sandoval faced the same problem: how to deal with the Indians who, after being baptized, were going back to their old rituals and were, therefore, falling into what the Catholic Church, to which they had sworn loyalty, considered idolatry. He was careful not to be blamed for the same excesses that Zumárraga had been removed from office, but this extra special zeal, together with the fact that he had many other problems of a different nature to deal with, amounted to only a handful of cases dealing with idolatry opened during his term (1544–47), some of which were never finished.[81]

---

81 With the arrival of Tello de Sandoval and the implementation of the New Laws endorsed by Bartolomé de Las Casas, problems started to occur. The people affected by these laws were the majority of the Spaniards in the colony, the conquistadores, who, now in their old age, did not see favorably this attempt to take their labor force away, a measure that threatened their economic stability once they had risked

Three cases were opened in 1544 against some Indians from Oaxaca: the caciques of Coatlán, the cacique and governors of Yanhuitlán, and some Indians accused of cannibalism (Sepúlveda and Herrera 1999: 40). Just to show how similar these cases were to those tried during Zumárraga's times, let me focus on the events that took place in one of them, in Yanhuitlán.

In this particular case more than one person was convicted: Don Domingo, cacique; and Don Francisco and Don Juan, the governors and encomenderos. The first one, Don Domingo Guzmán, was imprisoned in 1544, accused of practicing idolatry and of performing human sacrifices to the pagan idols that he, allegedly, worshipped. He was also accused of having married multiple times, one of them according to the old rites and, therefore, not in church. He was a thirty-five-year-old man who had been baptized almost twenty years before charges were ever pressed against him, an Indian who had even been confirmed and who took that opportunity to change his name from Alonso, as he had been known since his baptism, to Domingo, the name that he kept until his death (Sepúlveda and Herrera 1999: 65).

At the moment of his trial, Don Domingo was living with Doña Ana, and, though they were joined by the Catholic sacrament, he was notified not to live with her until the situation with his previous marriage could be resolved. However, he did not follow through and continued with his living arrangements as they were before the notification. He stayed in jail until December 1546, when he was released due to his poor health and sent back to his village, where he kept his possessions and remained as cacique until his death in 1558.

Together with the cacique, the two governors who operated in that territory were also accused of idolatry. The first one, Don Francisco, was obviously the most dangerous of the two, judging by the charges that were presented against him: polygamy and marrying by the old rites—but above all, he was accused of being a pagan priest, of performing sacrifices, of hiding other pagan priests like him from the colonial authorities, of hiding idols, of worshipping them, and so forth.

The other governor, Don Juan, was also accused of having multiple wives and of participating in the pagan ceremonies organized by Don Francisco and Don Domingo, but he was mainly seen as a follower of the other two and not so much as a main figure in the case. We do not know his final sentence (Sepúlveda and Herrera 1999: 68).

---

their lives to conquer those lands for the Crown. Bishop Zumárraga had to intervene in the matter and, together with Tello de Sandoval, managed to obtain a suspension of the order until the encomenderos could be heard before the Spanish Court. The representatives of the latter found the emperor, Charles V, at Mechlin on October 20, 1545. In virtue of the situation as explained to him, he modified the general tenor of the laws so that, while still correcting the principal abuses, they would not bear too heavily on the Spaniards in the colony.

Going back to Don Francisco, and precisely because of the bad influence that he had on the people surrounding him, he was also accused of being a bad example and of promoting this ill behavior among the Indians who lived nearby: "Que ha oído decir en público, en el dicho pueblo que cuando hace sus borracheras y fiestas del demonio, que el dicho don Francisco gobernador, es el que provee de lo necesario y da el esclavo para sacrificar, y que del esclavo que sacrifican comen la carne los indios que andan en las fiestas y comen carne humana, y es público esto"[82] (Sepúlveda and Herrera 1999: 131). For that reason Don Francisco was seen as an obstacle to the evangelization campaign, since he constantly encouraged his fellow Indians to disobey the orders coming from the Spaniards and turn to the rule of their ancestors, to the old rites in a twist similar to the Taki Onqoy movement, that was going to develop in Peru in the 1570s and of which the cacique Don Carlos had already been accused a couple of years before:

> Este testigo muchas veces le ha oido decir al dicho don Francisco y a todos los de su casa que los que fuesen a la iglesia con él no adorasen el sacramento del altar, que no era Dios, sino que adorasen los dioses de sus padres, que estaban antes en los cues, junto con la iglesia, porque ellos habían venido de Castilla, ni sabían las cosas de Dios, y que todos los domingos y fiestas el dicho don Francisco hacía a este testigo y a otros que fuesen a cavar y otras haciendas del campo, y que el dicho don Francisco comía carne todas las vigilias y cuaresmas, porque el dicho Francisco de las Casas se lo mandaba, diciéndole que la comiese porque era viejo.[83] (Sepúlveda and Herrera 1999: 180)

However, a remarkable difference appears in this case since, although what is proposed is an attempt to go back to what existed before the conquest, in this particular instance and as opposed to what happened in the Peruvian movement, the goal is not portrayed as a return to the old idols and places of worship (*huacas*, in the Peruvian case). On the contrary, in the proposal made by Don Francisco, we can see that the past has not been able to escape the contamination of the foreign elements, and instead of referring to the old divinities, the governor directly associates them with the Devil, just as the Catholic framework has taught him. He, therefore, sees the world according to the Catholic binaries (Good-Evil; God-Devil) and even

---

82 My translation: That has been heard in public in said village, that when parties and drinks in the ceremonies for the demon, that Don Francisco, the governor, said that he provides what is needed and offers a slave for the sacrifice, and that the Indians eat his human flesh and that this is public.

83 My translation: This witness has heard Don Francisco say many times that those who go to church with him should not worship the Host in the altar because it was not God, but that they should worship the gods of their parents, that were in the cues, next to the church, because those who had come from Castile knew nothing of God and that every Sunday and day of obligation, said don Francisco made this witness and others go to the countryside to dig and that Don Francisco ate meat everyday of fasting and during Lent, and he did so because Don Francisco ordered him to, arguing that he was old.

when he wants to escape this oppressive system he is trapped within, unable to see where he came from, rather, he is portrayed as "un viejo que es papa del demonio y adivino, y que habla con el demonio . . . les dice que no crean las cosas de Dios ni la doctrina sino que sirvan al diablo, porque los cristianos presto se han de acabar y se irán a Castilla, y que han de tornar a recibir al diablo, que no le enojen porque les matará y no lloverá"[84] (Sepúlveda and Herrera 1999: 123). For all these reasons, Don Francisco appears as a fierce enemy of the friars and their mission as well as all that they stood for.[85] However, in these particular circumstances, going against the friars was more than a resistance to convert to a new religion; it also implied a political stand, an alliance with the encomenderos, especially with Francisco de las Casas, that would not have occurred in the same terms before the New Laws were instituted. Therefore, this resistance was actually a step to having an active part in the struggle that Tello de Sandoval had come to face in the New World. What remains to be seen is whether the accusations against Don Domingo, Don Francisco, and Don Juan held any water or if, indeed, they were the result of their political confrontation with the friars (who controlled the Inquisition and its lines of action) and of their support of the encomenderos' vindications or at least to what degree they got a fair trial or if they got a much rougher treatment as a result of the political circumstances. However, we do not know what their final sentence looked like—only that Don Domingo was imprisoned for a couple of years and then released due to his poor health and that Don Francisco de las Casas was secluded in a convent in Mexico City forever and that he was never allowed back into his community or close to his relatives.[86]

---

84 My translation: An old man, who is the pope of the Devil and fortune-teller, and who talks to the Devil . . . tells him to believe neither in matters of God nor in the doctrine, but rather to serve the Devil, because Christians will soon go back to Castile and they should go back to the Devil, so that he doesn't get angry with them and punishes them with no rain and kill them.

85 "Es muy público y notorio, que los del dicho pueblo de Yanhuitlán son muy enemigos de los clérigos y frailes porque no les doctrinen y que ellos han revuelto y zizañado por donde echaron de allí a los frailes, y que porque otros pueblos comarcanos y los naturales de ellos han tomado la doctrina y aprendídola y la siguen y procuran de saber que los riñen y gritan y burlan de ellos porque lo hacen y que no hay pueblo en toda la tierra que de tan mal ejemplo, ni esté más en sus ritos y ceremonias, ni tomen tan mal la doctrina cristiana, como el dicho pueblo de Yanhuitlán." My translation: It is public that the people of Yanhuitlán are enemies of priests and friars and they don't want to be indoctrinated and that they have sent the friars away because all the other neighboring towns and peoples have taken the doctrine and learnt it and followed it and they fight with them and mock them because there is no other village all over the Earth that gives a worse example and that is more set in their rites and ceremonies, and that take the Christian doctrine as bad as they do as in the village of Yanhuitlán (Sepúlveda and Herrera 1999: 131–32).

86 This measure, the isolation of the idolater, was already recommended by one of the witnesses at the trial: "Que en verdad sino sacan de allí a don Francisco y no lo ponen en una prisión a donde se quede [sic] que mientras allí estubiere aproveche las reprehensiones y doctrina, porque él es que los impone a todos en que no oigan la predicación y que este testigo sabe y tiene por cierto que en toda la mixteca no hay pueblo ninguno de más mala gente de doctrinar que los de Yanhuitlán" (Sepúlveda and Herrera 1999: 127).

This case thus is clearly a reflection of the political atmosphere at the time and an evidence of the struggle that was taking place between the encomenderos and the friars in general and, more accurately, it is evidence of the conflict between the encomendero Francisco de las Casas, who was trying to protect his rights and privileges,[87] and the Dominicans who, led by Bartolomé de Las Casas, had initiated a campaign in protection of the Indians and in detriment to the status quo that had been kept so far, with the subsequent implications and threats that that meant for the Spanish landowner. We cannot forget that the area where the encomienda of Yanhuitlán was located was incredibly fertile and rich, which made the conflicts between the owners and the friars that much more aggressive and intensive: "Instalados encomendero y frailes en un mismo pueblo, y con jurisdicción en una misma área, 'la más fértil y rica,' pero con intereses diferentes y opuestos, pronto entraron en conflicto. El interés material del primero contra la tenacidad de los segundos, mostrada en la conversión de los indígenas y en la construcción de sus iglesias y conventos, además del carácter impetuoso y dominante de Las Casas, desembocaron en el proceso seguido a las autoridades indígenas de Yanhuitlán"[88] (Sepúlveda and Herrera 1999: 89). In this particular case the material interest of the encomenderos, desperate for the labor force in order to cultivate the land, made the conversion of the Indians and the respect for their rights extremely difficult, a situation that brought the opposition of the friars,

---

87 Francisco de las Casas received his encomienda directly from Cortés, who happened to be his wife's cousin, as a gesture for having brought to him the letters in which Charles V made Cortés governor of New Spain. Once in the colony, Francisco de las Casas was sent by Cortés to fight Olid, the leader of an expedition to Honduras and who had decided to declare his independence from Spain, setting out to conquer Honduras for himself. When Cortés learnt of Olid's rebellion, he sent Las Casas against him, who managed to defeat and capture Olid. Francisco de las Casas, caught in the middle of a conflict between Cortés and the First Audience, was accused of his death and sent to Castile. He was back in New Spain in 1527, but, fearing that he was going to be deprived of his privileges, including the aforementioned encomienda, due to his weak political situation, he decided to go to Spain in 1528 and ask for a Royal Decree that would protect his property. In his absence his encomienda was given to Diego de Porras. When the Second Audience was established, and once the New Laws had been superseded, some of the original encomiendas were returned to their original owners and some others were given to the Crown. That was the case of Yanhuitlán, which became a *corregimiento* (a territory normally populated by Indians and ruled by a *corregidor* named by the Real Audiencia) and was put under the care of Miguel Díaz de Aux. Francisco de las Casas continued fighting for the restitution of his encomienda. Finally, in 1534 the viceroy Antonio de Mendoza was ordered to return to las Casas the Indians that he had taken. The devolution was not completed until the end of 1536, and he was able to enjoy the privileges of his encomienda until his death in 1546. His eldest son, Gonzalo de las Casas, inherited the encomienda (Sepúlveda and Herrera 1999: 58–59).

88 My translation: Once the encomendero and the friars were settled in the same village and with jurisdiction over the same area, "the most fertile and rich," but with different and opposing interests, they soon had conflicts. The material interest of the former was against the tenacity of the latter, shown in the conversion of the natives and building of churches and convents. Together with the impulsive and dominant personality of las Casas, it became a court case against the native authorities of Yanhuitlán.

Dominicans in their majority, who were ready to fight the colonial system if it involved this treatment to the natives.

As we can see, since 1528, the year in which Zumárraga first arrived in New Spain, the situation had changed dramatically. The first expectations of a fast spread of Christianity and an easy extirpation of idolatry had been crushed by the hard evidence that surrounded the friars. The struggle for the conversion of the Indians became increasingly involved in the hegemonic aspirations of the Crown, an extreme that stirred many a conflict between friars and civil authorities.[89] The cases of dogmatizers began to appear more and more frequently and, in the midst of all this, both parties, Spaniards and Indians, had learned to turn the accusations of idolatry into a political mechanism. The moment of the first encounter was over and, now that the main protagonists knew each other, it was time for the negotiations to start. We will see some of them around the topic of the Virgin of Guadalupe in the following chapter.

---

89 Tello de Sandoval left New Spain in 1547, and with him left the last inquisitor that the colony was going to know for many years. In fact, the need for a permanent tribunal had been felt for quite some time but the delicate situation of the indigenous population, the main target of the Inquisition but also the main source of revenue for the empire in construction, made Phillip II wait until 1571 to establish a tribunal equipped to deal with the Indians. In the meantime, bishops and archbishops were in charge of dealing with the misbehaviors of the newly converted, but they were not granted the title of inquisitors (Greenleaf 1961: 17–20).

4

From Idolatrous to Marian

New Spain between Zumárraga and Montúfar

¿Acaso no estoy aquí,
yo que soy tu madrecita?[1]

These words, seemingly simple, are the key of an intricate scenario in which many factors play a substantial role: a shift of power from the Spanish clergy to the indige- nous peasantry, the imposition of the conquerors' religious beliefs, and the struggle to get settled in a new system where the different monastic orders could not find a point of agreement.

Little did Juan Diego, a common Indian, know that when he walked to Mass that day he was on his way to changing the story of Mexico as it was known so far, that his actions would be remembered for centuries, and that, from recently converted, he was going to end up becoming a saint, actually, the first indigenous American saint in the Catholic Church.

It is said that, in 1531, as Juan Diego walked at Tepeyac Hill, he was distracted by beautiful bird noises that preceded the first apparition of the figure who would later be identified as the Virgin of Guadalupe. She told him of her love for the people of Mexico and asked that the local bishop, Juan de Zumárraga, build a temple on that

---

1 This quote is taken from the *Nican Mopohua*, one of the two 1640s texts that popularized the legend of the 1531 apparition of the Virgin Mary as Our Lady of Guadalupe to St. Juan Diego (León-Portilla 2000: 133). I will be referring to it later in the chapter.

My translation: Am I not here, since I am your mother?

DOI: 10.5876/9781607328018.c004

spot. Juan Diego presented himself before him and explained the unusual request, though the bishop, unimpressed by the commoner, quickly dismissed him. Juan Diego reported his failure to the Virgin, but she insisted that he try again. The result was that he was once again rebuffed by the perplexed bishop, who said he would need a sign in order to comply.[2]

But when Juan Diego returned to his village he found that the uncle with whom he lived was seriously ill and in need of the last sacraments, so he took another route into town so he would not see the Virgin and be distracted from his duty to his uncle. Nevertheless, he met Mary again, who told him that he was free to visit the Bishop since his uncle was well again.

The Virgin then asked Juan Diego to gather some very special, out-of-season roses, which he would find at the top of the hill, and to carry them in his rough cactus fiber outer-garment, his *tilma*, to the Bishop. Once there he began to tell his story while unfolding the tilma, as the Bishop saw the wonderful image of Our Lady of Guadalupe stamped on it. This image, rather than the flowers, was the real sign for Bishop Zumárraga and the miracle performed by the Virgin in her fourth apparition.

News of the prodigy spread quickly, and the result was that the Aztecs, who had been reluctant to get involved in Christianity as the religion of their conquerors, the Spanish, flocked to the church. Since then, the miraculous image has been preserved in Mexico now for over four and a half centuries, and though such fiber garments usually disintegrate within a few years, Juan Diego's tilma has defied all attempts to give it a natural explanation.

Today the Guadalupe image adorns house exteriors and interiors, churches and home altars, taxis and restaurants. Our Lady of Guadalupe is celebrated in song and poetry, popular and sacred. Annually her shrine at Tepeyac is visited by millions of pilgrims from all different statuses and situations. But how did a borrowed image become a Christian symbol and later a source of national pride? How did Tonantzin (Aztec mother goddess) become Guadalupe? And how was this transition handled by the different administrations? What was at stake?

This chapter is a reflection on the use of the image of the Virgin in the process of conquest and colonization of New Spain. In it I will explore the apparitions of the Virgin of Guadalupe or, more accurately, the handling of her supposed apparitions to Juan Diego by the Zumárraga administration. Also, I will contrast this first treatment of the apparition with the actions of the archbishop to follow, Montúfar, and since the Virgin is said to have appeared in a place previously devoted to the cult

---

2   In the account of the traditional legend, I am following the text of the *Nican Mopohua*, written by Luis Laso de la Vega (in León Portilla 2000).

of a native divinity, I am particularly interested in the progression from idolatry to symbol of national identity.

Finally, I will be focusing on the use of the image of the Virgin in the process of colonization and evangelization of the transatlantic colonies at large, establishing an immediate antecedent in the use of the Virgen de Candelaria in the conquest of the Canary Islands, and continuing with the exploration of the previous intercession of the Virgin in the attempt of converting the Jews and Moors in Spain of the Reconquista, especially as portrayed in the *Cantigas de Santa María*, by Alfonso X (1959–72).

I have opened the chapter by sharing the main details of the foundational legend around the apparitions of the Virgin of Guadalupe; nevertheless, and in spite of Pope John Paul II's canonization of Juan Diego, the story's veracity has repeatedly been called into question.[3]

I have painted, in previous chapters, an image of Archbishop Juan de Zumárraga as a learned individual, one ready to face challenges, both in Spain and in the New World, and who left abundant testimonies of his diligence in the form of letters, catechisms, assorted books, memorials, and so on. He was remarkable in his careful way of producing trails of information, whether it be with other religious authorities in the colonies or with the emperor himself. In the light of this behavior, how are we to understand that there is not one single mention of his encounters with the Virgin of Guadalupe? Did he forget to record this event? And, even if he himself was not present during the apparition of the Virgin, did he forget to report the sightings by others? Certainly not. Then, what could explain this silence in a man who seemed to report everything and take note of everything? The only possible explanation, in my opinion, is that he was indeed not present in the episode involving the stamping of the Virgin in Juan Diego's *tilma*, nor was he a witness to it, though he is included in the miraculous account; rather, I am inclined to say that the foundational legend lacks true correspondence with the chronological development of New Spain and that the miraculous apparitions possibly did not even take place during Zumárraga's time, as I will explain later.

We have seen in the previous chapters that the situation of New Spain in the years following the arrival of the Spaniards and before the supposed apparition of the Virgin of Guadalupe were full of struggles against the "idolatry" of the Indians, as seen through the conquerors' eyes, as recorded by Motolinía: "Desde á poco tiempo vinieron á decir á los frailes, cómo escondían los Indios los ídolos y los ponian en los piés de las cruces, ó en aquellas gradas debajo de las piedras, para allí hacer que

---

3   Juan Diego was beatified on April 9, 1990, in the Vatican by Pope John Paul II and canonized on July 31, 2002, in the Basilica of Guadalupe, Mexico City, by the same pope. The homily presented by John Paul II during the canonization can be found in Appendix C.

adoraban la cruz y adorar al demonio, y querian allí guarecer la vida de su idolatría" (García Icazbalceta 1971a: 52).[4] In this context of resilient idolatry, would Zumárraga not have spread the news of the apparition of the Virgin if he had seen her? Wouldn't he have written about it and promoted her devotion? Would a man that spent his life trying to convert people into Christianity have kept these apparitions a secret? Although the answers to these questions would take us into the terrain of specula- tion, I think it is safe to believe that an episode of that magnitude would not have been left to oblivion and, though Zumárraga was not very impressionable and was quite a restrained man, I think that the encounter with the Virgin would have left a mark in his life and works, but it is simply not there. Zumárraga even went on to say that "Ya no quiere el Redentor del mundo que se hagan milagros, porque no son menester, pues está nuestra santa fe tan fundada por tantos millares de mila- gros como tenemos en el Testamento Viejo y Nuevo" (García Icazbalceta 1896: 25).[5] Would a person who has witnessed the miracle firsthand express himself in these terms? In my opinion it is not likely, especially in a context in which the opposite (the publicity of the miracle) would have been encouraged as a post-tridentian sign of Catholicism versus Reformation. But Zumárraga's silence was not unique to him. It was shared by his contemporaries, people who were in close connection with the, for the moment, bishop-elect and who did not refer to the apparitions of the Virgin either. I am thinking, for example, of the bishops of Oaxaca and Guatemala, who shared with Zumárraga the act of writing a letter to Charles V on November 30, 1537, and, of course, of the emperor himself, who was never informed of the fact that the Virgin of Guadalupe was a frequent visitor in his territories overseas. In fact, prior to 1555 there is no written evidence about any apparition in the Tepeyac, a silence that must be taken as evidence in itself of this apparition that never was.

The name of Guadalupe already had a history in the New World.[6] First inhab- ited by Arawak Amerindians and afterwards by the Caribe tribe, the island of

---

4 Also, let us remember Motolinía's account that I used as the opening of the third chapter.

> My translation: Recently, the friars said that the Indians hid idols and they put them at the feet of the crosses or in those stairs under the rocks to pretend that they were worshiping the cross while they worshipped the Devil and to hide their idolatry that way.

5 This statement belongs to the *Regla Cristiana*, dated in 1547, a document compiled and printed by direct orders of the Archbishop Zumárraga and made public during his administration. My translation: The Redeemer doesn't want more miracles in this world because they are not necessary, because our sacred faith is based on many thousands of miracles, both in the Old and the New Testament.

6 According to the *Nican Mopohua*, mentioned above, the Virgin identified herself as Guadalupe when she appeared to Juan Diego's uncle, Juan Bernardino. He was on his deathbed when Juan Diego set out to bring back a priest to hear his uncle's confession. It was when Juan Diego was gone that the Virgin of Guadalupe appeared to Juan Bernardino and cured him. Before leaving, she told him her name:

> Y que así la llamara,
> Así se nombrara,

Guadeloupe was finally "discovered" (or incorporated into the European imaginary) by Christopher Columbus, who, during his first trip in 1493, landed in this
island located in the eastern Caribbean Sea. He called it "Santa María de Guadalupe
de Extremadura," after the image of the Virgin Mary venerated at the Spanish monastery of Villuercas, in Guadalupe, Extremadura.

According to a medieval legend, the Spanish Guadalupe had appeared to a shepherd and led him to discover a wooden statue of herself that is now exhibited in the
Real Monasterio de los Jerónimos, in Guadalupe, Cáceres (Moffitt 2006: 50). The
shrine houses a statue (made of oak and measuring fifty-nine centimeters) reputed
to have been carved by Luke the Evangelist and given to Saint Leander, archbishop
of Seville, by Pope Gregory I. Later on, when Seville was taken by the Moors, a group
of priests fled northward and buried the statue in the hills near the Guadalupe River
in Extremadura, where it was discovered by the above-mentioned shepherd (Poole
1995: 23). According to the legend, the shepherd claimed that the Virgin Mary had
appeared to him and ordered him to ask priests to dig at the site of the apparition. It
was then, during the excavation, that the priests rediscovered the hidden statue and
built a small shrine around it, which evolved into the great Guadalupe monastery
and, later on, into a devotion that would cross the Ocean.

The curious aspect of the story is that, even from the configuration of its name,
the cult to Guadalupe shows its syncretic character, since it results from the combination of the Arabic word for *river* and that exists is many Spanish rivers still today
(Guadalhorce, Guadalmedina, Guadalquivir, Guadiana, etc.) and the Latin word
for wolf: *lupus*, creating a combination that could be translated as "Wolf River"
or "Wolf Creek" (Moffitt 2006: 50). This Virgin does, therefore, enter the scene
with a particular mission: that of bringing peoples together (even from the etymol-
ogy of her name, which combines Arabic and Latin), of erasing differences, and of
spreading Christianity to other cultures. In addition, Our Lady of Guadalupe is
one of three black *madonnas* in Spain (together with the Virgin of Montserrat in
Barcelona and Our Lady of Atocha in Madrid), adding, with this feature, another
dimension to her syncretic use both in the Spain of the Reconquista and in the
increasingly mestizo New World.

It was not until 1340 that the devotion to the Spanish Guadalupe became a
mass phenomenon due to the political support and financial endowment of the
monarchy. King Alfonso XI took a personal interest in the shrine's development,

---

La del todo doncella
Santa María de Guadalupe,
su preciosa imagen. (León-Portilla 2000: 157)

My translation: That she should be called / that she should be named / in all her maidenhood /
Santa María de Guadalupe / her beautiful image.

attributing his victory over the Moors at the Battle of Río Salado (October 24, 1340) to the Virgin's intercession. It was then through his initiative that the grandiose monastery was built and that visits to it were encouraged, becoming a pilgrimage center and the object of popular veneration. For these reasons it also became an influential site (Moffitt 2006: 50). Soon after its foundation, in 1386, the shrine was commended to the Hieronymites, who channeled the massive popular devotion to the figure into a more ordered cult.

This is the context for the formation of men such as Hernán Cortés himself, and other conquistadores of the New World (Pedro de Alvarado, the Pizarros, Gonzalo de Sandoval, etc.), whose *patria chica* (place of origin) was Cáceres and who had grown up permeated by this popular devotion as an important focus of their everyday life. It is, therefore, not surprising that the Spaniards brought their local devotion with them and that this cult was maintained in the New World.[7]

Long before the arrival of the Spanish conquering forces, the hill of Tepeyac had already been the destination of an ancient pilgrimage tradition centered around a pagan idol (as it would have been seen by the European invaders) named Tonantzin, venerated as the earth and fertility goddess, and also known as "Our Lady Mother." Therefore, the sights at Tepeyac may not have differed that much from the ones lived in Cáceres, had it not been for the fact that the Aztec profession of religion was threatened by an external enemy. In the midst of the Spanish conquista, the temple in the name of Tonantzin was destroyed and replaced by a Christian chapel.

This practice of destruction and replacement of symbols was not particularly new to the context of the conquest of the New World, but rather it had been a recurrent method used by innumerable cultures since remote times. Let us, for example, consider within Spain the layering of cultures that has given deserved fame to the Cathedral in Córdoba, a Latin-cross shape cut into the middle of the main Mosque, flanked by Arabic arches, and supported by Visigoth columns; or the Arabic garrison, Gibralfaro, still standing in Málaga over the remains of a Roman theater, and so forth. This modus operandi was also transferred to the New World, where the Cathedral of Mexico was placed within the walls of the Aztec Templo Mayor and where the "pagan idols" were substituted by Christian divinities.

Camiro Gutiérrez Zamora speculates about the possibility of a small temple having been built in the Tepeyac in the 1530s (therefore, under Zumárraga's administration) and devoted to a Virgin only identified as "la Virgen sacratísima"

---

7 To corroborate this imported character of the Virgin of Guadalupe in the New World, let us consider the fact that the Nahuatl language does not include the letters (or sounds for) "g" or "d" (Moffitt 2006: 49), which reveals the name of the Virgin as a borrowed element inserted in a very different phonological environment.

but with no other added denomination, as Torquemada corroborates in his *Monarquía Indiana*:

> Pues queriendo remediar este gran daño nuestros primeros religiosos, que fueron los que primero que otros entraron a vendimiar esta viña inculta y a podarla, para que sus renuevos y pámpanos hechasen fruto para Dios, determinaron de poner iglesia y templo en la falda de la dicha sierra, de Tlaxcallan, en un pueblo que se llama Chiauhtempa, que quiere decir a la orilla de la tierra húmeda o de la ciénaga, por serlo el sitio, y en ella constituyeron a la gloriosísima Santa Ana, abuela de Nuestro Señor, porque viniese con la festividad antigua, en lo que toca a la gloriosa celebración de su día, aunque no en el abuso y celebración idolátrica. En Tianhuizmanalco constituyeron casa San Juan Bautista; y *en Tonantzin, junto a México, a la Virgen sacratísima, que es nuestra Señora y Madre* y en estos tres lugares se celebran estas tres festividades, a las cuales concurren las gentes, en especial a la de San Juan; y hay muy grandes ofrendas aunque la mayor devoción ha faltado.[8] (Torquemada 1943–44: book X, ch. 7, my emphasis)

If we analyze this text by Torquemada, there is something that immediately calls our attention and that is the *deliberate* substitution of three indigenous deities by their, dare I say, Christian counterparts. Therefore, the cult to Toci (our grandmother, as it was stated by Torquemada earlier in the same chapter) was replaced by that of Santa Ana, Christ's grandmother; that of Telpuchtli, the Youth ("mancebo"), was substituted by Saint John, the Baptist; and finally, the cult of Tonan, ("our mother") was traded for that to the Virgin, Our Mother ("nuestra Señora madre").

Judging from this passage, the intentions of the missionaries seem crystal-clear: they wanted to use the pagan devotion to Tonantzin for their own purposes and channel this pagan devotion into a newly-found cult for the Virgin Mary in her role as the Mother of God, changing the goddess-mother of the Mexicans for the Christian Mother *per excellence*. In this case the correlation between this generic Christian Virgin and the previous Aztec goddess would have been fairly direct, since both advocacies were characterized the same way.

---

8 My translation: In order to remedy that great harm, our first friars, who were the ones who first tried to harvest in this uncultivated vineyard and trim it so that the new growths blossomed for God, they determined to set up a church in the slope of that mountain range of Tlaxcala, in a village named Chiauhtempa, that means, the wetlands or marshes, because that is the place, and there, they built in the name of the most glorious Saint Anna, grandmother of Our Lord, so that that her day coincided with the old celebration, although not in the spirit of the idolatrous celebration. In Tianhuizmanalco a house was built for Saint John the Baptist; and in Tonantzin, near Mexico, one for the very sacred Virgin, who is our Lady and Mother and in those three places these three festivities are celebrated and people gather, specially in Saint John's; and there were many big offerings, although a greater devotion is lacking.

This new site located at Tepeyac, previously dedicated to Tonantzin and now devoted to Guadalupe, was built in response to Indian idolatry and in order to facilitate the devotion of the Spaniards. It would have also been visited by the Indians who, led by habit, kept visiting the same places where their deities had resided before, not registering the fact that the devotion had been appropriated by the invaders or, precisely because of that, that is, in order to worship their deities in the appearances of being Christians.

But, together with this effort on the part of the first missionaries, also remarkable in Torquemada's quote is a general feeling of sadness that becomes more obvious in the last sentence ("la mayor devoción ha faltado": a greater devotion is lacking), a pessimism that points to a series of practices empty of heart-felt devotion, an apparent profession of faith devoid of meaning and still in debt to the pagan rites that preceded them. This sensation may also have been influenced by an earlier testimony pointing in the same direction in which Sahagún leaves us with a vivid impression of what that moment of transition must have felt like:

Cerca de los montes hay tres o cuatro lugares donde se solían hazer muy solemnes sacrificios, y que venían a ellos de muy lexas tierras. El uno de éstos es aquí en México, donde está un montezillo que se llama Tepeácac, y los españoles llaman Tepeaquilla, y agora se llama Nuestra Señora de Guadalope. En este lugar tenían un templo dedicado a la madre de los dioses que la llamavan *Tonantzin*, que quiere dezir "nuestra madre." Allí hazían muchos sacrificios a honra de esta diosa, y venían a ellos de más de veinte leguas de todas estas comarcas de México, y traían muchas ofrendas. Venían hombres y mugeres, y moços y moças, a estas fiestas. Era grande concurso de gente en estos días, y todos dezían "bamos a la fiesta de *Tonantzin*," y agora, que está allí edificada la iglesia de Nuestra Señora de Guadalope, también la llaman *Tonantzin*, tomada ocasión de los predicadores que a Nuestra Señora, la madre de Dios, llaman *Tonantzin*. De dónde haya nacido esta fundación de esta *Tonantzin*, no se sabe de cierto, pero esto sabemos de cierto, que el vocablo significa, de su primera imposición, a aquella *Tonantzin* antigua, y es cosa que se debería remediar, porque el propio nombre de la madre de Dios Sancta María, no es Tonantzin sino Dios *inantzin*. Parece ésta invención satánica para paliar la idolatría debaxo equivocación de este nombre *Tonantzin*. Y vienen agora a visitar a esta *Tonantzin* de muy lexos, tan lexos como de antes; la cual devoción también es sospechosa, porque en todas partes hay muchas iglesias de Nuestra Señora y no van a ellas, y vienen de lexas tierras a esta *Tonantzin*, como antiguamente.[9] (Sahagún 1990b: Book XI, appendix).

9   My translation: Near the hills there are three or four places where they used to do solemn sacrifices and they used to come from far away lands. One of those is here in Mexico, in a hill called Tepeácac and that the Spaniards call Tepeaquilla, and that is now called Our Lady of Guadalupe. In that place there used to be a temple dedicated to the mother of the gods who was called Tonantzin, that means "our mother."

This long quote is a vivid example of the pernicious syncretism that was over-whelmingly taking over New Spain in particular, and the colonies in general, a heterogeneous mixture of elements from both cultures with a lack of purpose and developing into a dangerous no-man's land. Sahagún, witness of the efforts carried out by the first Franciscans, cannot hide his concern when he has to, reluctantly, admit that their missionaries' teachings are having an effect that nobody desired. That way, instead of eradicating the Indian idolatry, the Christian devotion is appro-priated as a way to mask the old pagan habits, as a way to make fit into the main-stream practices that were clearly not to the liking of the Spanish forces. It is under this Christian disguise that the ancient pilgrimages to the sanctuary of Tonantzin can still take place and it is under this appearance of faithfulness that idolatry can still be fed. Sahagún, though, is aware of this strategy and, consequently, worried by the fact that other chapels equally dedicated to the Virgin are not visited that often; in fact, only the ones that used to be pagan temples are still centers of Indian devo-tion, a practice that he catalogues as suspicious.

Sahagún proposes, in the face of these events, to get to know the Indian reli-giosity deeply, as well as their way of life, as the last recourse to fight against this disguised idolatry:

7.

Ni conviene se descuiden los ministros de esta conversión con dezir que entre esta gente no hay más pecados de borrachera, hurto y carnalidad, porque otros muchos pecados hay entre ellos muy más graves y que tienen gran necessidad de remedio. Los pecados de la idolatría y de los ritos idolátricos, y suprestiçiones idolátricas y agüeros, y abusiones y cerimonias idolátricas, no son aún perdidos del todo. Para predicar contra estas cosas, y aun para saver si las hay, menester es de saber cómo las usavan en tiempo de su idolatría, que por falta de no saber esto en nuestra presencia hazen muchas cosas idolátricas sin que lo entendamos.[10] (Sahagún 1990b: Preface)

There used to be many sacrifices to honor this goddess and people came from many miles away from all the regions in Mexico and brought many offerings. Men, women, lads and lasses came to these celebra-tions. There was a multitude of people gathering in those days, all of the saying "we are going to the celebration of Tonantzin" and now that there is a church for Our Lady of Guadalupe there, they also call her Tonantzin. Nobody knows how this legend was born, but we know for sure that the word Tonantzin refers to that old Tonantzin and this is something that should be remedied because the proper name of Our Lord's mother, Saint Mary is not Tonantzin, but God inantzin. This seems to be a diabolic invention to ease idolatry under the mistaken name of Tonantzin. And now they come from far away, as far as before, and this devotion is also suspicious because there are many churches of Our Lady everywhere and they don't go to those, but they come from far away to this Tonantzin, just like they used to.

10   My translation: It is important that the ministers in charge of conversions don't ignore other sins besides drunkenness, theft and lust, because there are many others that need to be addressed. The sins of idolatry, omens and idolatrous superstitions are not entirely lost. To preach against these rites and to know if they persist, it is important to know how they used them in the time of their idolatry, because if we don't, they could use them in our presence without us knowing.

Here again, Sahagún insisted on the fact that this situation of satanic syncretism had to be remedied by advocating the thorough knowledge of the Mexicans, their language, and their way of life as the best tool, in the end, to understand their behavior and their thinking process, the ulterior motivations to actions that, otherwise, could not have been accurately interpreted.[11]

Sahagún's position in the fight against idolatry involved, first, knowledge about the so-called enemy but also, and this is an important component, a need to remedy this situation of syncretism that was working against the purpose of the missionaries. As a result, a need emerged to implement a break between the two religions, an imposed separation, a required distance that would avoid this dangerous transfer of devotions (according to the Christians). Therefore, Sahagún was a clear advocate for a radical break with other religions and became very wary of the phenomenon of translation and transfer.

Going back to the Tepeyac, O'Gorman, in his *Destierro de sombras*, suggests several possibilities for that first temple (O'Gorman 1986: 15). Thus, when the idol Tonantzin was removed, the possible scenarios were the following:

1. It is possible that there was no image of the Virgin in this first temple, a fact that García Icazbalceta can understand because of the lack of images in general at that time.[12]

2. In this first chapel it is possible that a generic image of the Virgin was used, one with no specific name or characteristics, that is, just an image of the Virgin with no particular link to a particular event or a region. This fact is corroborated by the testimony of Francisco de Salazar in response to the question number 6 in the *Información de 1556*, an inquiry ordered by Archbishop Montúfar into a sermon preached by Bustamante, the Franciscan provincial (I will go back to this document later in the chapter). In it, the witness says that "lo que sabe es que el fundamento que esta ermita tiene dende su principio fue el titulo de la madre de Dios, el qual á provocado á toda la cibdad á que tengan devocion en ir á rezar y encomendarse á ella."[13] (García Icazbalceta 1896: 115)

O'Gorman also considers the two other possibilities. First of all, that this first image was Our Lady of Guadalupe, from Extremadura, Spain, based on the

---

11 Sahagún collected his knowledge on pagan idolatries in a work entitled *Breve compendio de los ritos idolátricos que los indios de esta Nueva España usaban en tiempo de su infidelidad*, a work written in 1570 (Sahagún 1990a).

12 García Icazbalceta, in his *Carta acerca del origen de la imagen de Nuestra Señora de Guadalupe,* explains: "No sabemos en qué año se labró la ermita, ni qué imagen se puso en ella: tal vez ninguna, por ser entonces muy escasas" (García Icazbalceta 1896: 67, paragraph 68).

13 My translation: What we know for sure is that that chapel has been devoted to the mother of God from the beginning, which has moved the whole city to go there and pray and entrust themselves to her.

extended devotion that there was to this image among many of the conquistadores; and finally, it is possible that, from the beginning, the chapel at Tepeyac had the image of the Mexican Lady of Guadalupe, though this would be the weakest of the possibilities, only supported by the apparitionist scholars who believe that the stamped image of the Virgin of Guadalupe in Juan Diego's tilma was housed in the chapel supposedly built by Zumárraga from the beginning.[14]

In any case, and independently of what image (if any) was displayed in the first chapel at the Tepeyac, the nature of the phenomenon is not altered and conforms to what Poole calls "apparition genre" (Poole 1995: 22). By this, Poole understands a specific pattern, a formula that is recurrently repeated, in this case both in Spain and later across the Atlantic and that involves the same components each time, only with slight variations. Therein, the Virgin (or the Saint, as sometimes the case may be) appears to an individual and asks that a sanctuary be built in her name in that exact location. The person who sees the apparition is normally a poor person, marginalized and disenfranchised, and Poole adds that "in Spain, this could be a shepherd, a swineherd, a woodsman, or a charcoal burner. In America, the seer was more often an Indian, who not only represented the poor and oppressed but who also, like an Iberian herdsman, was closest to being a 'wild; person" (Pool 1995: 22). In most accounts of apparitions (that circulated in Early Modern Spain and were later transferred to the New World), the Virgin would identify herself, as happened in Juan Diego's story as told by Laso de la Vega's *Nican Mohopua*, and comfort the witness of the apparition in the overwhelming task that was required of him. Most of the narrative would then be occupied by the clash produced when a marginalized individual tries to influence the centers of power—in this case, the religious authorities—and by the disbelief of the latter. Finally, some proof is demanded, and, consequently, a miracle is produced. In the end, after the drama of rejection, the position of the poor prevails thanks to the intervention of the Virgin of Guadalupe, who gives comfort to the one in need.

These apparitions always take place in moments of great tension, whether it be the context of the Spanish Reconquista and the encounters with the infidels (Moors and Jews) in the Old Continent, or following the trauma of the "discovery" and invasion of the New Word. In any case, the apparition of the Virgin serves two purposes: that of bringing some relief to the conquered and behaving as a loving mother who has a tender touch in moments of distress, but also this same gesture is used to bring the infidels into the devotion of Mary; that is, it also has a political function by which the outsider is brought into the realm of the Christian conquering forces.

---

14 Camiro Gutiérrez Zamora (1996: 119–20) has written about this possibility in *El Origen del Guadalupanismo*, but he himself admits that his testimonies in this respect are rather weak.

INTERESTING

This double function had been established before in the *Cantigas* by Alfonso X, the Wise, which I will be studying in the next section.

The same sequence is reproduced exactly in the story of Juan Diego, a perfect example of a narrative that follows the tradition of the apparition genre. Nevertheless, this degree of faithfulness in following the established framework is what makes the story of Juan Diego suspicious, since it reveals it as a European product, one far from the native way of narrating and removed from the indigenous nature that was supposedly advocating it. Moffitt put it this way: "In sum, the populist cultural conventions that were going to exactly define the perceptual, even iconographic, revelations of *Nuestra Señora de Guadalupe* strictly belong to the Old World—the Iberian Peninsula—and not to *Nueva España* . . . The venerated icon of *Nuestra Señora de Guadalupe*—and once it is treated as a work of art, that is, something material and strictly of earthly origins—is simply a *pastiche* of wholly conventional, *European* iconographic motifs, all of which may be logically assigned to the manual and/or mental intervention of mere mortals" (45–46, 48–49). More specifically, the presentation of the Virgin of Guadalupe in Mexico is directly derived from "The Revelation of Saint John the Divine" (*Revelation* 12):

> 12:1 And there appeared a great wonder in heaven; a woman clothed with the sun, and the moon under her feet, and upon her head a crown of twelve stars: 12:2 And she being with child cried, travailing in birth, and pained to be delivered.
>
> 12:3 And there appeared another wonder in heaven; and behold a great red dragon, having seven heads and ten horns, and seven crowns upon his heads.[15]

OK. POINT?

If we were to compare this fragment with the opening paragraphs in Miguel Sánchez's account of the apparition written in 1648, we would see that the similarities are obvious:

---

15 This fact comes reinforced by the fact that it was believed that Our Lady of Guadalupe, in her apparition to Juan Diego's uncle, used the Nahuatl term *coatlaxopeuh*, which is pronounced "quatlasupe" and sounds very similar to the Spanish word "Guadalupe." *Coa* means "snake"; *tla* is the article "the"; and *xopeuh* means to "crush," so Our Lady of Guadalupe identified herself as "the one who crushes the snake," or the dragon, as it is suggested in this quote. This link between the Virgin of Guadalupe and the seven-head dragon is further explored by Miguel Sánchez (2010) in his *Imagen de la Virgen María Madre de Dios de Guadalupe*. In this text, partly responsible for creating the foundational legend that we all know today, the dragon becomes the image of the native idolatry, now defeated by the Virgin:

> Con esto digo, que este dragón es el demonio de la idolatría y gentilidad aqueste nuevo mundo, a quien tenía engañado . . . La idolatría en la gentilidad de México, tuvo su principo de siete naciones, que sacó el demonio de ciertas partes retiradas y lejos, que hoy llaman Nuevo México, y vinieron a poblar diversos sitios de toda ésta comarca . . . Luego si María Virgen es la más perfecta, viva y escogida imagen de Dios, y en aquesta su imagen de Guadalupe ha querido esmerarse, previniendo el dibujo en la tierra que le conquista, los nacidos en ella aunque tienen el general consuelo consigo en ser cada uno imagen de Dios, asegúrense venturosos cuando se vean acompañados de la Virgen de María, aparecida para defenderlos del dragón. (Torre Villar and Navarro de Anda 1982: 169 and 177)

NOTHING NEW ON THE VIRGIN OF GUADALUPE

Apareció estampado en el cielo un grande milagro, se descubrió esculpido un prodigioso portento, se desplegó en su lienzo retocada una imagen, era mujer vestida a todas luces, del sol toda envestida sin deslumbrarse, calzada de la luna sin divertirse, coronada de doce estrellas sin desvanecerse, estaba ya en aprietos del parto, que desmostraban sus clamores. Apareció al instante otra señal del cielo, era un dragón monstruo, disforme en cuantidad, sangriento en los colores, en la figura horrible, sustentaba siete cabezas y en ellas otras tantas coronas.[16] (Moffitt 2006: 124)

THE HELPING HAND DURING THE *RECONQUISTA*

As I mentioned above, the intervention of the Virgin Mary in times of distress does not start with the conquest of the New World but, rather, numerous are the episodes in which she assisted the Christian forces in their fight against the peninsular infidels during the process of *Reconquista* (years 711–1492).

The main collection of narratives around the figure and intervention of the Virgin Mary are, undoubtedly, the *Cantigas de Santa María*, collected by Alfonso X the Wise (King of Castile from 1252 until his death in 1284) and who summoned up in these narratives a wide array of aspects of Medieval everyday life. Included in this snapshot of the thirteenth century is the relationship between the three main groups living in the Iberian Peninsula, that is, Christians, Moors and Jews, and the legal regulations that were in place, available in the *Partidas*, also collected under the tutelage of the same king.

The *Cantigas*, or *Songs to the Virgin Mary*, is a collection of pictures of life that are put together with the purpose of making present the intervention of the Virgin Mary in normal life. There are 427 *cantigas* written in Galician-Portuguese with musical notation. The poems are, for the most part, about miracles attributed to the Virgin Mary. Of the more than 400 poems, approximately 15 percent are dedicated to Moors or Jews, or have them as protagonists, or, at least deal with issues around their presence together with the Christians. These songs are used, in my opinion, for the same purpose that Juan Diego's story is told in the midst of the struggle after the conquest of New Spain. In this case, in the colonies there is a need for a gesture that would mobilize people toward a devotion that was foreign and, in a parallel fashion, in the Spain of the *Reconquista*, an impulse was needed to facilitate the

---

16 My translation: It appeared, stamped in the sky, a great miracle, it was discovered, carved, a prodigious wonder, it was displayed, on a canvas, the image of a woman dressed in lights, covered by the sun but not blinded by it, wearing the moon in her shoes, crowned by twelve stars without fading: she was in the midst of labor pains as evident by her cry. And suddenly it appeared in the sky another sign, a monstrous dragon, disfigured in quantity, bloody in its colors, horrible in its shape with seven heads and as many crowns on them.

conversions of the infidels and their integration into the Christian system. There are, nevertheless, obvious differences between the two situations, not only in terms of chronology, but also otherwise. First, the fact that the *Cantigas* were a popular collection (some of the stories were already popular before they were included in the volume) reveals the presence of a specific culture that surrounds it, a preexistent propensity to trust the Virgin in cases of distress; that is, it creates an antecedent by which having the Virgin as a resource seems part of the options available. In this light we can understand that when a Christian needs a loan from a Jew and has no other backup, he uses the names of Jesus and the Virgin as cosigners in his loan (Alfonso X 1959–72: 25). In this circumstance the Jew, even rejecting the divinity of these two figures, decides to accept their names in the contract because he thinks highly of them, though he does not agree with their divinity. In the end, the story reveals the conversion of this Jew who, though he assured his disbelief in the beginning, he was nevertheless prone to Christianity, close to its teaching, and somewhat admiring of its figures, an inclination that is channeled into his final conversion. This way, the story puts on the table the transformation of the nonbeliever through the intervention of the Virgin herself, who does not hesitate to approach other peoples.

The same could be said about a Jewess who, moments before being "taken to be hurled from a high and rugged cliff" after having committed a crime, decides to take a chance with the Holy Virgin, and so she says: "If I remain alive and well, I will, without fail, become a Christian at once, before another day dawns" (Alfonso X 1959–72: 107). The Jewess "did not perish but fell clear of the rocks right at the foot of a fig tree" (Alfonso X 1959–72: 134), confirming the extraordinary power of the Virgin Mary. She converts immediately, manifesting that there was already in her an inclination to think of the Virgin, even when she belonged to a different religion, but she must have been close enough to the Christian doctrine, open enough to it that she would remember it in times of affliction.

There are a number of *cantigas* in which the Virgin rushes to the help of the needy, independent of their religion but, in contrast with the two cases already exposed, this time the people in need are also the innocent, the pure at heart, and not interested as in the previous cases. Among those poems, *cantiga 6* is especially remarkable. It tells the story of "a fatherless Jewish boy who, because he has learned to sing the 'Gaude Virgo Maria,'" and sings it everywhere, incurs the displeasure of the Jewish populace. One Jew, particularly enraged, takes the boy home with him, kills him, and hides his body in the basement. The boy's mother, invoking the Virgin's help, locates the boy, who has been resurrected. Supported by the rest of the Christians, they fall upon the Jews, throw the murderer into the furnace, and kill the rest mercilessly. In this cantiga the innocence of the Jewish boy, eventually killed and resurrected, contrasts with the cruelty of the Christians and the boy's mother who, not satisfied with only recovering the boy, take revenge to the extreme.[17]

In all these cases the cantigas present people who are not converted, Moors and Jews who still practice their religion and maintain their respective faiths but, in spite of this, manifest a clear closeness to the Christian divine figures, a respect, and, in some cases, admiration that leads them to interject the name of the Virgin, in particular, in moments of desperation. In the end the cantigas show the conversion of the main characters and, though we are never told whether this gesture carried with it the conversion of many others close to the new Christian, we are to suppose that it would produce a new group of people also favorably inclined to Christianity, just as the protagonists of the stories once were. In this sense, the effect intended by the cantigas and that of the story of Guadalupe certainly run parallel, and, although Juan Diego had already been baptized, he opened the door to the conversion of many who could identify with him and his indigenous past. This story made the Virgin present among the Indians, establishing a direct connection that drew multitudes to her new house.

There are other elements that are common to the two sets of stories. We talked above about the background of conflict that they both share since they were conceived under the influence of the Conquista and Reconquista, respectively. In the case of Spain, the Virgin actually participates directly in the fight and takes part with the Christians in their war against the infidels, just as Santiago de Compostela had also done in both military conflicts. This is evident in *Cantiga 28*, which relates the siege of Constantinople by the Moors. With the help of the Virgin, the ill-defended city is saved, and the Moors, overpowered by the newly invigorated Christian army, surrender their weapons and ask for baptism.[18]

In *Cantiga 345*, the Virgin, though she does not appear on the battlefield, looks after the Christian king, Alfonso X himself, in his dreams and tells him about the treason that he is being a victim of while he is away from his castle. As a consequence, the king returns home and puts a stop to the Moorish siege, also saving the image of the Virgin who alerted him.

These stories contrast with the one of Guadalupe in which, though the conquest does not appear in the first place, the legend of the apparition is definitely marked by it. In fact, the apparition is presented as the culmination of the conquest and the subsequent struggle for the establishment of Christianity in New Spain:

---

17 Also in this category we could include *Cantiga 167*, in which a Moorish mother prays to the Virgin for the resurrection of her son in spite the opposition of all her neighbors; or *Cantiga 205*, in which the Virgin intercedes to save the life of a Moorish woman and her son, who stand between the parapets of a castle being stormed by the Christians.

18 Something very similar is related in *Cantiga 165* about the siege of Tortosa.

Y a diez años
de que fue conquistada el agua, el monte,
la ciudad de México,
ya reposó la flecha, el escudo,
por todas partes estaban en paz
en los varios pueblos.
No ya sólo brotó,
ya verdea, abre su corola
la creencia, el conocimiento
del Dador de la vida, verdadero Dios.[19] (León-Portilla 2000: 93–94)

Following in this environment of confrontation, we have already mentioned above one of the most immediate consequences every time that the difference in religion becomes an issue: the substitution of the symbols of the conquered for those of conquering forces and, in the context we are looking at, the substitution of mosques by Christian churches in the Spain of the Reconquista and its counterpart in the New World: the replacement of native divinities by Christian figures.

Cantiga 229 focuses on the miracle performed by the Virgin in order to avoid the destruction of the church devoted to her in Vila-Sirga. The same topic centers the attention of the *Cantiga 292*, where the policy of substitution is stated: "When he [King Don Fernando] conquered some city from the Moors, he placed Her statue [the Virgin's] in the portico of the mosque." Slightly different is the situation discussed in *Cantiga 169*, where the emphasis is put on the conquering Moors rather than on the Christian forces. In this case it is the Moors who try to eliminate a church dedicated to the Virgin, and though they have all the rights for it (it is in their territory, and they have requested all the necessary permits), they do not dare go against the temple in case they become the object of the Virgin's wrath. Their respect for this borrowed symbol is made apparent.

In the Mexican case, the substitution of Tonantzin by a generic Immaculate is almost immediate: the pagan temple is replaced by a Christian church, and Christianity starts spreading among the indigenous population. But, in this case, and since the substitution is carried out without further consequences to the Spaniards, we are led to assume that the change was positive; that is, there were no punishments for the Spaniards or miraculous intervention of the pagan deities in order to avoid the substitution, allowing us to believe, according to the conquering eyes, that the Christian symbols were always meant to be there.

---

19 My translation: And ten years after it was conquered the water, the mountain, the city of Mexico, the arrow and the shield rested, they were at peace everywhere in several villages. Not only the greenery sprouted but also opened its corolla the belief, and the knowledge of the Giver of life, the true God.

Finally, there is a corpus of cantigas in which the image of the Virgin acquires relevance; that is, not the Virgin herself but her image, whether in the form of a statue or as a painting. Some of these poems show the severe punishments that are reserved for those who dare attack the image of the Virgin. In *cantiga 34*, a Jew steals an image of the Virgin. He takes it home, places it in his basement, and periodically insults it. The Virgin allows the Devil to murder the Jew for his actions. Meanwhile, a Christian finds the image and returns it to the glory that it deserves. In *Cantiga 99*, a parallel story is told in which the Virgin also administers death to the Moors who had desecrated her church and stolen her image.

Two cantigas, which are closely related to the events in the Tepeyac, deserve special mention. First, in *Cantiga 46*, an image of the Virgin comes to life in order to convince a Moor of her divinity and of the miracle of the incarnation of Christ in a woman. While the Moor is lost in wondering, the image of the Virgin starts coming to life. She is a pregnant woman, like Guadalupe, a mother trying, with open arms, to include more children within her protection. Finally, *Cantiga 27* is a definite example that finds echo in Juan Diego's story. In this case, Saint Peter requests that an image of the Virgin appear; that is, he does not ask for the incarnation of the Virgin herself but for her materialization in a painting that, displayed in front of a number of Jews, precipitates their conversion. These two cases have great resemblance with elements present in the story of Guadalupe, but there is something worth noticing: in both of these cases, and also in the case of Guadalupe in New Spain, the image (statue in *Cantiga 46* and painting in the other two) that comes to life is *no longer* a representation of the Virgin, a copy, but rather it is the Virgin herself, not a depiction but the divinity in the flesh and with characteristics that make her appear alive. But let us notice that this belief is completely contrary to that which the first missionaries (the Franciscans) had tried to teach the Indians, a line of criticism that would later be used by the Franciscan provincial—Bustamante—in his sermon against the Guadalupe devotion.

The same criticism could be used when approaching the cult of the Virgin of Candelaria in the Canary Islands. This episode, which resembles in many aspects the story of New Spain, was, undoubtedly, a precedent to it, not only in the strict chronological sense, though it took place a century before, but also in terms of being part of the same tradition, sharing in the apparition genre and in the corpus of hagiographic legends interrelated with the conquest. In the case of the Virgin of Candelaria, her story is intimately related to the conquest of Tenerife, where it appeared and from where it traveled to the New World, especially to Peru, where Candelaria, (also known as la Mamacha Candelaria or MamáCandi) is the patron saint of the city of Puno.

[handwritten: PROPHETIC/JUSTIFICATORY VALUE OF THE APPARITION]

The story of the apparition of the Virgen de Candelaria is made known by Fray Alonso de Espinosa, an accomplished scholar belonging to the Dominican Order. He had spent some time in Central America, in particular in Guatemala, where he read about the image before he found the opportunity to visit it (Espinosa 1907: vii).

According to Espinosa's *Guanches of Tenerife* (1594) second book, the image appeared in a cave near the seashore. It is there where two shepherds were trying to shelter their cattle when they noticed a strange reaction from the animals and, upon checking for the source of that behavior, saw the carved image:

> Two natives being on that coast, pasturing their flocks, having to cross that sandy beach and going towards the ravine, the sheep were frightened and turned back. One of the shepherds, believing that the sheep were alarmed because they saw people, and thinking they were some natives who wanted to steal their sheep (it being their custom to rob each other), went forward to make sure, looking towards that part of the ravine. He then saw the holy image, which was on its feet, upon a rock. Being a person who was unaccustomed to similar visions, he set himself, not without fear, to consider the matter. There, seeing an infant in her arms, it seemed to him that it was a woman, though strange to him as regarded colour and clothes. (1907: 47)

Espinosa does not point to the exact year of these events but ventures an approximation: around the year 1400, about a hundred years before the evangelization of the island.

This fact, the apparition of the Virgin in a land of nonbelievers, has, on the one hand, the appeal of spreading the Christian religion to people not familiarized with the Gospel (to the point that they doubted her divine character and tried to harm the statue), but also, it has the added connotation of making the evangelization of the Guanches and, therefore, the arrival of the Spanish conquering forces, part of a divine plan announced by the Virgin herself. This way, the colonization of the island becomes just and necessary, a small price to pay in order to introduce the Canaries into Christianity.[20]

---

20 The same *motif* would be used in 1648 when Miguel Sánchez, in his *Imagen de la Virgen María Madre de Dios de Guadalupe*, presents the conquest of New Spain as part of a divine plan and even announced by a sign from the sky, making the arrival of the Spaniards just, necessary, and providential:

> En el cielo apareció una señal. Muchas se vieron en él antes de conquistarse aquesta tierra en su ciudad de México, evidentes pronósticos de lo que sucedió, porque en años muy anteriores a la ocasión, brotaba el cielo ardientes globos y abrazados cometas, que a luces claras del día, de tres en tres desde el oriente volaban al occidente, rociando con centellas los aires, que cada una, si no era rayo que mataba, era relámpago que confundía a los mexicanos moradores, conociendo en esto cercana la destrucción de aquella monarquía, permitiéndolo Dios como en segundo Egipto de bárbara gentilidad...]No sería mucho confrontase Dios con aquellas señales, las que se vieron en México antes de su conquista. (Torre Villar and Navarro de Anda 1982: 165).

Here again, following the formula established by the apparition genre, the statue is found by poor people, non-converted (as was the norm in the stories found in the *Cantigas*), even called infidels, as Moors and Jews had been called for centuries in the Spain of the Reconquista ("The holy relic was in possession of the infidels," Espinosa 1907: 56), unlikely emissaries chosen by the sacred image to intercede in her name, people who did not even know what sort of supernatural element they were looking at:

> One of them had a *Tabona*, a dark smooth stone, which when sharpened against another similar stone, becomes like a razor, and is used for lancing and bleeding. Holding this stone he came to the holy image, intending to cut one of her fingers, to satisfy his ignorance and see if she could feel. Putting the finger of the image over his own he began to cut, and found himself deceived, for he cut his own fingers, without doing any harm to the fingers of the image. But he persevered, and began again, always cutting his own fingers until the blood ran down, and he rolled over. The fingers of the holy image remained unharmed, without any mark on them. These were the first two miracles that Our Lady worked, for the good of the natives, on themselves. (Espinosa 1907: 48)

Here again we have two aspects that resemble the Juan Diego story. On the one hand, it is important to notice that, as happened in the last two *cantigas* we looked at (*Cantigas 27 and 46*), the apparition is not of the Virgin herself but of an *image of the Virgin*. This is also true in respect to the last apparition of the Virgin of Guadalupe, the one that takes place in Juan Diego's tilma, and though the other three are of the Virgin encarnated, it is this last one that remains as the example of a living image and that confirms her divinity.[21] But this fact becomes a threat, a point of confusion in the fight against the idolatry of the natives, a crossroads where everything melts since the image ceases to be the representation of the divine to become the divine itself. Also, because of the intrinsic divinity of the Candelaria's image, it is said not to be man made (just like the Virgin of Guadalupe) but, rather, "brought to this island by the ministry of angels, and that it was the work of their hands. For it is not possible that a work so fine and perfect should have been carved by mortal hands, as well as regards design, shape, colours and inscription" (Espinosa 1907: 51–52). So far, the formulaic apparition genre established by Poole (1995: 22) has been followed in Tenerife: the Virgin appeared in a natural landscape and was apparent to the animals too, creating an immediate connection with the land that she chose. Also, she is seen by an individual, in this case, two who were poor, marginalized, infidel natives in this setting and who had to face the authorities in her name. That is exactly what

---

21 On the living properties of the Virgin of Guadalupe, there are innumerable sources. See, for example, Jody Brant Smith (1983).

happens in the Candelaria story, and, though she does not request anything (she does not ever utter a word or communicate in any way), her apparition, which took place before the arrival of the Spaniards, is reported to the landowner. Nevertheless, and contrary to what Zumárraga supposedly did, this Lord "much astonishment for what he heard, desired to see the thing described by the shepherds" (Espinosa 1907: 49). I think that would have been a more likely reaction in the bishop-elect too.

As happened to Juan Bernardino, Juan Diego's uncle, the Virgen de Candelaria also performs miraculous healings, winning with them the respect of the witnesses: "On putting their hands on the image preparatory to raising it, a miraculous thing happened. The injuries of both were healed and made sound, to the great admiration of all present, who, with shouts and whistling applauded the deed, and were pleased and delighted at the benefit thus conferred. The Lord and his followers concluded that the woman must be something supernatural, having such power to take away health and to restore it. With this they recovered their valour, losing their feeling of terror" (Espinosa 1907: 50–51). But this is where the similarities end. Contrary to what is established by Poole, the Virgen de Candelaria does not request that a hermitage be built in her name, although she obtains the same effect: "Having gone the distance of an arquebus shot and a little more, the image being light, and the carriers being strong men of great force, they were yet obliged to rest and ask for help. For this reason, after the country had become Christian, there was founded on the same spot a small hermitage called *del Socorro*, which had always been much venerated and frequented" (Espinosa 1907: 53). Poole talks about the presence of an emissary, a person who would speak for the Virgin, and though the two shepherds establish the first connection, in Espinosa's story there is one more character, Antón, and he becomes the emissary. He is described as a converted individual, "instructed in the faith and baptized," chosen by God as "the tongue of these people" (Espinosa 1907: 56), that is, a person in between, a representative of the Guanches but one who is also able to connect, through the Gospel, with the Spaniards:

> Finally he came to the territory of Guimar. As he came in Spanish clothes, the natives thought he was one of those who made inroad on them, and approached him in a hostile manner. But the boy Anton spoke to them in their own language and appeased them. Being received, he went to the house of the Lord to give an account of the reason of his coming, and to answer any questions that might be put to him. The Lord thought that, as this boy had traveled in other lands and among other people, he might have some knowledge of what the woman was who was in his house. So the Lord took Anton to where the holy image was. When Anton saw it he went down on his knees, put his hands together, and made signs that everyone present should do the same. (Espinosa 1907: 57)

Antón, therefore, lives the moment of *anagnorisis* on behalf of everybody else who surrounds him: the Spaniards, who realize that the natives have been personally touched by God and the Virgin; and the natives, who recognize, through Antón, the honor of this presence and live the awakening of their faith:

> The fame of this was spread abroad. It was told, in all parts of the island, that the woman who had appeared in the kingdom of Guimar was the mother of the sustainer of the world, to whom they confessed, and whom they looked upon as God. They came from all parts to the dedication of the cave, and a great concourse of people assembled. They ordered festivals, rejoicings, dances and displays of agility, with races, hurling of lances and other exercises, showing much agility and dexterity, good dispositions, and all the force that each one could display. It was decided to enact a law that the people should assemble here, so many times a year, in honour of the Mother of God, for their rejoicings and dances (for they knew no other way of showing veneration.) (Espinosa 1907: 58–59)

The Virgen de Candelaria remained in the cave, now called San Blas, where Antón lived and devoted his life to her service, as an antecedent of what the future was to hold for Juan Diego.

In sum, in both cases, the Canaries and New Spain, the extirpation of idolatry became a process with two stages: one that involved marginalizing or, in some cases, eliminating the regional native devotions, that is, reducing their religiosity to something exotic, accessorial, unimportant, that could, therefore, be eliminated or ignored without further consequences. In both cases, in the Spaniards' view, the natives are considered "infidels," that is, lacking religion, Christian religion that is, rather than owners of a vast variety of religious references. They are, for that reason, described in the negative, as ignorant people "not accustomed to reverence nor worship gods, not to treat divine things" (Espinosa 1907: 53).

Second, we witness the replacement of the symbol—the appearance of the Virgin, in this case—in order to fill the vacuum left by the pagan devotion, the introduction of a new reference that, undoubtedly, links religion and politics and brings the natives into the Christian Church. This change that, on the surface, operates only on an emotional level is also destined to make the natives into Christians and, from there, into subjects, fully participant (though from the periphery in all the extension of the word) in the European imaginary or, at least, in the capacity that the dominating cosmology had in mind of them.

Nevertheless, in the case of New Spain the transition was not so clearly established. It actually had a middle step in which the first friars, trying to work against the native resistance to change, attempted a middle ground in which the native deity was *like* the

Christian one; that is, Tonantzin was then seen as a preparation for the Marian devotion that was presented as the ultimate goal, as we already saw in Sahagún's text above. This middle-land is what I will make the focus of the next section.

THE EMERGENCE OF THE APPARITION

After the death of Zumárraga in 1548, there was a period of three years in which Mexico did not have a bishop appointed. Finally, Alonso de Montúfar, a Dominican, was appointed in 1551, but he did not arrive to his new position until 1554, leaving the see in Mexico empty for a total of six long years.

Montúfar was sixty when he was appointed to the archbishopric of New Spain. He was extremely well learned and had a past as a theological consultant of the Inquisition; therefore, he was very familiar with issues surrounding the fight for orthodoxy in the Catholic religion and practice in the aftermath of Trent (Poole 1995: 58).

As I mentioned above, there is no written evidence of the apparition of Guadalupe until 1555. This date, of course, would put us at the very beginning of Montúfar's administration, since he had arrived just a year before.

O'Gorman establishes that the apparition must have happened between November 6, 1555, and September 6, 1556, leaving a period of ten months in between (O'Gorman 1986: 21). The reasoning behind this conclusion is as follows: When the First Provincial Council of Mexico opened (on November 6, 1555), there was no mention of any apparition of the Virgin of Guadalupe, or of any other event of this nature. This silence is loud enough for O'Gorman, who assumes that, if the apparition had taken place, it would have been recorded in the most comprehensive meeting that had taken place in Mexico so far, not allowing for the possibility of a choice to the contrary (O'Gorman 1986: 118n10). On this matter, Poole does not attach the same importance to the fact that Guadalupe was not mentioned in the *Concilio*, considering it "local devotion centered in Mexico City" and thus, inappropriate for the agenda of the provincial council (Poole 1995: 251n46). But let us notice that O'Gorman does not refer, with his chronological interval, to the apparition of the Virgin of Guadalupe. However, he does refer to the apparition of her image, that is, the placement of it in the hermitage at the Tepeyac, eliminating any possibility of any miraculous event and opening the door to talk about a manipulation of the legend.

In any case, what is not debatable is that there is no evidence of the existence either of the apparition or of the image of the Mexican Guadalupe anywhere in New Spain until September 6, 1556, when Montúfar himself included this topic in a sermon that he preached in the Cathedral of Mexico.[22]

---

22 We do not have the text of the sermon preached by Montúfar, but the gist of it can be reproduced from the data collected in the *Información de 1556*, an investigation that Montúfar himself launched to clarify

On that occasion, the archbishop opened his address with the formula "Beati oculi qui vident quae nos videtis," a quote from Luke 10:23 by which Montúfar introduced the theme of marvel into the lives of the people who listened to him.[23] With this opening, the archbishop wanted to make known how lucky they were, witnesses of a miraculous event, touched by the grace of Christ, who, as a sign of his love for his church in the Indies, would not hesitate to send the Virgin, his Mother. Therefore, this devotion finds open support from the religious authorities who want to promote these practices among the Spaniards and spread it among the Indians: "Él [Montúfar] procuró de persuadir a todo el pueblo a devoción de nuestra Sra., diciendo cómo su hijo precioso en muchas partes *ponía devoción* a la imagen de su Madre preciosa en los pueblos y en los despoblados, y para esto señaló a nuestra Sra. de la Antigua y de los Remedios, y nuestra Sra. de los Reyes dentro de la iglesia mayor de Sevilla, y nuestra Sra. de Monserrat y de la Peña de Francia, y nuestra Sra. del Orito [*sic*]" (Torre Villar and Navarro de Anda 1982: 51, my emphasis).[24] We can see that, according to Montúfar, the image of the Virgin had been "placed" in this context not at random, but purposely "placed" there by the specific plan designed by Christ himself. And, with such a sponsor, who could doubt it (O'Gorman 1886: 70)? Nevertheless, right from this statement, we are made aware of the possibility of a manufactured apparition born to satisfy precisely the effect that Montúfar outlines: the increase in the devotion of both Spaniards and Indians.

However, Montúfar himself included his own limits in the same sermon, reminding himself of the ordinances made by the *Concilio Laterense* that, in one session established "dos cosas, so pena de excomunión al sumo potífice reservada: la una, que nadie infamase a los prelados, y la otra, que ninguno predicase milagros falsos ni inciertos" (Juan Salazar's testimony in the *Información de 1556*, Torre Villar and Navarro de Anda 1982: 51).[25] This way, Montúfar gave his future opponents the argument that they would need to criticize him. Why would he do this? What would be his intention? O'Gorman offers as the only possible explanation that Montúfar really believed that the miracle was true (O'Gorman 1986: 71), but (and this is a major change) the only miracle that is ever mentioned in the *Información*

---

the contents of a sermon by Fray Francisco de Bustamante, the Franciscan provincial who attacked Montúfar's sermon. I will refer to it later.

23 We know that Montúfar opened his sermon with this quote through the testimony of Gonzalo de Alarcón (García Icazbalceta 1896: 120)

24 This statement is part of Juan Salazar's testimony in the *Información de 1556*. My translation: He tried to persuade everyone of the devotion to Our Lady saying that her precious son spread devotion to the image of her precious Mother in many places and deserted areas, and for this he referred to Our lady of Antigua and of the Remedios and Our Lady of the Reyes inside the main church in Seville and Our Lady of Monserrat and de la Peña in France and Our Lady of Orito.

25 My translation: Two things, under penalty of excommunication reserved to the Holy Father: one, that nobody slander the prelates, and the other, that nobody preach false or unconfirmed miracles.

de 1556 had nothing to do with the story we opened the chapter with, that is, with the traditional account of Juan Diego's encounters with the Virgin of Guadalupe. It actually dealt with a cattle farmer who felt cured as he walked near the site at the Tepeyac.[26] This miracle is also referred to in a letter that the viceroy of New Spain, Martín Enríquez de Almanza, sent to King Phillip II. The letter says the following:

> Fecha de San Lorenzo el Real, a 15 de mayo de 1575, sobre lo que toca a la fundación de la ermita de nuestra Señora de Gudalupe, y que procure con el arzobispo que la visite.
>
> Visitalla y tomar las cuentas, siempre se ha hecho por los prelados; y el principio que tuvo la fundación de la iglesia que ahora está hecha, lo que comúnmente se entiende es que el año de 1555 o 1556 estaba allí una ermitilla, en la cual estaba la imagen que ahora está en la iglesia, y que un ganadero que por allí andaba, publicó haber cobrado salud yendo a aquella ermita, y empezó a crecer la devoción de la gente, y pusieron nombre a la imagen nuestra señora de Guadalupe, por decir que se parecía a la de Guadalupe de España.[27] (Torre Villar and Navarro de Anda 1982: 149)

This document, that confirms the miracle at the Tepeyac, is also useful in confirming the approximate timing proposed by O'Gorman: 1555 or 1556, in any case, very far from the proposed 1531 in the foundational legend.

Other testimonies, now coming from the text of the *Información de 1556* proper, can help us confirm the same timing. The first evidence is born from the fact that even when Zumárraga was supposed to be a direct participant in the story of the miracle, a direct witness of it, he is only mentioned in the above-mentioned document and, that time, not even by his name:

> Dijo, que este testigo, como vecino que es de esta ciudad, por el trato y conversación que en ella tiene, vio de mucho tiempo a esta parte, así en el tiempo del *sor. arzobispo pasado como del presente*, ir mucha gente a las huertas, así hombres como mujeres, y a ellas llevar muy buen repuesto de comida y cena, donde en algunas partes que este testigo se halló, vio jugar y hacer otros excesos, y que después acá que se divulgó la devoción de nuestra Sra. de Guadalupe ha cesado mucha gente de lo que tiene dicho, y que ya no se platica otra cosa en la tierra si no es ¿dónde queréis que vamos?,

---

26 By the way, there is no evidence that this man's name was Juan Diego.

27 My translation: The Royal site of St Lawrence, May 15th, 1575, regarding the foundation of the chapel of Our Lady of Guadalupe and the archbishop's visit.

> Visit it and take account, which has always been done by the prelates; and the seed of the foundation of the church that is now built, it is commonly attributed to a little chapel that was there in 1555 or 1556, that held the image that is now in the church, and that a cattle farmer who was around made public that he had healed by going to that chapel and people's devotion started to grow and named the image Our Lady of Guadalupe because it had resemblance with the Guadalupe in Spain.

vámonos a nuestra Señora de Guadalupe: que le parece a este testigo que está en Madrid.[28] (Torre Villar and Navarro de Anda 1982: 53)

This testimony is, in my opinion, very effective. First, it shows the persistence of Indian idolatry, alive even in spite of the efforts of many friars who had worked hard in the process of evangelization of the natives. Second, it corroborates the miracle referred by the cattle farmer, and, what is more important, it does not mention any other miraculous event, silencing the supposedly famous apparitions of the Virgin. Finally, this text very clearly establishes the devotion for Guadalupe as a phenomenon belonging to Montúfar's administration and nonexistent before that. It states that although the native idolatry had been alive in the outskirts of the cities, both during Zumárraga's and Montúfar's administration, it is in the term of the second when many people had abandoned those illicit practices *due to* the newly found devotion to Guadalupe. This fact clearly makes it a phenomenon attached to Montúfar and, by the same token, very unlikely before 1554.

To this fact we must add two more references that within the *Información de 1556* catalogue the devotion as "new," in the case of Alonso Sánchez de Cisneros (Torre Villar and Navarro de Anda 1982: 61) and the image of the Virgin as one painted yesterday ("pintada ayer," Torre Villar and Navarro de Anda 1982: 71). These references do not mention a year in particular. But even if "yesterday" only means *recently*, that is still a far cry from 1531.

Following this line of thought, it is not reasonable to believe that the image of the Virgin of Guadalupe, neither the Spanish one nor the Mexican, would have been in the temple at the Tepeyac; rather, it is much more likely that there was no image at all, or maybe a generic Immaculate, allowing then for the possibility of the placement of the Mexican Guadalupe in a date close to the year of the *Información*, that is, around 1554 or 1555 (i.e., some twenty-three years after what the foundational legend assures), judging for these references to a "recent" image (Gutiérrez Zamora 1996: 124).

The last evidence that I would like to bring into discussion has to do with a comment made by Bachiller Salazar when he is trying to talk about the pillars that hold the foundation of the hermitage. The mere fact that anybody would have to look for the basics around which the devotion of Guadalupe is sustained if, in reality, she had appeared four times would be outrageous (Torre Villar and Navarro de Anda 1982: 58). Therefore, if we reverse this logic, the foundation of the Guadalupe shrine

---

28 My translation: This witness, neighbor of this villa and by the knowledge he has, said that for a long time, during the time of the last archbishop and also the current one, that many people went to the orchards, men and women, carrying food and dinner where this witness saw people play and commit other excesses and, after the devotion to Our Lady of Guadalupe was made public, many people have stopped doing that and there is no conversation other than Where do you want to go? Let's go to Our Lady of Guadalupe, that according to this witness, it must be in Madrid.

should have been the story of Juan Diego, the four apparitions, and the healing of Juan Bernardino, and so there would be no reason to be questioning what the foundation of the devotion was in 1556. Is it possible that the apparitions were completely forgotten in twenty-five years? Is it possible that nobody had news from them and that they had never heard of Juan Diego? I must say that in the light of this testimony, it does not seem likely that the apparitions ever took place or that Zumárraga, or his administration, was in any way involved. Neither are there any remarks of the divine character of the painting, and so we must conclude that the legend around the apparitions and Juan Diego's story were born at a later date.

The reaction to Montúfar's sermon did not take long, and only two days later, on September 8, 1556—the day on which the Catholics celebrate the Nativity of the Virgin Mary and also the feast of Our Lady of Guadalupe in Extremadura (Spain)—Fray Francisco de Bustamante, Franciscan provincial in New Spain, delivered a sermon of his own in response to Montúfar's. Unfortunately, the text of this sermon is lost, but we can partially reproduce it based on the testimonies given by the witnesses of it and collected in the *Información de 1556*.

Bustamante chose to deliver his sermon on an important day, according to the Catholic calendar, assuring that way that the president and the oidores de la audiencia (the judges) would be present. There were a number of points that Bustamante wanted to make and, in our case, for being interested in the idolatry of the Indians, we will start there. Bustamante was concerned with the fact that the archbishop had promoted the devotion for the Virgin of Guadalupe and encouraged the reverence of the image as miraculous and the site as sacred. In the Franciscan's opinion, this devotion, formulated as Montúfar had, was confusing for the natives and could ruin many previous efforts:

> Lo primero que dijo que una de las cosas más perniciosas para la buena cristiandad de los naturales, que se podían sustentar, era la devoción de nuestra Sra. de Guadalupe, porque desde su conversión se les había predicado que no creyesen en imágenes, sino solamente en Dios y en nuestra Sra. . . . porque les habían dado a entender en sus sermones que las imágenes eran de palo y de piedra, y que no se habían de adorar, mas de que estaban por semejanza de las del cielo, y que los indios eran tan devotos de nuestra Sra. que la adoraban y que pasaban mucho trabajo para quitarles esa aquella opinión, y que visto ahora que aquella imagen hacía milagros, aunque no estaba ninguno averiguado, que se pasaría mucho trabajo de aquí en adelante en quitarles la opinión que tenían de adorar la imagen de nuestra Sra.[29] (Torre Villar and Navarro de Anda 1982: 44)

---

29 My translation: He began by saying that one of the most dangerous things that could be done against the good Christianity of the natives was to promote the devotion to Our Lady of Guadalupe because since their conversion they had been told not to believe in images, but only in God and Our Lady . . . because we had taught them in our sermons that images were made of wood and stone and should not

This passage, rich in meaning, can give us the keys to a number of aspects. First of all, it confirms both Bustamante's and Sahagún's fears: the Indians are not differentiating their pagan idolatry from the Christian sacred figures; rather, they are worshiping, within the Catholic practices, saints and virgins *as if they were* pagan deities.

This fact is confirmed by other sources of the time, such as G. Mendieta (1973: Book II; chapter IX and Book III, chapter XIII) and Torquemada (1943–44: Book XV, chapter XXIII), among others. It is also specifically addressed in the *Información de 1556* as a response to what the archbishop had said in his sermon and told by the second witness interviewed: "Dijo que el arzobispo mi señor estaba muy engañado en pensar que estos indios no eran devotos de nuestra Sra., porque los que los trataban entendían ser tanta su devoción, que *la adoraban por Dios* y que antes era necesario en esto irles a la mano y dárselo a entender" (Torre Villar and Navarro de Anda 1982: 44, my emphasis).[30] According to this statement, we have to understand that the archbishop had a very superficial knowledge of the natives because, otherwise, he would have realized that the Indians did worship the Virgin Mary but not as such, rather as a blurry sacred figure with mixed characteristics from the pagan Tonantzin and the ideas that the missionaries were trying to convey about God. Syncretism, therefore, had proved to be a very dangerous way of introducing the Indians to Catholicism, a road in no-man's land where the natives have already lost the continuity of their way of life but at the same time are unable to participate in the European one with no ties attached. Therefore, the natives have substituted one image for another but have not changed the mindset behind it *[+ COMMON]*

As we mentioned above, Sahagún proposed a radical rupture of this dangerous *[FEATURE OF CATHOLIC DEVOTION]* continuity (between Tonantzin and Guadalupe), but Bustamante's worry was that by attaching miracles to the image of Guadalupe, the Indians would not be able to disassociate the magical component from the Christian devotion to which they were being introduced. In fact, if we look at the *Información de 1556*, we get the impression that the natives were approaching the Virgin as an idol, as a magical figure, and not as something they were faithful to. Thus, they *asked* for things and expected an immediate, direct response, thinking that that was the nature of miracles: something you can order at your convenience. There is no intention to wait for an afterlife reward. This attitude is evident in Juan de Masseguer's testimony, one of the witnesses interrogated for the *Información*: "Preguntado si ha ido algunas veces

[SPECULATION]

---

be worshipped, but only in that they resemble what is in heaven, and that the Indians were very devout to Our Lady and we have worked really hard to correct that opinion and if it was stated that that image performed miracles, although none of them were confirmed, that it would be very difficult to teach them not to worship the image of Our Lady.

30 My translation: He said that the archbishop was very mistaken to think that the Indians were not devout to Our Lady because the ones he knew had such devotion that they worshipped her as God and that it was necessary to make them understand.

a la dicha ermita de nuestra Sra. dijo: Que más de veinte veces, y ayer particular-mente fue allá a llevar una niña hija suya, que estaba mala de tos, que se ahogaba, y la encomendó allá a nuestra Sra. y dio su limosna; y le hizo decir una misa; y bendito Dios, la niña está buena" (Torre Villar and Navarro de Anda 1982: 70).[31] As we can see in this passage, there is no mention of faith, trust, or willingness to wait. The expectation is for the miracle to work on demand or else the devotion to the Virgin would be in serious danger: "Les daban a entender [a los indios naturales de esta tierra] que aquella imagen de nuestra Sra. de Guadalupe hacía milagros, y como algunos indios cojos, ciegos o mancos iban a ella con aquel propósito y no tornaban sanos, antes peores con el cansancio del camino, lo tenían por burla, y que sería mejor que se procurase de quitar aquella devoción, por el escándalo de los naturales" (Torre Villar and Navarro de Anda 1982: 49).[32] To this, Bustamante requests in his sermon that the miracles that are attributed to the Virgin of Guadalupe be checked, researched, and proved, for the benefit of all in the community, but Montúfar could only testify to the extended devotion awakened at the Tepeyac, no specific miracles, apparitions, healings, or miraculous stamping on Juan Diego's tilma: "Su señoría no predicaba milagro ninguno de los que algunos decían haber hecho la dicha imagen de nuestra Sra. . . . ni hacía caso de ellos, porque no tenía información hecha de ellos . . . que los milagros que su señoría predicaba de nuestra Sra. de Guadalupe era la gran devoción que toda esta ciudad ha tomado a esta bendita imagen, y los indios también" (Torre Villar and Navarro de Anda 1982: 51).[33] Bustamante, in spite of his harsh criticism of Montúfar's sermon and policy, is quick to insist on the fact that he does not want to take away the devotion for the Virgin from the natives but rather to free the devotion from pagan elements. In order to do this, the Franciscan pro-vincial saw it necessary to clarify the origin of the image that, according to the testi-mony of Sánchez de Cisneros and that of Juan de Massenguer, was recently painted

31 My translation: Asked if he has gone sometimes to the chapel of Our Lady, he said that more than twenty times and that yesterday in particular he took one of his daughters there because she had a bad cough and was getting choked and that he entrusted her to Our Lady and gave some alms and had a Mass in her honor and that, thank God, the girl has healed.

32 My translation: It was understood [by the Indians of that land] that that image of Our Lady of Guadalupe performed miracles and, since some disabled, blind or amputee Indians went there to be healed and nothing changed, they thought it was a mockery, and that it would be better to eradicate that devotion, to avoid the protest of the Indians.

33 My translation: His lordship did not preach about any miracles of those that Our Lady was said to have performed, nor did he pay any attention to them because they had not been researched . . . because those miracles of Our Lady were the big devotion that that town hads taken to that blessed image, including the Indians.

Su señoría no predicaba milagro ninguno de los que algunos decían haber hecho la dicha imagen de nuestra Sra. . . . ni hacía caso de ellos, porque no tenía información hecha de ellos . . . que los milagros que su señoría predicaba de nuestra Sra. de Guadalupe era la gran devoción que toda esta ciudad ha tomado a esta bendita imagen, y los indios también.

by an Indian by the name of Marcos. This way Bustamante completely erases the divine nature of the painting and establishes it as a work of art with human origin.

The reaction to this statement, especially delivered in front of many authorities of the time, should have been extraordinary, but in fact there were only three brief mentions of little scandal in the *Información de 1556*, a very mild response to such a daring accusation.[34] In fact, Torre Villar and Navarro de Anda assure us that the scandal was probably born from the discrepancy between Montúfar and Bustamante, that is, from having two high religious authorities encourage different behaviors, rather than because Bustamante had rejected the divine origin of the painting (1982: 110). In the end Bustamante suffered barely any consequences, and his accusations were never rejected.[35] In fact, the *Información* was opened in case Bustamante needed to be reprimanded, but it was never finished and, therefore, a punishment was never issued (Torre Villar and Navarro de Anda 1982: 47). Let us stop here for a moment. What are the implications of this laxity? Was his accusation so well known that Montúfar did not think it was worth going against? Did it, in the end, really matter to the multitudes that were already visiting the shrine? Gutiérrez Zamora concludes that the archbishop must have known about the origin of the image and decided that, for that reason, Bustamante's accusations did not deserve any reprimand: "El arzobispo sabía de las circunstacias que rodeaban a la imagen, pues de no ser así imagínense ustedes el escándalo que se hubiera armado al respecto, de lo que no quedó constancia alguna en la *Información de 1556*" (Camiro Gutiérrez Zamora 1996: 123).[36] Following this reasoning, O'Gorman concludes that, based on all the evidence, it was Montúfar who orchestrated the placement (not miraculous apparition any more) of the image of the Virgin of Guadalupe in the hermitage of Tepeyac, a hypothesis that O'Gorman backs up with two main arguments: First, the archbishop did not establish the divine origin of the image when he had the chance, that is, during his sermon or even later on, during the *Información* that he ordered against Bustamante. In fact, Montúfar did not refer to the apparitions at any point and looked at the devotion of the people as the main source of this devotion rather than at the miraculous events. Second, Montúfar did not offer any opposition to Bustamante's statements—that is, he did not investigate the possible participation of the Indian Marcos, or even call him to

---

34 The witnesses who talked about this mild scandal were Juan de Mesa, Bachiller Salazar, and Juan de Massenguer.
35 In fact, Bustamante was allowed to remain in his job, and later he was even reelected to it. See Mendieta (1973: Book IV, chapter 42): "Fue electo en noveno provincial el prudentísimo Fr. Francicos de Bustamante, de la provincia de Castilla ... Y cumplido su oficio [Fray Francisco de Toral] fue reelegido segunda vez por undécimo provincial el mesmo Fr. Francisco de Bustamante. Mas al segundo año el vino recado de España para que fuese comisario general, lo cual fue causa que acortase el capítulo."
36 My translation: The archbishop knew the circumstances surrounding the image, because if not, imagine the scandal that would have been raised, of which there was no evidence in the *Información de 1556*.

testify; he did not ask the witnesses about this possibility or register their possible astonishment; and he did not punish Bustamante in any way. In fact, he did not even finish the investigation.

Bearing all this in mind, we can conclude that first, the archbishop Montúfar knew that the image was not of supernatural or divine origin and was not surprised when the Indian Marcos was named as the producer of it;[37] second, Zumárraga had nothing to do with the story of Guadalupe: he was not present, and he did not participate in it; and third, the legend including Juan Diego was a product constructed much later (in fact in the 1640s).[38]

With all these facts in hand, there is one question remaining. Whom does the legend benefit? So, who could have been interested in promoting this second part in the strategy to eradicate the native idolatry? In other words, if the Indians rejected the Christianized Tonantzin and embraced an indigenous-friendly Virgin of Guadalupe, who would win in the change? I am afraid that the answer to all these questions is the same: the archbishop Montúfar, ultimate promoter of the devotion.

With this change, Montúfar managed to achieve two goals: on the one hand, he warmed the hearts of the Indians, who were now not only allowed but encouraged to worship Guadalupe the same way that they had the pagan Tonantzin, falling exactly into the dangers that Sahagún and Torquemada had pointed out, in this middle-land where the continuum between the two divinities was purposely blurred; and second, with this gesture, Montúfar attracted the Indians toward the Episcopal institution, that is, the centralized church as opposed to the missionary orders and established a fierce competition in relation to the Franciscans,

---

37 In fact, O'Gorman goes on to say that the archbishop possibly commissioned the image himself (O'Gorman 1986: 148).

38 There are two texts considered responsible for the elaboration of the foundational legend. The first of the two was written by Miguel Sánchez (1594–1674), a priest, writer, and theologian from New Spain. His text, entitled *Imagen de la Virgen María Madre de Dios de Guadalupe*, is considered by many as the first written documentation of the 1531 apparition of the Virgin Mary as Our Lady of Guadalupe and, though there are earlier references to it, Sánchez's text contributed a great deal to the creation of the myth and the foundational legend as we know it today. It was written in Spanish and mostly directed to the *criollos* living in New Spain. In it, the story of Guadalupe becomes short instances among long paragraphs of biblical interpretation. This fact separates this text widely from another account published in 1649. This one was written by Luis Laso de la Vega, the vicar of Guadalupe. This account was entitled *Huei tlamahuiçoltica omonexiti in ilhuicac tlatocaçihuapilli Santa María totlaçonantzin Guadalupe in nican huei altepenahuac Mexico itocayocan Tepeyacac*, Nahuatl for "By a great miracle appeared the heavenly queen, Saint Mary, our precious mother of Guadalupe, here near the great altepetl of Mexico, at a place called Tepeyacac." The title is generally shortened to *Huei tlamahuiçoltica* and translated as "The Great Happening"). This text, as opposed to Sánchez's, was written in Nahuatl and intended for the common folk. For this reason this style is very different from the one published the year before. In de la Vega's, the biblical material that was predominant in *Imagen de la Virgen María* is entirely missing, and it only consists of a simple story focused on the four apparitions of Guadalupe. There are also other differences regarding the number of miracles included.

who, so far, had had the monopoly over the natives' evangelization.[39] With these two achievements, Montúfar was well on his way toward the introduction of clerics, instead of missionaries, and also toward favoring the institution that he directed in detriment of the old *doctrinas*. It is, therefore, not surprising that a Franciscan—Bustamante—would raise his voice in disagreement with this policy, especially when there was news that Montúfar needed to charge the Indians (the tithe or *diezmo*) for the costs originating in the change. Bustamante was afraid, as many others were, that the natives would think that the push for their conversion was not without interest and, that, in fact, the Gospel was being sold to them, creating an obstacle for the natives' conversion (O'Gorman 1986: 130).

This *diezmo* had to be approved by the king, which is the reason why Bustamante chose to deliver his sermon in front of the members of the audiencia (judges), therefore trying to use the state as an Episcopal mechanism of control:

> Que mirasen los que allá iban lo que hacían, porque era en gran prejuicio de los naturales, y que fuera bien al primero que dijo que hacía milagros, le dieran cien azotes, y al que lo dijere de aquí en adelante, sobre su ánima le diesen doscientos, caballero en un caballo, y que encargaba mucho el examen de este negocio al visorrey y audiencia, y que *aunque el arzobispo dijese otra cosa*, que por eso el rey tiene jurisdicción temporal y espiritual, y *esto encargó mucho a la audiencia*; y también dijo que no era bien predicarlo en púlpitos, primero que estuviesen verificados en ellos y de los milagros que se decía había hecho; había muchas personas de calidad presentes.[40] (Torre Villar and Navarro de Anda 1982: 43, my emphasis)

Montúfar's appetite for control seems stronger than his care for the natives and, though his encouragement of the Virgin of Guadalupe's devotion put the Indians closer to the idolatry that was being fought by the missionaries, he delivered his sermon regardless in the pursuit of a stronger position in the archbishopry and in the campaigns of evangelization. Montúfar had, as a backdrop, the long tradition of the "apparition genre" already present in the campaigns developed in the Spain of the Reconquista. This reference was full of parallels in terms of converting the

---

39 There is a reference to Montúfar acting like a *tigre fiero* (fierce tiger) against the Franciscans that can be found in the letter that Fray Jerónimo de Mendieta sent to Bustamante on January 1562. This letter follows the confrontation between the Franciscans and the archbishop Montúfar. It can be read in García Icazbalceta (1971b: vol. II, 542).

40 My translation: Those who went there should think about what they were doing because it was very detrimental for the natives, and that the first one who said that miracles were performed should be lashed a hundred times and from now on, whoever repeated should be lashed two hundred times and that the viceroy should be on top of this matter even if the archbishop said a different thing, because the king has temporal and spiritual jurisdiction, and he entrusted the *Audiencia* with this as well; and he also said that it shouldn't be preached from the pulpits; first the miracles had to be confirmed and they, very sure of them; there were very many important people present.

other—facing multiple challenges such as different religions, ways of life, race, and so on—combined in the process of establishing a political hegemony. Therefore, using European *topoi* in a story immersed in the European tradition, Montúfar allows (O'Gorman would say that he created) a pagan symbol, a Christianized pagan idol (Tonantzin) to become the basis for a native-friendly Guadalupe. According to the previous quote, Montúfar should have received 200 lashes for his behavior.[41]

In conclusion, and going back to the plasticity that I hope has been attached to the concept of idolatry throughout this book, I believe that this chapter, and the behavior it shows, is a sound representation of how idolatry is in the eye of the beholder. It is not a behavior or a mindset; it is not a group of practices or a set of features. It is not even defined by the object and/or figure to which the worship is directed. As this chapter shows, idolatry is defined in terms of position: position toward the center of power, position with respect to the decision-making point, and, in our case, position in relation to empire. In this sense, the more the popular beliefs grow closer to the teachings of the empire, the less idolatry there is, a progression that Montúfar saw from afar and used to the benefit of the Spanish Catholic Church (although not necessarily its orthodoxy) and its establishment in the New World. That way, in spite of the transfer of elements from one set of practices to the next, Montúfar saw it convenient to allow a syncretism much despised by the missionary orders in the name of the ultimate goal of community of cult with the newly converted. By encouraging this transfer (inspired in the interventions of the Virgin Mary in the context of the Spanish Reconquista), the second archbishop of New Spain opened a door for that previously irreducible excess of indigenous culture to be incorporated into the Catholic mainstream and put the first stone in the creation of a myth that, nowadays, has become the banner of Mexican identity.[42]

---

41 Actually, according to the previous quote, the first cattle farmer should have been punished with a hundred lashes whereas Montúfar himself would be eligible for two hundred.

42 This gesture was at least enough to help Sahagún have a change of heart, since, in 1570, he is willing to write that the strongest of idolaters, those of Mexico, had surrendered to the Catholic faith:

> Conviene tras lo ya dicho, dar relación a Vuestra Santidad de cómo los muros de Jericó han caído a la voz de las trompetas evangélicas: que es que los más fuertes idólatras de este Nuevo Mundo, que son los habitadores de esta Nueva España (en especial de la gran ciudad de México), se han rendido a la santa fe católica de la Iglesia Romana y van de cada día aprovechando en el cristianismo. (Sahagún 1990b: 4).

> My translation: I am reporting to your holiness that the walls of Jerico have fallen to the sound of the trumpets of the Gospel: the greatest idolaters in this world, the peoples of New Spain (in particular the ones in the City of Mexico) have surrendered to the Catholic faith of the Roman Church and are growing in their Christianity.

5

Conclusion

En muchas de sus fiestas tenian costumbre de hacer bollos de masa, y estos de muchas maneras, que casi usaban de ellos en lugar de comunion de aquel dios cuya fiesta hacian; pero tenian una que mas propiamente parecia coumunion, y era por Noviembre ... cantaban y decian, que aquellos bollos se tornavan carne de Tezcatlipoca, que era el dios ó demonio que tenian por mayor, y á quien mas dignidad atribuian; y solo los dichos muchachos comian aquellos bollos en lugar de comunion, ó carne de aquel demonio; los otros Indios procuraban de comer carne humana de los que morian en el sacrificio, y esta comian comunmente los señores principales, y mercaderes, y los ministros de los templos; que á la otra gente baja pocas veces les alcanzaba un bocadillo. Despues que los Españoles anduvieron de guerra, y ya ganada México hasta pacificar la tierra, los Indios amigos de los Españoles muchas veces comian de los que mataban, porque no todas veces los Españoles se lo podían defender, sino que algunas veces, por la necesidad que tenian de los Indios, pasaban por ello, aunque lo aborrecian (Motolinía, *Historia de los Indios de Nueva España*, in García Icazbalceta 1971a: 23–24).[1]

---

1   My translation: In many of the festivities it was accustomed to make loaves of bread, of many different kinds, and they used them as communion wafers for the god whose festivities those were; and it was around November ... they sang and said that those loaves turned into Tezcatlipoca's flesh, who was the god or the devil that they had in the greatest regard; and only the young lads ate them instead of the communion bread, or flesh of that demon; the other Indians ate human flesh from the ones who had been sacrificed and lords, merchants, and ministers from the temple ate of it, because the lowly people hardly got a bite. After the fight with the Spaniards, from the conquest of Mexico until its appeasement, the

DOI: 10.5876/9781607328018.c005

In the context of sixteenth-century New Spain, idolatry was more than a theoretical concept. As can be seen in the preceding quote and as I hope to have shown throughout these pages, idolatry was very much a present reality, one that could determine the life or death of particular individuals and groups, settle or create conflicts, and intricately related to hegemony and domination.

There are a number of reasons why the concept of idolatry is fascinating to me in the particular context in which I have presented it. In the midst of the Reformation and Counter-Reformation debates, the "discovery" of the New World posed innumerable questions about how to integrate the *other*, how to deal with difference at various levels. It is here where the concept of idolatry reveals its true value: in being what was needed in different contexts and instances, in other words, in being malleable, adaptable.

As we have seen throughout this book, idolatry was not created to deal with the American *other,* and, though it was frequently used in this context, its application to other infidels had already been seen in the Spain of the Reconquista, when Vicente Ferrer preached against the idolatrous Moors and Jews. Idolatry thus became an accusation that could be adapted according to the particular group that was in the eye of the accuser, rather than tied to a specific set of practices. In this same spirit, the concept could be used by the Reformers to accuse the Catholics and by the latter to refer to the pagan Indians, and though the activities of those groups were of a radically different nature, idolatry was the label used to engulf them all.

From this point of view, idolatry becomes useful in its plasticity, in its adaptability. Idolatry is then a relative term marked by social and cultural coordinates, a polyvalent term that can find meaning in very different contexts. For these reasons, though I have tried to offer my own definition of idolatry, it was my intention to keep its multiplicity of meanings alive, and therefore I have presented idolatry as those beliefs and practices that do not conform to those of the hegemonic power and become, for this reason, sinful, erroneous, and false. In this sense I believe that the behaviors and the policies installed in the New World mirrored the ones that had already proved effective in the fights against Moors and Jews in Spain and, though the two contexts evolved differently, the antecedent made of Spain a cultural laboratory that later found its echo in the Canary Islands and in the New World.

Described this way, idolatry becomes the door that opens the possibility to include the *other*, if only as a peripheral value, as an exotic element that, from the outside, reinforces the practices of the center in a gesture that was used as effectively

---

Indians that had befriended the Spaniards often ate from whom they had killed, but not always, because they Spaniards tried to stop it, but, because of the need that the Indians had, they sometimes allowed it, although they abhorred it.

in Europe as it was in the Americas. It marks a position relative to the hegemonic power, and, as a result, it denotes an attitude of superiority toward those practices named idolatrous and, therefore, out of the mainstream. Idolatry, then, stands for coloniality without qualms." ?

But, at the same time, in the context of colonial Mexico, idolatry—or, should I say, the control over the idolatry of the Indians—became a battlefield in which many different interests were at stake. Far from what could be thought, not all efforts were directed in one same direction and not all the colonizing forces worked as one. Many groups attempted different initiatives, and the difficult communication with the central administration did not help avoid contradictory attempts. At the center of this crossroads, the fight against idolatry put on the table the conflict between the military interests and those of the missionaries, between the missionaries themselves and the civil administrators, and created a landscape of confusion from which the newly converted needed to learn.

This is the context in which the first archbishop in Mexico, Juan de Zumárraga, developed his ministry. His challenges were multiple. Not only did he have to establish an institution in a land that was not receptive to the invaders, but he also had to maintain orthodoxy among the Spaniards who, far from home, relaxed in their habits. Therefore, for the archbishop, not only the Spaniards had to be monitored but also the Indians, whose idolatries seemed resistant to all sorts of initiatives. As we saw above, the right balance between the religious orthodoxy and the political interest of the Crown was not easy to find, and the archbishop ended up losing his battle and the jurisdiction over the Indians. His struggles are related in the second and third chapters.

Chapter 4 is the culmination of the evolution presented. Having shown how malleable idolatry can be and how it can address different practices or even the same behaviors viewed from different perspectives, the legend of the Virgin of Guadalupe is the perfect example of this no-man's land. It illustrates the conflict within the missionary orders, the fight for the control over the Indians' conversion, and it shows how, as Motolinía wrote in his quote above, some Spaniards considered that the ends justified the means. The construction of this legend also shows how idolatry could be and, in fact, was manipulated to achieve particular results, in this case, the adherence of the Indians; and how idolatry can be disguised as popular piety if the hegemonic power is willing to present it that way. Indian idolatry was then used as a tool to incorporate them into the Christian world and, more important, as Spanish subjects. We have gone full circle, from the extirpation of idolatry to its use by the institution, from paganism to canonization. A legend was created not for the salvation of the Indians but for that of the Spanish empire. Maybe that was the real miracle that took place at the Tepeyac.

Appendix A

Traslado de ciertas Ordenanzas fechas por el Audiencia Real
insertas en una provisión sellada con el sello real

(Carreño 1944: Doc. 60, 130–5, my emphasis)

Don Carlos por la divina clemencia, Emperador semper augusto, Doña Juana su madre y el mismo Don Carlos por la misma gracia, Reyes de Castilla, de León, de Aragón, de las dos Sicilias, de Jerusalén, de Navarra, de Granada, de Toledo, de Valencia, de Galicia, de Mayorcas, de Sevilla, de Cerdeá, de Córdoba, de Córcega, de Murcia, de Jaen, de los Algarbes, de Algecira, de Gibraltar, de las Islas de Canaria, de las Indias, Islas e Tierra Firme del mar Océano, Condes de Barcelona y de Flandes y de Tirol, etc. Por cuanto hasta agora no se ha dado noticia a los indios naturales desta Nueva España, de algunas cosas que han de saber y tener, demás y allende de las que se les han enseñado y enseñan por los religiosos que entienden en su conversión, y de los que han de guardar, complir y ejecutar por los gobernadores, alcaldes, alguaciles que en nuestro nombre hasta agora se han proveído y proveerán por el nuestro Visorrey de la Nueva España en los pueblos y lugares de indios della, y porque nuestra intención y voluntad es que los dichos indios se aparten y quiten de hacer de cometer ningunos delitos y excesos, y se les dé a entender en qué cosas y casos los hacen y cometen en ofensa de Dios nuestro Señor para que mejor vengan en conocimiento de nuestra santa fe católica, que es la principal intención que tenemos y deseamos, y no pretendan inorancia, visto y platicado por el dicho nuestro Visorrey y Presidente e Oidores de la nuestra Abdiencia y Candelería Real que reside en la ciudad de México de la Nueva España, fué acordado que para el remedio dello y orden que se debe de tener para loque de yuso se hará mención, que debíamos mandar dar esta nuestra carta en la dicha razón, e nos tovímoslo por bien, y por la presente mandamos que demás y allende que a los indios naturales desta Nueva España se les dé a entender lo que en nuestra carta contenido y sean amonestados que no vayan contra el tenor della, agora y de aquí adelante los gobernadores, alcaldes, alguaciles que así están, son y fueren proveídos por el dicho nuestro Visorrey en los pueblos de indios en el uso y ejercicio de sus cargos y en la ejecución desta nuestra provisión, guarden y cumplan y ejecuten tengan la forma y orden siguiente:

Primeramente ordenamos y mandamos que a los indios desta Nueva España así a los que están en nuestra real cabeza como encomendados en personas particulares se les dé a entender, digan, *hagan saber que han de creer y adorar en un solo Dios verdadero, y dejar e olvidar de los ídolos que tenían por sus dioses y adoraciones, que hacían a piedras y al sol y luna, o a otra cualquier criatura y que no hagan ningunos sacrificios ni ofrecimientos a ellos, con apercibimiento que el que lo contrario hiciere, si fuere cristiano, averiguándose ser verdad algunas cosas dello, mandaremos y por la presente mandamos, que por la primera vez le sean dados luego cient azotes públicamente y le sean cortados los cabellos; y por la segunda vez sea traído ante los dichos nuestro Presidente e Oidores con la información que contra él hobiere, para que se proceda contra él conforme a justicia; e si no fuere cristiano, sea preso y luego azotado y llevado ante guardián, deán o prior de iglesia más cercana donde haya persona eclesiástica, para que por él sea exhortado e informado de lo que le conviene saber para venir en conocimiento de Dios Nuestro Señor y de su santa fe católica y se salvar.*

De lo contenido en este capítulo los dichos gobernadores, alcaldes, alguaciles tenga muy gran vigilancia e cuidado informándose si algún indio o india de tal lugar do así fueren gobernadores, alcaldes, alguaciles van y pasan contra el tenor dél.

Iten si alguno no quisiere ser cristiano, que no le admitan ni reciban a dicho oficio alguno ni dignidad en el tal pueblo ni en otro; y así lo son y quieran ser, que lo azoten y trasquilen; e si contra nuestra religión cristiana algo dijere o publicare, sea traído preso ante los dichos nuestros Presidente y Oidores de la dicha nuestra Audiencia con la información para que sea gravemente castigado.

Que el que una vez fuere baptizado no se baptize otra, porque es muy grave pecado, e si lo hiciere con la información sea traído preso a la cárcel desta Corte.

Iten que el indio o india que después de ser baptizado idolatrase o llamare a los demonios, ofreciéndoles copal, o papel, o otras cosas, por la primera vez que sea preso y luego le azoten y traquilen públicamente; y por la segunda sea traído como dicho es a la dicha nuestra Audiencia con la información que contra él hobiere.

Iten, que el indio o india cristiano que no se quisiere confesar cuando lo manda la Santa Madre Iglesia, que sea preso y azotado públicamente; e si dos años estuviere sin querer confesar, sea traído como dico es para que se haga en el caso, justicia.

Que el que después de ser baptizado estuviere amancebando con una o muchas mujeres, sea exortado primero para que las deje; y no las dejando, sea preso y azotado luego públicamente.

Que el indio que, siendo casado a ley y bendición, tuviere manceba, sea exortado que la deje, y no la dejando sea azotado públicamente después de preso; e si fure la india casada y tuviere aceso carnal con otro hombre, el marido lo denuncie si quisiere; y si diere información dello, sean ambos presos y traídos a la dicha nuestra Audiencia con la información que el tal marido tuviere para que sean puestos en la cárcel desta Corte y se le haga justicia al marido.

Otro sí, que el indio o india que siendo casado a ley y bendición se casare otra vez, que sean presos y luego sean azotados públicamente y herrados con un hierro caliente a manera de Q en la frente y pierda la mitad de sus bienes para la nuestra cámara y fisco y se entregue a la primera mujer o marido; y para que esto se ejecute conforme a justicia, sean traídos a la cárcel desta Corte a buen recaudo con la información que contra él hobiere.

Que el que el día de domingo o fiestas de guardar no viniere a la doctrina cristiana o a misa o a sermón, si lo hobiere, por la primera vez esté dos días en la cárcel y por la segunda sea azotado, no teniendo justo impedimento.

Que los que encubrieren la afinidad o consantguinidad al tiempo que se hace el examen para los desposar o casar, sean azotados públicamente, si ambos lo supiesen; y si no, el que lo supiere; y el casamiento que se deshaga y para ello trayan a los tales casados o desposados ante el Obispo del Obispado que fuere para que sabida la verdad pública, provea en ello lo que sea justicia.

Iten que el que se emborrachare con vino de Castilla o de la tierra, de cualquier calidad que sea, lo prendan y luego le sean dados cient azotes públicamente por la primera vez; y por la segunda le azoten y trasquilen y si más veces lo hiciere, sea traído a la dicha nuestra Abdiencia.

El indio o india que hiciere alguna hechicería, echando suertes o naipes o en otra cualquier manera, sea preso y azotado públicamente, y sea atado a un palo en el tianguis donde esté dos o tres horas con una coroza en la cabeza, y la mesma pena se de a los alcahuete o alcahuetas.

Que el padre o madre que diere su hija para que la tengan por manceba sea preso y con la información le traigan a la cárcel desta Corte.

El que matare a otro en cualquier manera o comiere carne humana, sea preso y con la información le trayan preso a la cárcel desta Corte y lo mesmo hagan al que corrompiere aguna moza virgen y al que pecare en el pecado nefando contra natura, y de lo contenido en este capítulo tengan muy gran cuidado y solicitud para prender los culpados.

La india que tomare patli para echar lo que tuviere en el vientre y la persona que se lo diere o aconsejare sean presas, y con la información traídas a la cárcel desta Corte.

Que los indios e indias que no estuvieren enfermos no se bañen en baños calientes, so pena de cient azotes y que estén dos horas atados en un palo en el tianguis y si se lavaren en agua públicamente delante de mcuhas personas, descubriendo las partes vergonzosas, sean reprendidos para que no lo hagan más.

El marido o la mujer que no hicieren vida maritable de consumo que sean compelidos a ello y para que lo hagan sean presos, y queriéndolo hacer, sean sueltos.

Que los indios cristianos que fallecieren sean enterrados y los lleven en andas con la cruz delate; y los que con él furen vayan en procesión, rogando a Dios Nuestro Señor haya misericordia de su ánima y se procure questando malos se confiesen, haciéndolo saber al religioso más cercano.

Que el indio o india que tañendo a la Ave María no se hincare de rodillas, que cea reprendido y lo mesmo se haga, si pasando por delante de la cruz o otra imagen no hiciere acatamiento; pero si por menosprecio dejare de hacer alguna de las dichas cosas, que sea azotado públicamente.

Que ninguno hurte ni tome lo ajeno; e si lo hiciere, le den cient azotes públicamente por la primera vez, e si lo hiciere segunda vez, sea traído a la cárcel desta Corte con la información.

Iten que ninguno haga a otro esclavo de nuevo, por manera alguna; e si lo hiciere, con la información sea traído preso a la cárcel desta Corte.

Que ninguno juergue al pator ni al batey, so pena de cient azotes y para se los dar, sea preso; e si fuere principal, que esté quince días preso en la cárcel de pueblo do lo hiciere.

Otro sí: que ninguno sea osado de contrahacer cacao, ni echar agua en la miel so pena que por la primera vez sea azotado y trasquilado y por la segunda sea traído preso a la cárcel desta Corte con la información, y así mismo sea traído preso si falsificare moneda.

Iten que ningún indio ande en hábito de india; y si se tomaren en estos hábitos, que sean presos y luego azotados públicamente y trasquilados y los tengan en el tiangues atados tres horas a un palo con aquellos hábitos.

Que ninguna india no sea osada de echarse sobre otra como varón, e si lo hiciere, le den de azotes y tresquilen públicamente.

Que ninguno tenga detenido o encerrado a otro por causa alguna contra su voluntad, porque tiene gran pena; e si lo hiciere sea preso y traído a la cárcel desta Corte con la información.

Iten que ninguno sea osado de se echar carnalmente conmadre e hija; y si lo hicieren, sea preso y con la información traído a la cárcel desta Corte, para que se haga justicia.

Otro sí: que ninguno quite ni ponga mojones, porque es grave delito. Si alguno hiciere, sea preso y traído a la cárcel desta Corte con la información.

Iten que ninguno por su autoridad tome tierra, casa o heredad que otro posea, sino que lo pida ante la justicia; e si lo hiciere, que sea preso y le den de azotes y le manden que deje lo que así tomó a la persona que lo tenía para que sea suyo.

Que niguno dé veneno para matar a otro porque, aunque no muera, es gran delito. Si así lo hiciere, sea preso y con la información traído para que se haga justicia.

Otro sí: que ningún cacique, gobernador ni principal, ni otra persona alguna sea osado de tomar al tameme que se alquila, lo que le dan por su trabajo e si alguno lo hiciere, que le quiten el oficio que tuviere y torne lo que tomó con el doble al tameme; e si no tuviere oficio, le azoten por ello.

Que los dichos gobernadores, alcaldes, alguaciles provean cómo en los pueblos se dé el mantenimiento necesario al español que por él pasare, a los cuales mando lo paguen sin le hacer maltratamiento so pena de diez pesos para la nuestra cámara por cada vez que lo hicieren y con apercibimiento que les hacemos que a su costa inviaremos un alguacil desta Corte para que los trayan preson a la cárcel della; y mandamos a los dichos gobernadores, alcaldes y alguaciles, que muestren este capítulo al tal español no esté de dos días arriba, yendo de paso en el tal pueblo so la dicha pena.

Lo cual todo que dicho es, han de dar a entender en su lengua y ejecutar los dichos alguaciles en los pueblos que no estuvieren por Nos nombrados o por el nuestro Visorrey en nuestro nombre, gobernadores o alcaldes, porque habiendo éstos, ellos son los que lo han de hacer, y por su mandado lo han de complir los dichos alguaciles, a los cuales todos y cada uno dellos mandamos que den a entender a los macehuales y naturales de sus pueblos que si algún español, cacique o principal, o otra cualquier persona daño o maltramiento les hiciere, o tributos de más de los que están tasados les llevaren, se vengan a quejar ante el nuestro Visorrey, y por él serán oídos y se les hará justicia, porque sepan que nos nuestros vasallos y los queremos mucho, deseamos su salvación y conservación, y mandamos al dicho nuestro Visorrey que así lo haga y cumpla, y así mismo les diga que han de tener mucho acatamiento y reverencia a los Obispos que son sus prelados, y a los religiosos porque son ministros de Dios y les enseñan la doctrina cristiana para que vengan en su conocimiento, que es el mayor bien que les pueden hacer, y para que lo suso dicho venga a noticia de todos, mandamos que tres veces en el año junten todas las gentes de sus pueblos y subjetos y les den a entender esto por buenas lengua intérpretes porque nadie pueda pretender inorancia. Dada en la ciudad de México a diez días del mes de junio de mil e quinientos y treinta y nueve años.

Appendix B

Text of the Edict of Expulsion of the Spanish Jews

(Beinart 2002: 49–54)

Don Fernando e Donna Ysabel . . . al prinçipe don Juan nuestro muy caro y muy amando hijo e a los ynfantes, prelados, duques, marqueses, condes, maestres de las hordenes, priores, ricos omes, comendadores, alcaydes de los castillos y casas fuertes de los nuestros trynos e sennorios, e a los conçejos regidores, alcaides, alguasiles, merinos, caualleros, escuderos, ofiçiales, e omes buenos de la muy noble e leal cibdad de Auyla e de las otras çibdades e villas e lugares de su obispado, e de los otros arçobispados e obispados e dioçesis de los dichos nuestros reynos e sennorios, e a las aljamas de los judios de la dicha cibdad de Auila e de todas las dichas çibdades e villas e lugares de su obispado e de todas las otras çibdades e villas e lugares de los dichos nuestros reynos e sennorios e a todos los judios e personas syngulares dellos asy variones como mugeres de cualquier hedad que sean e a todas las otras personas de qualquier estado, dignidad, preeminençia, condiçion que sean, a quien lo de yuso en esta nuestra carta contenydo atanner puede en qualquier manera, salud e gracia. Bien sabedes o deuedes saber que porque no fuemos ynformados algunos malos christianos que judaysauan e apostotuan de nuestra santa fe catolica, de lo qual era mucha cabsa la comunicaçion de los judios con los christianos; en las cortes que hesimos en la cibdad de Toledo el anno pasado de mill e quatroçientos e ochenta annos, mandamos apartar a los dichos judios en todas las cibdades, villas e lugares de los nuestros reynos e sennorios e dalles juderias e lugares apartados done biuyesen, es perando que con su apartamiento se remediaria, e otrosy ouymos procurado e dado horder como se hiziese ynquisiçion en los dichos nuestros reynos e sennorios,

DOI: 10.5876/9781607328018.c007

la qual como sabeys, ha mas de dose annos que se ha fecho e fase, e por ella se han fallado muchos culpantes segun es notorio e segun somos ynformados de los ynquisidores e de otras muchas personas religiosas e ecylesiasticas e seglares, consta e paresçe el grand danno que a los christianos se ha seguido y sigue de la partiçipaçion, conversaçion, comunicaçion que han tenido e tienen con los judios, los quales se prueua que procuran sienpre por quantas vias e maneras pueden de subvertir e substraer de nuestra santa fe catolica a los fieles christianos e los apartar della e atraer e pervertir a su dannada creençia e opinion ynstruyendolos en las çerimonias e observançias de su ley, haziendo ayuntamientos donde se leen e ensennan lo que han de creer e guardar segun su ley procurando de çcircunçidar a ellos e a sus fijos, dandoles libros por donde rezasen sus oraçiones e declarandoles los ayunos que han de ayunar e juntandose con ellos a leer e ensenarles las estorias de su ley, notyficandoles las pacuas nates que vengan, avisandoles de los que en ellas han de guardar e haser, dandoles e leuandoles de su casa el pan çençenno e carnes muertas con çerimonias, ynstruyendoles de las cosas que se han de apartar, asy en los comeres como en las otras cosas por observançia de su ley, e persuadioendoles en quanto pueden a que tengan e guarden la ley de Muysen e hasiendoles entender que non ay otra ley ni verdad, saluo aquella, lo qual consta por muchos dichos e consfisiones asy de los mismos judios commo de los que furein peruertidos y engannados por ellos, lo qual ha redundado en gran danno detrimento e obprobio de nuestra santa fe catolica. Y commo quiera que de mucha parte desto fuemmos ynformados antes de agora por muchos y conesçemos quel remedio verdadero de todos estos dannos e yncovinientes estaua en apartar del todo la comunicaçion de los dichos judios con los christianos e echarlos de todos nuestros reynos, quisimonos contentar con mandarlos salir de todos la çibdades e villas e lugares de Andaluzia, donde paresçia que quello nastaria para que los otros de las otra cibdades e villas e lugares de los nuestro reynos e sennorios çesasen de hazer e cometer los susodicho; y porque somos ynformados que aquello ni las justiçias que se han fecho en elgunos de los dichos judios que se han hallado muy culpantes en los dichos crimines e delitos contra nuestra santa fe catolica, no basta para entero remedio para obuiar e remediar commo cese tan grand adprobio y ofensa de la fe y religion christiana porque cada dya se halla y paresçe que los dichos judios creçen en continuar su malo e dannado proposito a donde biuen conversan, y porque no aya lugar de mas ofender a nuestra santa fe, asy en los que hasta aqui Dios ha querido guardar commo en los que cayeron, se emmendaron e reduzieron a la santa madre yglesia, lo qual segun la flaqueza de nuestra humanidad e abstuçia e subgestyon diabolica que contino nos guerrera, ligeramente podria acaesçer sy la cabsa principal desto no se quita, que es echar los dichos judíos de nuestros reynos, porque cuando algun graue e detestable crimen es cometydo por algunos de algun colegio e vuniversidad es rason quel tal colegio e universidad sean disoluidos e anichilados e los menores por los mayores e los unos por los otros. Et que aquellos que pervierten el bien e honesto bevir de la ciudades e villas e por contagio pueden dannar a los otros sean espelidos de los pueblos e aun por otras mas leues cabsas que sean el danno de la republica, quanto mas por el mayor de los crimines e mas peligroso e contagioso commo lo es este. Por ende nos con el consejo y paresçer de algunos prelados e grandes caualleros de nuestros reynos e de otras personas de çiençia e conçiençia de nuestro consejo aviendo avido osbre ello muchas deliberaçion, acordamos de mandar salir todos los dichos judíos e judías de nuestros reynos e que jamas tornen ni bueluan a ellos ni a algunos dellos. Y sobre ello mandamos dar esta nuestra carta por la qual manadamos a todos los judios e judias de qualquier hedad que sean que biuen e moran e estan en los dichos nuestros reynos e sennorios, asy los naturales delos commo los non naturales que en qualquier manera e por qualquier cabsa ayan venido e estan en ellos, que fasta en fin del mes de jullio primero que viene deste presente anno, salgan de todos los dichos nuestros reynos e sennorios con sus fijos e fijas e criados e criadas e familiares judios, asy grandes commo pequennos de qualquier hedad que sean e no sean osados de tornar a ellos ni estar en ellos ni en parte alguna dellos, de biuienda ni de paso ni en otra manera alguna so pena que sy lo non fisyeren e cunpileren asy, e fueren hallados estar en los dichos nuestros reynos e sennorios o venir a ellos en cualquier manera, yncurren en pena de muerte e confiscaçion de todos sus bienes para la nuestra camara e fisco, en las quales penas yncurran por ese mismo fecho e derecho syn otro proçeso ni declaraçion. E mandamos e defendemos que ningunas ni algunas personas de los dichos nuestros reynos de qualquier estado, condiçion[,] dignidad que sean, non sean osados de reçebir reçebtar ni acojer ni defender ni tener publica ni secretamente judio o judia, pasado el dicho termino del fin de jullio en adelate para syenpre jamas en sus tierras ni en sus casas ni en otra parte alguna de los dichos nuestros reynos e sennorios so pena de perdimiento de todos sus bienes, vasallos e fortalesas e otros heredamientos. E otrosy, de perder qualesquier merçedes que de nos tengan, para la nuestra camera e fisco. E porque los dichos judios e judias puedan durante el dicho tienpo fasta en fin del dicho mes de jullio mejor disponer de sy e de sus bienes e hasienda, por la presente los tomamos e reçebimos so nuestro seguro e anparo e dendidimiento real, e los aseguramos a ellos o a sus bienes para que durante el dicho tienpo fasta el dicho dia fin del dicho mes de jullio, puedan andar e estar seguros e puedan entrar e vender e trocar e enagenar todos sus bienes muebles e rayses, e disponer dellos libremente a su voluntad e que durante el dicho tyenpo no les sea fechomal ni danno ni desaguisado alguno en sus personas ni en sus bienes contra justiçia, so las penas en que cahen e yncurren los que quebrantan nuestro seguro real. E asy mismo damos licencia e facultad a los dichos judíos e judías que puedan sacar fuera de todos los dichos nuestros reynos e sennorios, sus bienes e hasienda por mar e tierra con tanto que no saquen oro ni plata ni moneda amonedada ni las otras cosas vedadas por las leyes de nuestros reynos saluo en mercaderias, e que non sean cosas vedadas, o en canbios. E otrosy, mandamos a todos los conçejos, justiçias, regidores, caualleros, escuderos, ofiçiales, e omes buenos de la çibdad de Auyla o de las otras çibdades e villas e lugares de nuestros reynos e sennorios e a todos nuestros vasallos, subditos naturales que guarden e cunplan e fagan guardar e cunplir esta nuestra carta e todo lo en ella contenydo, e den e fagan dar todo el fauor e ayuda que para ello fuere menester, so pena de nuestra merçed e de confiscaçion de todos sus bienes e ofiçios para la nuestra camara e fisco. E porque esto pueda venir a notiçia de todos e ninguno pueda pretender ynorançia, mandamos que esta nuestra carta sea apregonada por la plaças e lugares acostunbrados desa dicha çibdad e de las principales çibdades e villas e lugares de su obispado, por pregon e ante escriuano publico. E los vunos ni los otros no fagades ni fagan ende al por alguna (manera), so pena de la nuestra merçed e priuaçion de los ofiçios e confiscaçion de los bienes, a cada vno de los que lo contrario fisyeren. E demas mandamos al ome que les esta nuestra carta mostrar, que los enplase que parescan ante nos en la nuestra corte doquier que nos seamos, del dia que los enplasar, fasta quinse dias primeros syguientes so la dicha pena so la qual mandamos a qualquier escriuano publico que para esto fuere llamado, *que de ende al que se la mostrare,* testimonio sygnado con su sygno porque nos sepamos commo se cunple nuestro mandado. Dada en la nuestra çibdad de Granada, a XXXI dias del mes de março anno del nasçimiento de nuestro Sennor Ihesuchristo de mill e cuatroçientos e nouenta e dos annos. Yo el rey.—Yo la reyna.—Yo Johan de Coloma secretario del rey e de la reyna nuestros sennores la fize screvir por su mandado.—Registrada, Alaua—Almaçan, chançeller.

TRANSLATION OF THE EDICT OF EXPULSION OF THE SPANISH JEWS

Don Fernando and Doña Isabel . . . to the Prince don Juan, our very dear and much beloved son, and the Infantes, prelates, dukes, marqueses, counts, masters of the orders, priors, *ricoshombres,* commanders, *alcaides* of the castles and citadels of our realms and dominions, and to the councilors, governors, *alcaldes, alguaciles, merinos, caballeros, escuderos,* officials, and good men of the very noble and loyal city of Avila and the other cities and boroughs and places of its bishopric, and of the other archbishoprics and bishoprics and dioceses of the said realms and dominions, and to the synagogues of the Jews of the said city of Avila and of all said cities and boroughs and places in its bishopric and of all the other cities and boroughs and places in our said realms and dominions and to all the Jews and individual persons among them, as well men and women, of whatever age they may be, and to all the other persons of whatever religion, estate, dignity, pre-eminence, condition they may be, to whom that contained below in this our edict pertains or may pertain in any manner, greetings and grace. You know well, or ought to know, that because we were informed that in our realms there were some bad Christians who Judaized and apostatized from our holy Catholic faith, whereof the chief cause was the communication between the Christians and the Jews; in the Cortes which we convened in the city of Toledo in the past year of one thousand four hundred and eighty years, we ordained that the said Jews should be set apart in all cities, boroughs, and places of our realms and dominions and to give them Jewish quarters and separate places where they might dwell, hoping that which this separation [the matter] would be corrected, and in addition we took care and gave an order whereby inquiries should be made in our said realms and dominions, which, as you know, has been done for more than twelve years and is being done, and by it many offenders have been revealed, as it is known and as we are informed, by the Inquisition and many other religious persons and, both churchmen and laity. Thereby is established and made manifest the great damage to the Christians which has resulted and results from the participation, conversation, communication which they have held and do hold with the Jews, of whom it is proved that they always attempt by whatever ways and means they can to subvert and detract faithful Catholics from our holy Catholic faith and separate them from it and attract and pervert them to their cursed belief and opinion, instructing them in the ceremonies and observances of their law, convening assemblies where they read to them what they must believe and observe according to their law, taking care to circumcise them and their sons, giving them books from which they can recite their prayers and declaring the fasts which they have to fast and joining with them to read and to teach them stories of their law, notifying them of the Passover before its date, informing them about what they must observe and do, giving them and removing from their houses the unleavened bread and the meat that has been slaughtered according to their rite, teaching them about what they must avoid in foods and other things to observe in their religion, and in persuading them as best they can to keep and observe the Law of Moses, and in giving them to understand that there is other religion or truth save that, and this is proved by the many declarations and confessions both of the Jews themselves and also of those who were corrupted and deceived by them. And all of this has brought great damage and injury to our Catholic faith. And although most of this was known to us before, and we knew that the true remedy for all this harm and damage was to separate the said Jews from all communication with the Christians and to expel them from our kingdom, it was our wish to be content with ordering them to leave all the cities, boroughs, and places in Andalusia, where it appeared that they had caused the most damage, in the belief that this would be sufficient for those in the other cities, boroughs, and places in our realms and dominions to cease doing and committing the above. And whereas we are informed that neither that nor the punishments that have been given to some of those said Jews, who were discovered to be great offenders in these sins and transgressions against our holy Catholic faith, are sufficient as an entire remedy, to prevent and ensure the cessation of so great a dishonour and offence against the Christian faith and religion, because every day it is discovered and made manifest that the said Jews continue ever more active in their evil and harmful purpose in every place where they dwell and have dealings, and so that there may be no place for further offence against our holy faith, both in those whom until now God has chosen to preserve, and in those who have stumbled fallen into sin, and removed themselves from Holy Mother Church, which because of the weakness of our human character and the diabolical cunning and subterfuge which constantly makes war against us, could easily happen unless the principal reason for it is not removed, which is to expel the said Jews from our kingdoms, for when a crime is committed by someone in some society or corporation it is right that such society or corporation should be dissolved and eliminated, and that the few should be punished because of the many and the ones because of the others. And that those who corrupt the good and honest life of the cities and boroughs by their contagion may harm others be driven out of the settlements, even for other lesser causes that are harmful to the state, the more so for the greatest crimes and the most dangerous of infections, as this is. Hence we, with the counsel and in the regard of certain prelates and grandees and caballeros of our realms and other persons of wisdom and consciousness in our council, having considered the matter with much deliberation, are agreed in ordering that all the said Jews and Jewesses of our realms shall leave and never return nor come back to them or to any of them. And upon this we order that this our edict be given by which we order that all Jews and Jewesses of whatever age they may be who live and dwell and are in our said realms and dominions, as well the native-born among them as those not native-born who in no manner and for any reason have come and are in them, that by the end of the next month of July that comes in the present year they shall leave all our said realms and dominions with their sons and daughters and servants and maidservants and Jewish followers, as well the great as the small, of whatever age they may be, and that they do not dare return to them or to be in them or any part of them, whether dwelling or in transit or in any other manner, under the penalty that if they not do so and comply, and are found to be in our said realms and dominions or to come to them in any manner, they incur the punishment of death and the confiscation of all their property to our exchequer and treasury, and these penalties are incurred by that same fact and law with no other trial nor sentence no declaration. And we command and prohibit that any or all persons in our said realms, of whatsoever estate, condition, dignity they may be, dare to receive, shelter, or assist or keep publicly or secretly a Jew or Jewess, after the said date of the coming end of July and hereinafter in their lands or houses or in any other part of our said realms and dominions on pain of loss of all their possessions, vassals, and citadels and other hereditaments. And moreover, to lose any favours which they may have from us, for the benefit of our exchequer and treasury. And so that the said Jew and Jewess during the said time until the end of the said month of July may better dispose of themselves and of their possessions and effects, for the present we take and place them under our security and royal protection and defence, and we assure them, to them and to their possessions, so that during the time until the said days at the end of the month of July, they may go and be safe and may enter and sell and trade and transfer all their property moveable and immoveable, and dispose thereof in accordance to their wish, and that during the said time no one may do them evil or damage nor injustice to their persons nor to their possessions against justice, under the penalty to which are subject those who trespass against royal security.

Moreover we give permission and facility to the said Jews and Jewesses that they may remove from all our realms and dominions, their property and effects by sea and land as long as they do not remove gold nor silver nor coined money nor the other things prohibited in the laws of our realms save for items of merchandise that are not forbidden or commerce in bills of exchange.

And in addition, we order all the councilors, justices, governors, officials, and good men of the said city of Ávila or of the other cities and boroughs and places in our realms and dominions and to all our vassals, being natural subjects, that they observe and fulfill, and cause to be observed and fulfilled, this our edict and all things therein contained, and give and cause to be given all aid and support that shall be needful thereof, on pain of loss of our favour and the confiscation of all their property and offices to our exchequer and treasury. And so that this may come to the attention of everyone, and that no one may claim ignorance, we ordain that this our edict be cried aloud in the squares and customary places of the said city and the principal cities and boroughs and places of its bishopric, by proclamation and before the public notary. And let neither the ones nor the others henceforth do otherwise in any manner, on pain of loss of our favour and deprivation of their offices and the confiscation of their property for each one of those who shall act contrary thereto. And moreover we order that the man who shall show whom this our edict shall summon, that he shall order them to appear before our court wherever we may be, within the fifteen days next following the day that he shall summon them, on the said pain of punishment according to which we order every notary public who may be called for this purpose to give thereupon to the man who shall show it to him, and attestation sealed with his seal, so that we may know how our edict is enforced. Given in our city of Granada, the thirty-first of the month of March in the year of the birth of our Lord Jesus Christ of one thousand four hundred and ninety-two years. I the king.—I the queen.—I Juan de Coloma, secretary of the king and queen, our lords, caused it to be written by their command.—Registered, Álava.—Almazán, chancellor.

Appendix C

CANONIZATION OF JUAN DIEGO CUAUHTLATOATZIN

HOMILY OF THE HOLY FATHER JOHN PAUL II

MEXICO CITY, WEDNESDAY JULY 31, 2002

1. *"I thank you, Father . . . that you have hidden these things from the wise and understanding and revealed them to babes; yea, Father, for such was your gracious will" (Mt 11:25–26).*

Dear Brothers and Sisters,

These words of Jesus in today's Gospel are a special invitation to us to praise and thank God for the gift of the first indigenous Saint of the American Continent.

With deep joy I have come on pilgrimage to this Basilica of Our Lady of Guadalupe, the Marian heart of Mexico and of America, to proclaim the holiness of Juan Diego Cuauhtlatoatzin, the simple, humble Indian who contemplated the sweet and serene face of Our Lady of Tepeyac, so dear to the people of Mexico.

I am grateful for the kind words of Cardinal Norberto Rivera Carrera, Archbishop of Mexico City, and for the warm hospitality of the people of this Primatial Archdiocese: my cordial greeting goes to everyone. I also greet with affection Cardinal Ernesto Corripio Ahumada, Archbishop Emeritus of Mexico City, and the other Cardinals, as well as the Bishops of Mexico, of America, of the Philippines and of other places in the world. I am likewise particularly grateful to the President and the civil Authorities for their presence at this celebration.

Today I address a very affectionate greeting to the many indigenous people who have come from the different regions of the country, representing the various ethnic groups and cultures which make up the rich, multifaceted Mexican reality. The

DOI: 10.5876/9781607328018.c008

Pope expresses his closeness to them, his deep respect and admiration, and receives them fraternally in the Lord's name.

What was Juan Diego like? Why did God look upon him? The Book of Sirach, as we have heard, teaches us that God alone "*is mighty; he is glorified by the humble*" (cf. *Sir* 3:20). Saint Paul's words, also proclaimed at this celebration, shed light on the divine way of bringing about salvation: "*God chose what is low and despised in the world . . . so that no human being might boast in the presence of God*" (1 *Cor* 1:28,29).

It is moving to read the accounts of Guadalupe, sensitively written and steeped in tenderness. In them the Virgin Mary, the handmaid "*who glorified the Lord*" (*Lk* 1:46), reveals herself to Juan Diego as the Mother of the true God. As a sign, she gives him precious roses, and as he shows them to the Bishop, he discovers the blessed image of Our Lady imprinted on his *tilma*.

"The Guadalupe Event," as the Mexican Episcopate has pointed out, "meant the beginning of evangelization with a vitality that surpassed all expectations. Christ's message, through his Mother, took up the central elements of the indigenous culture, purified them and gave them the definitive sense of salvation" (14 May 2002, No. 8). Consequently Guadalupe and Juan Diego have a deep ecclesial and missionary meaning and are a model of perfectly inculturated evangelization.

"*The Lord looks down from heaven, he sees all the sons of men*" (*Ps* 33:13), we recited with the Psalmist, once again confessing our faith in God, who makes no distinctions of race or culture. In accepting the Christian message without forgoing his indigenous identity, Juan Diego discovered the profound truth of the new humanity, in which all are called to be children of God. Thus he facilitated the fruitful meeting of two worlds and became the catalyst for the new Mexican identity, closely united to Our Lady of Guadalupe, whose mestizo face expresses her spiritual motherhood which embraces all Mexicans. This is why the witness of his life must continue to be the inspiration for the building up of the Mexican nation, encouraging brotherhood among all its children and ever helping to reconcile Mexico with its origins, values and traditions.

The noble task of building a better Mexico, with greater justice and solidarity, demands the cooperation of all. In particular, it is necessary today to support the indigenous peoples in their legitimate aspirations, respecting and defending the authentic values of each ethnic group. Mexico needs its indigenous peoples and these peoples need Mexico!

Beloved bothers and sisters of every ethnic background of Mexico and America, today, in praising the Indian Juan Diego, I want to express to all of you the closeness of the Church and the Pope, embracing you with love and encouraging you to overcome with hope the difficult times you are going through.

At this decisive moment in Mexico's history, having already crossed the threshold of the new millennium, I entrust to the powerful intercession of Saint Juan Diego the joys and hopes, the fears and anxieties of the beloved Mexican people, whom I carry in my heart.

Blessed Juan Diego, a good, Christian Indian, whom simple people have always considered a saint! We ask you to accompany the Church on her pilgrimage in Mexico, so that she may be more evangelizing and more missionary each day. Encourage the Bishops, support the priests, inspire new and holy vocations, help all those who give their lives to the cause of Christ and the spread of his Kingdom.

Happy Juan Diego, true and faithful man! We entrust to you our lay brothers and sisters so that, feeling the call to holiness, they may imbue every area of social life with the spirit of the Gospel. Bless families, strengthen spouses in their marriage, sustain the efforts of parents to give their children a Christian upbringing. Look with favour upon the pain of those who are suffering in body or in spirit, on those afflicted by poverty, loneliness, marginalization or ignorance. May all people, civic leaders and ordinary citizens, always act in accordance with the demands of justice and with respect for the dignity of each person, so that in this way peace may be reinforced.

Beloved Juan Diego, "the talking eagle"! Show us the way that leads to the "Dark Virgin" of Tepeyac, that she may receive us in the depths of her heart, for she is the loving, compassionate Mother who guides us to the true God. Amen.

After the celebration, before imparting the final blessing the Holy Father said:

At the end of the canonization of Juan Diego, I want to renew my greeting to all of you who have been able to take part, some in this basilica, others in the nearby areas and many others by means of radio and television. I warmly thank all those I have met in the streets for their affection. In this new saint you have a marvellous example of a just and upright man, a loyal son of the Church, docile to his Pastors, who deeply loved the Virgin and was a faithful disciple of Jesus. May he be a model for you who are so attached to him, and may he intercede for Mexico so that it may always be faithful! Take to all Mexicans the message of this celebration and the Pope's greeting and love for them all!

Appendix D

Chronology

	Spain and Europe	New World
711	End of Visigoth rule. The coming of Islam	
c. 1140	*Poema del Mio Cid*	
1252–84	Alfonso X, the Wise.	
1326	The Pope John XXII publishes a bull entitled *Super Illius Specula*, in which he asserts that diabolic acts are real.	
1376	Eimeric's *Directorium Inquisitorum* is published.	
1391	Pogrom in Seville. The mob is encouraged by Ferran Martínez, archdeacon.	
1469	Wedding of Ferdinand of Aragon and Isabella of Castile.	
1478	The Inquisition in Castile.	
1484	The new Inquisition in Aragon.	
1487	*Malleus Maleficarum*, by Sprenger and Kramer, is published.	
	Publication of Fray Hernando de Talavera's *Católica impugnación*.	

DOI: 10.5876/9781607328018.c009

	Spain and Europe	New World
1492	Nebrija's grammar.	Christopher Columbus's first voyage.
	Order of expulsion of the Jews from Spain.	
1493	Fray Hernando de Talavera's *Oficio de la toma de Granada* is first performed.	
1494		Treaty of Tordesillas, which divided the world outside of Europe between Spain and Portugal.
1506	Death of Christopher Columbus. Cardinal Cisneros assumes the regency of Spain.	
1516	Cisneros's death. Charles V rules Spain.	
1517	Luther (1483–1546) published his ninety-five theses on the door of the Wittenberg Castle's Church.	
1519–26		Hernán Cortés (1485–1547) conquers Mexico and writes his *Cartas de relación*.
1524	The Indies Council is created in Spain.	Francisco Pizarro (1475–1541) starts exploring Peru.
1525	Battle of Pavia. Frances I of France is captured by Charles V.	
1527		Fray Bartolomé de Las Casas (1474–1566) starts publishing his *Historia de las Indias* (1527–61)
1528		Juan de Zumárraga arrives in New Spain as bishop-elect.
1529	Martín de Castañega publishes his *Tratado de las supersticiones y hechicerías*	Charles V names Hernán Cortés governor of New Spain.
1531		Supposed apparition of the Virgin of Guadalupe to Juan Diego.
1532	Publication of *The Prince*, by Machiavelli.	
1533		First play performed in the New World, *Ejemplo del Juicio Final*, seen in Mexico.
1535		Arrival in Mexico of the first viceroy, Don Antonio de Mendoza.
		Zumárraga becomes apostolic inquisitor in New Spain.

Spain and Europe	New World
1538 — Pedro Ciruelo publishes *A Treatise Reproving All Superstitions and Forms of Witchcraft*.	Foundation of the University of Santo Domingo (first in America).
1539	Performances of *La conquista de rodas* and *La Conquista de Jerusalén*.
	Don Carlos, cacique of Texcoco, is tried and executed by the Inquisition.
1541	Fray Toribio de Motolinía (1495?–1569) writes his *Historia de los indios de la Nueva España*.
1542	Las Casas's New Laws of Indies are approved.
1543	Indian Inquisition is ended in New Spain
1545 — Council of Trent starts (1545–63)	
1544–47	Visitor General Francisco Tello de Sandoval receives commission as apostolic inquisitor.
1548	Death of Zumárraga, first bishop in New Spain.
1552	Fray Bartolomé de Las Casas (1474–1566) publishes his *Brevísima relación de la destrucción de las Indias*.
	Francisco López de Gómara (1511–72?) publishes his *Historia general de las Indias*.
1553	Pedro Cieza de León (1518–1560) publishes the first part of *Crónica del Perú*.
1554	Alonso de Montúfar becomes the second bishop of New Spain
1555	First Provincial Council of Mexico
1556 — Carlos V (1517–56) is succeeded by his son Philip II (1556–98).	Bishop Montúfar gives a sermon encouraging the devotion of the Virgin of Guadalupe.
	Bustamante, the Franciscan provincial, responds to the bishop's sermon.
	Francisco López de Gómara (1511–72?) publishes his *Historia general de las Indias*.

Spain and Europe	New World
1560	Fray Bernardino de Sahagún (1500–1590) writes his *Historia general de las cosas de Nueva España* (1560–69).
1568	Bernal Díaz del Castillo (1495–1584) writes his *Verdadera historia de la conquista de la Nueva España*.
1571 Battle of Lepanto against the Turks.	Phillip II establishes the Inquisition in New Spain and Peru.
1572	Death of Alonso de Montúfar, bishop of New Spain.
1573	Cristóbal de Molina, a Spanish friar, writes his chronicle *Narratives of the rites and laws of the Incas*.
1590	José de Acosta (1539–1600) publishes *Historia moral y natural de las Indias*.
1594 Espinosa's *Guanches of Tenerife* is published in Seville.	
1595 Pedro de Ribadeneyra's *Tratado de la religión y virtudes que debe tener el príncipe cristiano para governar y conservar sus Estados. contra lo que Nicolás Machiavelo y los políticos de este tiempo enseñan.*	
1598 Death of Phillip II. His son, Phillip III, becomes king of Spain (1598–1621).	
1605 Miguel de Cervantes Saavedra (1547–1616) publishes the first part of *Don Quijote de la Mancha*.	
1607	First English settlement in America in Jamestown, Virginia.
1609 Due to a decree by Philip III, the *moriscos* are expelled from Spain.	The Inca Garcilaso de la Vega (1539–1616) publishes *Comentarios reales*. Auto-de-fé in Lima, Peru, instigated by the priest Francisco de Avila.
1619 Lope de Vega (1562–1635) publishes *Fuente Ovejuna*.	
1621 Death of Philip III. Philip IV becomes king of Spain (1621–65).	
1635 Calderón de la Barca (1600–1681) publishes *La vida es sueño*.	

	Spain and Europe	*New World*
1640	Diego de Saavedra Fajardo (1584–1648) publishes *Empresas políticas o Idea de un príncipe político cristiano*.	
1648		Publication of Miguel Sánchez's *Imagen de la Virgen María*, considered the first written account of the 1531 apparition of the Virgin Mary as Our Lady of Guadalupe.
1649		Luis Laso de la Vega, the vicar of Guadalupe, writes a Nahuatl version of the apparition of the Virgin of Guadalupe: *Huei tlamahuiçoltica*.
1651	First appearance of *El criticón* (1651–57) by Baltasar Gracián (1601–58).	Sor Juana Inés de la Cruz is born in México (1651–95)
1665	Death of Philip IV. His son, Charles II, takes the throne of Spain (1665–1700).	
1700	Charles II dies without heir.	

References

Acosta, J. 1894. *Historia natural y moral de las Indias*. Madrid: Anglés.

Acosta, J. 2002. *Natural and Moral History of the Indies*. Durham, NC: Duke University Press. https://doi.org/10.1215/9780822383932.

Agamben, Giorgio. 1998. *Homo Sacer: Sovereign Power and Bare Life*. Stanford, CA: Stanford University Press.

Aguado, A., R. Capel, and T. Glez, et al., eds. 1994. *Textos para la historia de las mujeres en España*. Madrid: Cátedra.

Alberro, S. 1988. *Inquisición y sociedad en México, 1571–1700*. Mexico City: Fondo de Cultura Económica. https://doi.org/10.4000/books.cemca.2601.

Alberro, S. 1999. *El águila y la cruz: Orígenes religiosos de la conciencia criolla. México, siglos XVI–XVII*. Mexico City: Fondo de Cultura Económica.

Albó, X. 1996. "Jesuitas y culturas indígenas: Perú 1568–1606. Su actitud, métodos y criterios de aculturación." *America Indigena* 26 (3): 249–308.

Albornoz, C. 1971. *Las informaciones de Cristóbal de Albornoz: Documentos para el estudio del Taki Onqoy*. Ed. Luis Millones. Cuernavaca, Mexico: Centro Intercultural de Documentación.

Alfonso X. 1959–72. *Cantigas de Santa María, Coimbra*: Por ordem da Universidade.

Alfonso X. 2000. *Songs of Holy Mary of Alfonso X, the Wise: A Translation of the Cantigas de Santa María*. Trans. Kathleen Kulp-Hill. Tempe: Arizona Center for Medieval and Renaissance Studies.

DOI: 10.5876/9781607328018.c010

Alfonso X. 2001. *Las Siete Partidas*. Ed. Robert I. Burns. Trans. Samuel Parsons Scott. Philadelphia: University of Pennsylvania Press.

Amador de los Ríos, J. 1875–76. *Historia social, política y religiosa de los judíos de España y Portugal*. Madrid: Impr. de T. Fortanet.

Anderson, P. 1974. *Lineages of the Absolutist State*. London: N.L.B.

Andrien, K. J. 1991. *Transatlantic Encounters: Europeans and Andeans in the Sixteenth Century*. Berkeley: University of California Press.

Anghie, A. 1996. "Francisco de Vitoria and the Colonial Origins of International Law." *Social and Legal Studies: Law and Postcolonialism* 5 (3): 321–36. https://doi.org/10.1177/096466399600500303.

Aracil Varón, M. B. 1999. *El teatro evangelizador: Sociedad, cultura e ideología en la Nueva España del siglo XVI*. Roma: Bulzoni.

Aranguren, José Luis. 1957. *Catolicismo y protestantismo como formas de existencia*. Madrid: Revista de Occidente.

Archivo Arzobispal de Lima (AAL). N.d.a. "Legajo I, expediente IX: Causa de capítulos seguidos contra el doctor Francisco de Avila, cura de la doctrina de San Damián y anexos." "Sección documental de capítulos (1600–1898)." Manuscrito. Folios 46–84.

Archivo Arzobispal de Lima (AAL). N.d.b. "Legajo III, expediente 6: Lampas y San Luis de Matara, 1620." "Sección documental de capítulos (1600–1898)." Manuscrito.

Archivo Arzobispal de Lima (AAL). N.d.c. "Legajo XVII, expediente 2: Quinti, 1649." *Sección documental de causas criminales (1600–1898)*.Manuscrito.

Archivo Arzobispal de Lima (AAL). N.d.d. "Legajo XXVI, expediente 7: Huarochirí–San Lorenzo de Quinti-Los Reyes, 1670." "Sección documental de causas criminales (1600–1898)." Manuscrito.

Archivo General de la Nación. 1912. *Procesos de indios idólatras y hechiceros*. Mexico City: Archivo General de la Nación.

Archivo General de la Nación. 1949. *Libro primero de votos de la Inquisición de México: 1573–1600*. Mexico City: Archivo General de la Nación.

Arias, S., and R. Marrero-Fente. 2014. *Coloniality, Religion and the Law in the Early Iberian World*. Nashville: Vanderbilt University Press.

Aristotle. 1932. *Politics. London: W. Heinemann*. New York: G. P. Putnam.

Arriaga, P. J. 1999. *La extirpación de la idolatría en el Pirú* (1621). Ed. Henrique Urbano. Cuzco, Peru: Centro de Estudios Regionales Andinos "Bartolomé de Las Casas."

Arrillaga, R. 1993. *Grandeza y decadencia de España en el siglo XVI*. Mexico City: Porrúa.

Arróniz, O. 1979. *Teatro de evangelización en Nueva España*. Mexico City: Universidad Nacional Autónoma de México.

Baskin, W. 1972. *Dictionary of Satanism*. New York: Philosophical Library.

Bataillon, M. 1966. *Erasmo y España: Estudios sobre la historia espiritual del siglo XVI.* Mexico City: Fondo de Cultura Económica.

Batllori, M. 1979. *Del descubrimiento a la independencia: Estudios sobre Iberoamérica y Filipinas.* Caracas: Universidad Católica Andrés Bello.

Baudot, Georges. 1995. *Utopia and History in Mexico: The First Chroniclers of Mexican Civilization, 1520–1569.* Boulder: University of Colorado Press.

Bauman, Zygmunt. 1998. "Allosemitism: Premodern, Modern, Postmodern." In *Modernity, Culture and the Jew*, ed. Bryan Cheyette and Laura Marcus, 143–56. Stanford, CA: Stanford University Press.

Beinart, H. 1981. *Conversos on Trial: The Inquisition in Ciudad Real.* Jerusalem: Magnes Press, Hebrew University.

Beinart, Haim. 2002. *The Expulsion of the Jews from Spain.* Portland: Littman Library of Jewish Civilization.

Bernand, C., and S. Gruzinski. 1992. *De la idolatría: Una arqueología de las ciencias religiosas.* Mexico City: Fondo de Cultura Económica.

Bonilla, L. 1962. *Historia de la hechicería y de las brujas.* Madrid: Biblioteca Nueva.

Bonnassie, P. 2001. *Las Españas medievales.* Barcelona: Crítica.

Boyer, P., and Stephen Nissenbaum. 1996. *Salem Possessed: The Social Origins of Witchcraft.* Cambridge, MA: Harvard University Press.

Briggs, R. 1996. *Witches and Neighbours: The Social and Cultural Context of European Witchcraft.* New York: Penguin Books.

Burkhart, L. M. 2001. *Before Guadalupe: The Virgin Mary in Early Colonial Nahuatl Literature.* Albany, NY: Institute for Mesoamerican Studies, University at Albany: Distributed by University of Texas Press.

Calderón de la Barca, P. 1979. *Mística y real Babilonia.* Berlin: Walter de Gruyter. https://doi.org/10.1515/9783111389622.

Calderón de la Barca, P. 1994. *La aurora en Copacabana.* Ed. Ezra S. Engling. London: Tamesis.

Calvin, J. 1844. *Institutes of the Christian Religion.* Trans. John Allen. Philadelphia: Presbyterian Board of Publication.

Camiro Gutiérrez Zamora, A. 1996. *El origen del guadalupanismo: Fue Montúfar, y no Zumárraga, el padre de la devoción a la Virgen de Guadalupe.* Mexico City: EDAMEX.

Carreño, A. 1944. *Un desconocido cedulario del siglo XVI perteneciente a la Catedral Metropolitana de México.* Mexico City: Ediciones Victoria.

Carreño, A. 1950. *Don Fray Juan de Zumárraga: Teólogo y editor, humanista e inquisidor; documentos inéditos.* Mexico City: Editorial Jus.

Carrillo, F. 1990. *Cronistas que describen la colonia: Las relaciones geográficas, la extirpación de idolatrías.* Lima: Editorial Horizonte.

Caro Baroja, J. 1961. *Los judíos en la España moderna y contemporánea*. Madrid: Arión.

Caro Baroja, J. 1967. *Vidas mágicas e Inquisición*. 2 vols. Madrid: Taurus.

Caro Baroja, J. 1969. *Las brujas y su mundo*. Madrid: Alianza Editorial.

Caro Baroja, J. 1972. *Inquisición, brujería y criptojudaismo*. Barcelona: Ariel.

Castañeda Delgado, P., and Hernández Aparicio. 1989. *La inquisición de Lima*. Madrid: Deimos.

Castro, A. 1948. *España en su historia: Cristianos, moros y judíos*. Buenos Aires: Editorial Losada.

Ceballos, D. L. 1994. *Hechicería, brujería e inquisición en el Nuevo Reino de Granada: Un duelo de imaginarios*. Medellín, Colombia: Editorial Universitaria Nacional.

Cervantes, F. 1994. *The Devil in the New World: The Impact of Diabolism in New Spain*. New Haven: Yale University Press.

Céspedes, V. 2000. *Las glorias del Mejor Siglo: Teatro colonial. Siglos XVI–XVII. Antología general del teatro peruano*. Vol. 2. Lima: Pontificia Universidad Católica del Perú.

Chauvet, F. 1949. "Fray Juan de Zumarraga, Protector of the Indians." *Americas* 5 (3): 283–95. https://doi.org/10.2307/977658.

Chávez, E. 2006. *Our Lady of Guadalupe and Saint Juan Diego: The Historical Evidence*. Lanham, MD: Rowman and Littlefield Publishers.

Cheyette, Bryan, and Laura Marcus, eds. 1998. *Modernity, Culture and the Jew*. Stanford, CA: Stanford University Press.

Cieza de León, P. 1943. *Del señorío de los incas*. Ed. Alberto Mario Salas. Buenos Aires: Ediciones argentinas "Solar."

Cieza de León, P. 1984. *Crónica del Perú*. Ed. Franklin Pease. Lima: Pontificia Universidad Católica del Perú, Fondo Editorial: Academia Nacional de la Historia.

Cieza de León, P. 1986. *Descubrimiento y conquista del Perú*. Edited by Carmelo Sáenz de Santa María. Madrid: Historia 16.

Ciruelo, P. 1977. *A Treatise Reproving All Superstitions and Forms of Witchcraft*. Rutherford, NJ: Fairleigh Dickinson University Press,.

Ciruelo, P. 1977. *Reprobación de las supersticiones y hechicerías*. Barcelona: Glosa.

Cobo, B. 1990. *Inca Religion and Customs: Historia del Nuevo Mundo. Capítulo 11–12*. Translated and edited by Roland Hamilton. Austin: University of Texas Press.

Columbus, C. 1984. *Textos y documentos completos: Relaciones de viajes, cartas y memoriales*. Ed. Consuelo Valera. Madrid: Alianza Editorial.

Columbus, C. 1986. *Los cuatro viajes: Testamento*. Edited by Consuelo Varela. Madrid: Alianza Editorial.

Congreso Internacional de Historia de América, Congreso Internacional. 1994 (1992). *El Reino de Granada y el Nuevo Mundo / V Congreso Internacional de Historia de América, mayo de 1992*. 5th ed. Granada: Diputación Provincial de Granada.

Cortés, H. 2004. *Cartas de relación*. Mexico City: Porrúa.

Covarrubias Orozco, S. 1611. *Tesoro de la lengua castellana o española*. Madrid: Turner.

Cuevas, M. 1921–28. *Historia de la iglesia en México*. Tlalpam, D.F., Mexico: Asilo Patricio Sanz.

Cuevas, M. 1975. *Documentos inéditos del siglo XVI para la historia de México*. Mexico City: Porrúa.

Cursos de Verano de El Escorial. 1996. *Historia silenciada de la mujer: La mujer española desde la época medieval hasta la contemporánea. Directed by Alain Saint-Saëns*. Madrid: Editorial Complutense.

Daraul, A. 1962. *Witches and Sorcerers*. London: Frederick Muller Limited.

Davies, T. 1944. *El Siglo de Oro Español*. Zaragoza, Spain: Ebro.

Dean, C. 1999. *Inka Bodies and the Body of Christ: Corpus Christi in Colonial Cuzco*. Durham, NC: Duke University Press.

Deyermond, A. 1980. *Edad media: Historia y crítica de la literatura española*. Vol. 1. Ed. Francisco Rico. Barcelona: Crítica.

Díaz del Castillo, B. 1999. *Historia de la verdadera conquista de la Nueva España*. Madrid: Castalia Didáctica.

Diccionario de Autoridades. 1964. Madrid: Real Academia Española.

Diccionario de literatura Española. 1972. Madrid: Revista de Occidente.

Diccionario enciclopédico Espasa. 1978. Madrid: Espasa-Calpe.

Domínguez Ortiz, A. 1978. *Historia de los moriscos: Vida y tragedia de una minoría*. Madrid: Revista de Occidente.

Dopico Black, G. 2001. *Perfect Wives, Other Women: Adultery and Inquisition in Early Modern Spain*. Durham, NC: Duke University Press. https://doi.org/10.1215/97808 22383079.

Dussel, Enrique D. 1992. *1492, El encubrimiento del otro: Hacia el origen del "mito de la modernidad": Conferencias de Frankfurt, Octubre de 1992*. Santafé de Bogotá, Colombia: Ediciones Antropos.

Duverger, C. 1996. *La conversión de los indios de la Nueva España*. Mexico City: Fondo de Cultura Económica.

Duviols, P. 1977. *La destrucción de las religiones andinas: Conquista y colonia*. Trans. Albor Maruenda. Mexico City: Universidad Nacional Autónoma de México.

Duviols, P. 2003. *Procesos y visitas de idolatrías: Cajatambo, siglo XVII*. Lima, Perú: Instituto Francés de Estudios Andinos: Pontificia Universidad Católica del Perú.

Echevarría, B. 1998. "La Compañía de Jesús y la primera modernidad de América Latina." In *Barrocos y modernos: Nuevos caminos en la investigación del Barroco iberoamericano*, ed. Petra Schumm, 49–65. Madrid: Iberoamericana.

Eimeric, N., and F. Peña. 1983. *El Manual de los Inquisidores*. Barcelona: B.U.M.A.

Eire, C. M. N. 1979. *Idolatry and the Reformation: A Study of the Protestant Attack on Catholic Worship in Germany, Switzerland and France, 1500–1580*. New Haven.

Eire, C. M. N. 1986. *War against the Idols: The Reformation of Worship from 1993 to Calvin*. Cambridge: Cambridge University Press. https://doi.org/10.1017/CBO9780511528835.

Eliade, Mircea, ed. 1987. *Encyclopedia of Religion*. New York: Macmillan.

Elizondo, V. P., A. Deck, and T. Matovina. 2006. *The Treasure of Guadalupe*. Lanham, MD: Rowman and Littlefield Publishers.

Elliott, J. 1964. *Imperial Spain, 1469–1716*. New York: St. Martin's Press.

El Saffar, R. 1989. "Anxiety of Identity: Gutierre's Case in *El Médico de su Honra*." In *Studies in Honor of Bruce W. Wardropper*, ed. Dan Fox, Harry Sieber, and Robert TerHorst, 105–24. Newark, Del.: Juan de la Cuesta.

Erasmus, D. 1953. *The Praise of Folly*. Ed. Leonard F. Dean. New York: Hendricks House; Farrar, Straus.

Erasmus, D. 1963. *The Enchiridion*. Ed. and trans. Raymond Himelick. Bloomington: Indiana University Press.

Espinosa, A. 1907. *The Guanches of Tenerife, the Holy Image of Our Lady of Candelaria, and the Spanish Conquest and Settlement*. London: Hakluyt Society.

Fernández-Armesto, F. 1982. *The Canary Islands after the Conquest: The Making of a Colonial Society in the Early Sixteenth Century*. New York: Oxford University Press.

Fernández-Armesto, F. 1987. *Before Columbus: Exploration and Colonization from the Mediterranean to the Atlantic 1229–1492*. Philadelphia: University of Pennsylvania Press. https://doi.org/10.1007/978-1-349-18856-7.

Fernández-Armesto, F. 1991. *Columbus*. Oxford: Oxford University Press.

Fernández-Armesto, F. 1995. *The European Opportunity*. Aldershot, UK: Variorum.

Fernández, M. 1989. *La Sociedad Española en el Siglo de Oro*. Madrid: Gredos.

Fernández-Santamaría, J. A. 1986. *Razón de estado y política en el pensamiento español del Barroco (1595–1640)*. Madrid: Centro de Estudios Constitucionales.

Ferrer, V. 2002. *Sermonario de San Vicente Ferrer*. Ed. Francisco M. Gimeno and Luz Mandigorra Llavata Maria. Valencia: Ajuntament de Valencia.

Flint, Valerie I. J. 1994. *The Rise of Magic in the Early Medieval Europe*. Princeton, NJ: Princeton University Press.

Flores, F. 1985. *El Diablo en España*. Madrid: Alianza.

Foucault, M. 2003. *Society Must Be Defended: Lectures at the Collège de France, 1975–76*. New York: Picador.

Frazer, J. G. 1951. *The Golden Bough*. New York: MacMillan Company.

Freedberg, D. 1989. *The Power of Images: Studies in the History and Theory of Response*. Chicago: University of Chicago Press.

García-Arenal, M. 1978. *Inquisición y moriscos: Los procesos del Tribunal de Cuenca.* Madrid: Siglo Veintiuno Editores.

García Cabrera, J. C. 1994. *Ofensas a Dios, pleitos e injurias: Causas de idolatrías y hechicerías, Cajatambo, siglos XVII–XIX.* Cuzco: Centro de estudios regionales andinos Bartolomé de Las Casas.

García Icazbalceta, J. 1881. *Don fray Juan de Zumárraga, primer obispo y arzobispo de México.* Mexico City: Andrade y Morales.

García Icazbalceta, J. 1896. *Obras.* Mexico City: Imp. de V. Agüeros, editor.

García Icazbalceta, J. 1929. *Biografía de d. fr. Juan de Zumárraga, primer obispo y arzobispo de Mexico.* Madrid: Aguilar.

García Icazbalceta, J. 1947. *Don fray Juan de Zumárraga, primer obispo y arzobispo de México.* Ed. de Rafael Aguayo Spencer and Antonio Castro Leal. México: Porrúa.

García Icazbalceta, J. 1952. *Investigación histórica y documental sobre la aparición de la Virgen de Guadalupe de México.* Mexico City: Ediciones Fuente Cultural.

García Icazbalceta, J. 1971a. *Colección de documentos para la historia de México.* Mexico City: Kraus Reprint.

García Icazbalceta, J. 1971b. *Nueva colección de documentos para la historia de México.* Nendeln, Liechtenstein: Kraus Reprint.

Garcia Soormally, M. 2011. *Magia, hechicería y brujería: Entre La Celestina y Cervantes.* Sevilla: Renacimiento.

Garrido Aranda, A. 1979. *Organización de la Iglesia en el Reino de Granada y su proyección en Indias, siglo XVI.* Sevilla: Escuela de Estudios Hispano-Americanos.

Garrido Aranda, A. 1980. *Moriscos e indios: Precedentes hispánicos de la evangelización en México.* Mexico City: Universidad Nacional Autónoma de México.

Giles, Mary E. 1999. *Women in the Inquisition: Spain and the New World.* Baltimore: Johns Hopkins University Press.

Gisbert, T. 1999. *El paraíso de los pájaros parlantes: La imagen del otro en la cultura andina.* La Paz: Plural Editores: Universidad Nuestra Señora de La Paz.

González de Eslava, F. 1998. *Coloquios espirituales y sacramentales.* Mexico City: Universidad Nacional Autónoma de México, Instituto de Investigaciones Filológicas, Centro de Estudios Literarios.

González Obregón, Luis, ed. 1910. *Proceso inquisitorial del cacique de Texcoco.* Mexico City: Archivo General de la Nación.

González Rodríguez, P. 1996. "La acción educativa de España en el Perú: El virrey Toledo y la promoción del indio (1569–1581)" *Archivo Ibero-americano* 56 (January–June): 221–22, 191–278.

Gossy, M. 1989. *The Untold Story.* Ann Arbor: University of Michigan Press.

Gracia Boix, R. 1991. *Brujas y hechiceras de Andalucía*. Córdoba, Spain: Real Academia de Ciencias, Bellas Artes y Nobles Artes.

Greenleaf, R. 1961. *Zumárraga and the Mexican Inquisition, 1536–1543*. Washington, DC: Academy of American Franciscan History.

Greer, Margaret R. 1991. *The Play of Power: Mythological Court Dramas of Calderón de la Barca*. Princeton, NJ: Princeton University Press.

Greer, Margaret R. 2006. "The Politics of Memory in *El Tuzaní de la Alpujarra*, 113–30." In *Reality in Early Modern Spain*, ed. Richard Pym. Woodbridge, UK: Tamesis.

Greer, Margaret R. 2007. *Rereading the Black Legend: The Discourses of Racism in the Renaissance Empires*. Ed. Margaret R. Greer, Walter Mignolo, and Maureen Quilligan. Chicago: University of Chicago Press.

Griffiths, N. 1998. *La cruz y la serpiente: La represión y el resurgimiento religioso en el Perú colonial*. Trans. Carlos Baliñas Pérez. Lima: Fondo Editorial de la Pontificia Universidad Católica del Perú.

Gruzinski, S. 1991. *La colonización de lo imaginario: Sociedades indígenas y occidentalización en el México español. siglos XVI–XVIII*. Mexico City: Fondo de Cultura Económica.

Gruzinski, S. 1993. *The Conquest of Mexico: The Incorporation of Indian Societies into the Western World, 16th–18th Centuries*. Trans. Eileen Corrigan. Cambridge: Polity Press; Oxford: Blackwell Publishers.

Gruzinski, S. 1994. *La Guerra de las imágenes: De Cristóbal Colón a "Blade Runner" (1492–2019)*. Mexico City: Fondo de Cultura Económica.

Gruzinski, S. 2001. *Images at War: Mexico from Columbus to Blade Runner (1492–2019)*. Trans. Heather MacLean. Durham, NC: Duke University Press. https://doi.org/10.1215/9780822383116.

Guamán Poma, F. 1956–66. *Primer nueva coronica y buen gobierno*. Lima: Editorial Cultura, Dirección de Cultura, Arqueología e Historia del Ministerio de Educación Pública del Perú.

Guibovich Pérez, P. 1998. *En defensa de Dios: Estudios y documentos sobre la Inquisición en el Perú*. Lima: Ediciones del Congreso del Perú.

Guibovich Pérez, P. 2000. *La inquisición y la censura de libros en el Perú virreinal (1570–1813)*. Lima: Fondo Editorial del Congreso del Perú.

Guiley, R. 1999. *The Encylopedia of Witches and Witchcraft*. New York: Checkmark Books.

Hampe Martínez, T. 1996. *Cultura barroca y extirpación de idolatrías: La biblioteca de Francisco de Ávila, 1648*. Cuzco: Centro de Estudios Regionales Andinos Bartolomé de las Casas.

Harrison, S. 1980. "Magic in the Spanish Golden Age." *Renaissance and Reformation* 4:47–64.

Horcasitas, F. 1974. *El Teatro náhuatl: Épocas novohispana y moderna*. Prólogo de Miguel León-Portilla. Mexico City: Universidad Nacional Autónoma de México, Instituto de Investigaciones Históricas.

Jáuregui, C. 2005. *Canibalia: Canibalismo, calibanismo, antropofagia cultural y consumo en América Latina*. Córdoba, Spain: Casa de las Américas.

Kamen, H. 1983. *Spain, 1469–1714: A Society of Conflict*. London: Longman.

Kamen, H. 1985. *Inquisition and Society in Spain in the Sixteenth and Seventeenth Centuries*. Bloomington: Indiana University Press.

Kamen, H. 2003. *Empire: How Spain Became a World Power; 1492–1763*. New York: Perennial.

Kieckhefer, R. 1989. *Magic in the Middle Ages*. New York: Cambridge University Press.

Kirk, S., and S. Rivett. 2014. *Religious Transformation in the Early Modern Americas*. Philadelphia: University of Pennsylvania Press.

Kohut, K. 2000. *La formación de la cultura virreinal. Frankfurt: Vervuert*. Madrid: Iberoamericana.

Kors, Alan C., and Edwards Peters. 1972. *Witchcraft in Europe: 1100–1700: A Documentary History*. Philadelphia: Pennsylvania University Press.

Kramer, H., and J. Sprenger. 1975. *Malleus Maleficarum*. Buenos Aires: Orión.

Lafaye, J. 1999. *Quetzalcóatl y Guadalupe: La formación de la conciencia nacional*. Mexico City: Fondo de Cultura Económica.

Las Casas, Bartolomé de. 1967. *Apologética historia sumaria*. Ed. Edmundo O'Gorman. Mexico City: UNAM.

Lasso de la Vega, L. 1998. *The Story of Guadalupe: Luis Laso de la Vega's Huei tlama-huiçoltica of 1649*. Stanford, CA: Stanford University Press; Los Angeles: UCLA Latin American Center Publications, University of California.

León Portilla, M. 2000. *Tonantzin Guadalupe: Pensamiento náhuatl y mensaje cristiano en el "Nicān mopōhua."* Mexico City: Colegio Nacional: Fondo de Cultura Económica.

Levack, B. 1995. *La caza de brujas en la Europa Moderna*. Madrid: Alianza.

Levillier, R. 1935. *Don Francisco de Toledo, supremo organizador del Perú; su vida, su obra (1515–1582)*. Buenos Aires: Espasa Calpe.

Levinson, Brett. 2005. "On Netanyahu's *The Origins of the Inquisition in Fifteenth Century Spain*: Does the Inquisition Justify Zionism?" *Journal of Spanish Cultural Studies* 6 (3): 245–58. https://doi.org/10.1080/14636200500312169.

Lewis, Laura A. 2003. *Hall of Mirrors: Power, Witchcraft, and Caste in Colonial Mexico*. Durham, NC: Duke University Press. https://doi.org/10.1215/9780822385158.

Lisi, F. L. 1990. *El tercer concilio limense y la aculturación de los Indígenas sudamericanos: Estudio crítico con edición, traducción y comentario de las actas del concilio provincial celebrado en Lima entre 1582 y 1583*. Salamanca: Universidad de Salamanca.

Lisón Tolosana, C. 1992. *Las Brujas en la historia de España*. *Madrid*. Temas de Hoy, Col.: Historia de la España Sorprendente.

Lopes Don, P. 2006. "Franciscans, Indian Sorcerers, and the Inquisition in New Spain, 1536–1543." *Journal of World History* 17 (1): 27–48. https://doi.org/10.1353/jwh.2006.0025.

López de Gómara, F. 1987. *La conquista de México*. Madrid: Historia 16.

López de Gómara, F. 1991. *Historia general de las Indias y Vida de Hernán Cortés*. Caracas, Venezuela: Biblioteca Ayacucho.

Lunenfeld, M. 1977. "Isabella I of Castile and the Company of Women in Power." *Historical Reflections: Réflexions Historiques* 4 (2): 207–29.

Lupher, D. 2003. *Romans in a New world: Classical Models in Sixteenth-Century Spanish America*. Ann Arbor: University of Michigan Press.

Luther, M. 1878. *The Table Talk of Martin Luther*. Translated and edited William Hazlitt. London: G. Bell.

Luther, M. 1999. *Luther's Works, vol. 43: Devotional Writings II*. Ed. J. J. Pelikan, H. C. Oswald, and H. T. Lehmann. Philadelphia: Fortress Press.

Lynch, J. 2012. *New Worlds: A Religious History of Latin America*. New Haven: Yale University Press.

MacCormack, S. 1991. *Religion in the Andes: Vision and Imagination in Early Colonial Peru*. Princeton, NJ: Princeton University Press.

Machiavelli, N. 1992. *The Prince*. Ed. Robert M. Adams. New York: W.W. Norton.

Mackay, A. 1987. *Society, Economy and Religion in Late Medieval Castile*. London: Variorum Reprints.

Madox, O. 1973. *The Book of Witches*. New Jersey: Rowman and Littlefield.

Mair, Lucy. 1969. *Witchcraft*. New York: McGraw-Hill Book Company.

Mannarelli, M. E. 1998. *Hechiceras, beatas y expósitas: Mujeres y poder inquisitorial en Lima*. Lima: Ediciones del Congreso del Perú.

Mariana, Juan de. 1699. *The general history of Spain: From the first peopling of it by Tubal, till the death of King Ferdinand, who united the crowns of Castile and Aragon; With a continuation to the death of King Philip III*. London: Sare.

Martín, L. 2001. *La conquista intelectual del Perú: El Colegio jesuita de San Pablo, 1568–1767*. Barcelona: Editorial Casiopea.

Martín de Castañega. 1946. *Tratado muy sutil y bien fundado de las supersticiones*. Madrid: Sociedad de Bibliófilos Españoles.

Martín del Río, S. J. 1991. *La magia demoníaca: Libro II de las Disquisiciones Mágicas*. Ed. Jesús Moya. Madrid: Hiperión.

Martín Soto, R. 2000. *Magia e Inquisición en el Antiguo Reino de Granada (Siglos XVI–XVII)*. Málaga: Arguval.

Marwick, M. 1970. *Witchcraft and Sorcery*. Melbourne: C. Nicholls and Company Ltd., Penguin Books.

Marzal, M., ed. 1994. *El rostro indio de Dios*. Mexico City: Centro de Reflexión Teológica. Universidad Iberoamericana, Centro de Integración Universitaria.

Mauss, M. 1972. *A General Theory of Magic*. Londres: Routledge and Kegan.

Medinaceli, X., et al. 2001. *El discurso de la evangelización del siglo XVI*. La Paz, Bolivia: Instituto de Estudios Bolivianos, Facultad de Humanidades y Ciencias de la Educación de la Universidad Mayor de San Andrés.

Mendieta, G. [1870] 1973. *Historia eclesiástica indiana*. Mexico City: Antigua librería; Madrid: Atlas.

Merediz, E. M. 2004. *Refracted Images: The Canary Islands through a New World Lens. Transatlantic Readings*. Tempe: Arizona Center for Medieval and Renaissance Studies.

Michelet, J. 1987. *La bruja*. Barcelona: Akal.

Mignolo, Walter. 2003. *The Darker Side of the Renaissance: Literacy, Territoriality, and Colonization*. Ann Arbor: University of Michigan Press. https://doi.org/10.3998/mpub .8739.

Mignolo, Walter. 2005. *The Idea of Latin America*. Malden, MA: Blackwell Pub.

Millones, L. 1987. *Historia y poder en los Andes centrales: Desde los orígenes al siglo XVII*. Madrid: Alianza.

Millones, L. 1995. *Perú colonial: De Pizarro a Tupac Amaru II*. Lima: COFIDE.

Mills, K. 1994. *An Evil Lost to View?: An Investigation of Post-Evangelization Andean Religion in Mid-Colonial Peru*. Liverpool: University of Liverpool, Institute of Latin American Studies.

Mills, K. 1996. "Bad Christians in Colonial Peru." *Colonial Latin American Review* 5 (2): 183–218. https://doi.org/10.1080/10609169608569890.

Mills, K. 1997. *Idolatry and Its Enemies: Colonial Andean Religion and Extirpation, 1640–1750*. Princeton, NJ: Princeton University Press.

Moffitt, J. 2006. *Our Lady of Guadalupe: The Painting, the Legend and the Reality*. Jefferson, NC: McFarland.

Molina, Cristóbal de. 1989. *Fábulas y mitos de los Incas*. Madrid: Historia 16.

Monten, J., and R. Collier. 1999. "The Sermons of Francisco de Avila." Working paper no. 29 Durham, NC: Duke–University of North Carolina Program in Latin American Studies.

Montúfar, A. 1964. *Ordenanzas para el coro de la catedral mexicana, 1570*. Madrid: Porrúa Turanzas.

Motolinía, T. 1996. *Memoriales: Libro de oro (MS JGI 31)*. Ed. Nancy Joe Dyer. Mexico City: El Colegio de México, Centro de Estudios Lingüísticos y Literarios.

Mullett, M. 1999. *The Catholic Reformation*. London: Routledge.

Mumford, J. 2000. "Clara's Miccinelli Cabinet of Wonders: Jesuits, Incas and the Mysteries of Colonial Peru." *Lingua Franca* (February): 36–45.

Murray, M. 1986. *El Dios de los brujos*. Mexico City: Fondo de Cultura Económica.

Nagel Bielicke, F. 1994. "El aprendizaje del idioma náhuatl entre los franciscanos y los jesuitas en la Nueva España." *Estudios de Cultura Nahuatl* 24:419–41.

Nebrija, A. 1946. *Gramática castellana*. Madrid: Ediciones de Cultura Hispánica, Instituto de Cooperacion Iberoamericana.

Nesvig, M. 2005. *Popular Religion in Mexico*. Albuquerque: University of New Mexico Press.

Netanyahu, B. 1999. *Los orígenes de la inquisición en la España del siglo XV*. Barcelona: Crítica.

Newall, V. 1974. *Encyclopedia of Witchcraft and Magic*. New York: Hamlyn.

Nirenberg, D. 1996. *Communities of Violence Persecution of Minorities in the Middle Ages*. Princeton, NJ: Princeton University Press.

Ocaña, D. 2000. *Comedia de Nuestra Señora de Guadalupe y sus Milagros: Teatro Colonial; Siglos XVI–XVII. Antología General del Teatro Peruano*. Vol. 2. Pontificia Universidad Católica del Perú.

O'Gorman, E. 1958. *Invención de América: El universalismo de la cultura de Occidente*. Mexico City: Fondo de Cultura Económica.

O'Gorman, E. 1986. *Destierro de sombras: Luz en el origen de la imagen y culto de Nuestra Señora de Guadalupe del Tepeyac*. Mexico City: Universidad Nacional Autónoma de México.

Pagden, A. 1982. *The Fall of Natural Man: The American Indian and the Origins of Comparative Ethnology*. Cambridge: Cambridge University Press.

Pagden, A. 1995. *Lords of All the World: Ideologies of Empire in Spain, Britain and France 1500–1800*. New Haven, CT: Yale University Press.

Pavia, M. 1947. "Magic and Witchcraft in the Literature of the Siglo de Oro, Especially the Drama." PhD Diss., University of Chicago.

Pearl, J. 1998. *The Crime of Crimes: Demonology and Politics in France, 1560–1620*. Waterloo, ON: Wilfrid Laurier University Press.

Peña Echeverría, F. J. 1998. *La razón de estado en España: Siglos XVI–XVII. Antología de textos*. Madrid: Tecnos.

Pereña, L., V. Abril, C. Baciero, et al. 1988. *Inculturación del indio*. Salamanca: Universidad Pontificia de Salamanca.

Pérez de Colosía Rodríguez, M. I. 1984. *Auto Inquisitorial de 1672: El criptojudaismo en Málaga*. Málaga, Spain: Diputación Provincial.

Pérez Luna, J. A. 2001. *El inicio de la evangelización novohispana: La obediencia.* Mexico City: Colección Biblioteca del INAH.

Perry, M., and A. Cruz. 1991. *Cultural Encounters: The Impact of the Inquisition in Spain and the New World.* Berkeley: University of California Press.

Phelan, J. L. 1970. *The Millennial Kingdom of the Franciscans in the New World.* Berkeley: University of California Press.

Polo de Ondegardo, J. 1916. *Los errores y supersticiones de los indios, sacadas del tratado y averiguación que hizo el licenciado Polo: Informaciones acerca de la religión y gobierno de los Incas. Colección de libros y documentos referentes a la historia del Perú.* Vols. 3–4. Lima: Sanmarti.

Poole, S. 1995. *Our Lady of Guadalupe: The Origins and Sources of a Mexican National Symbol, 1531–1797.* Tucson: University of Arizona Press.

Prescott, W. H. 2001. *History of the Conquest of Mexico.* New York: Modern Library.

Pulgar, F. 1943. *Crónica de los reyes católicos.* Madrid: Espasa-Calpe.

Ragnow, M., and W. Phillips. 2011. *Religious Conflict and Accommodation in the Early Modern World.* Minneapolis: Center for Early Modern History, University of Minnesota.

Ramos, G., and H. Urbano. 1993. *Catolicismo y extirpación de idolatrías: Siglos XVI–XVII; Charcas, Chile, México, Perú.* Cuzco: Centro de estudios regionales andinos "Bartolomé de las Casas."

Ribadeneyra, P. 1927. *Obras escogidas del padre Pedro de Rivadeneira, con una noticia de su vida y juicio crítico de sus escritos por don Vicente de la Fuente.* Madrid: Hernando.

Ricard, R. 1986. *La conquista espiritual de México: Ensayo sobre el apostolado y los métodos misioneros de las órdenes mendicantes en la Nueva España de 1523–24 a 1572.* Trans. Angel María Garibay. Mexico City: Fondo de Cultura Económica.

Rico, F. Marzo 1994. "Sorceress, Love Magic, and the Inquisition Linguistics." *Modern Language Association of America* 109 (2): 207–31. https://doi.org/10.2307/463117.

Río, M. 1991. *La magia demoníaca.* Madrid: Hiperión.

Ríos Izquierdo, P. 1995. *Mujer y sociedad en el Siglo XVII. Madrid.* Horas y Horas, Colombia: Mujeres en Madrid.

Robbins, R. H. 1991. *Enciclopedia de la brujería y demonología.* Madrid: Debate.

Rodríguez Solís, E. 1930. *Historia de la prostitución en España y América.* Madrid: Biblioteca Nueva.

Rojas Garcidueñas, J. 1935. *El teatro de Nueva España en el siglo XVI.* Mexico City: Imprenta de Luis Álvarez.

Roth, C. 1989. *La inquisición española.* Barcelona: Martínez Roca.

Ruiz Medrano, E., and S. Kellog. 2010. *Negotiation within Domination: New Spain's Indian Pueblos Confront the Spanish State.* Boulder: University Press of Colorado.

Saavedra Fajardo, D. 1976. *Empresas políticas: Idea de un príncipe político-cristiano*. Madrid: Nacional.

Sahagún, B. 1990a. *Breve compendio de los ritos idolátricos que los indios de esta Nueva España usaban en tiempo de su infidelidad*. Mexico City: Lince.

Sahagún, Bernardino de. 1990b. *Historia general de las cosas de Nueva España*. Madrid: Historia 16.

St. Thomas Aquinas. 1989. *Summa Theologiae*. London: Eyre and Spottiswoode.

Sánchez, Miguel. 2010. *Imagen de la Virgen María, madre de Dios de Guadalupe, milagrosamente aparecida en la Ciudad de México*. Alicante, Spain: Biblioteca Virtual Miguel de Cervantes.

Sánchez Ortega, M. H. 1992. *La mujer y la sexualidad en el antiguo régimen: La perspectiva inquisitorial*. Madrid: Akal Universitaria.

Sandoval, P. 1955–56. *Historia de la vida y hechos del emperador Carlos V*. Ediciones Atlas. Vol. 81. Madrid: Atlas.

San Pedro, Juan de. 1992. *La persecución del demonio: Crónica de los primeros agustinos en el Norte del Perú (1560)*. Mexico City: Centro Andino y Mesoamericano de Estudios Interdisciplinarios (C.A.M.E.I.).

Schroeder, S., and S. Poole. 2007. *Religion in New Spain*. Albuquerque: University of New Mexico Press.

Schwaller, J. 2000. *The Church in Colonial Latin America*. Wilmington, DE: SR Books.

Schwaller, J. 2011. *The History of the Catholic Church in Latin America: From Conquest to Revolution and Beyond*. New York: New York University Press.

Seed, Patricia. 1993. "'Are These Not Also Men?': The Indians' Humanity and Capacity for Spanish Civilisation." *Journal of Latin American Studies* 25 (3): 629–52. https://doi.org/10.1017/S0022216X00006696.

Segura, C. 1993. *Árabes, judías y cristianas: Mujeres en la Europa Medieval*. Ed. Celia del Moral. Granada: Universidad de Granada, Seminario de Estudios de la mujer.

Sepúlveda, J. 1941. *Tratado sobre las justas causas de la guerra contra los indios*. Mexico City: Fondo de Cultura Económica.

Sepúlveda y Herrera, M. T. 1999. *Procesos por idolatría al cacique, gobernadores y sacerdotes de Yanhuitlán, 1544–1546*. Mexico City: Instituto Nacional de Antropología e Historia.

Silverblatt, I. 1987. *Moon, Sun, and Witches: Gender Ideologies and Class in Inca and Colonial Peru*. Princeton, NJ: Princeton University Press.

Silverblatt, I. 1988. "Political Memories and Colonizing Symbols: Santiago and the Mountain Gods of Colonial Peru." In *Rethinking History and Myth: Indigenous South American Perspectives on the Past*, ed. Jonathan D. Hill, 174–94. Urbana: University of Illinois Press.

Silverblatt, I. 2000. "The Inca's Witches: Gender and the Cultural Work of Colonialization in Seventeenth-Century Peru." In *Possible Pasts: Becoming Colonial in Early America*, ed. Robert Blair St. George, 109–30. Ithaca, NY: Cornell University Press.

Simpson, L. 1966. *Many Mexicos*. Berkeley: University of California Press.

Smith, J. 1983. *The Image of Guadalupe: Myth or Miracle?* Garden City, NY: Doubleday.

Smith, J. 1994. *The Image of Guadalupe*. Macon, GA: Mercer University Press in association with Fowler Wright Books.

Sten, M., et al. 2000. *El teatro franciscano en la Nueva España: Fuentes y ensayos para el estudio del teatro de evangelización en el siglo XVI*. Mexico City: Facultad de Filosofía y Letras, UNAM.

Surtz, R. 1979. *The Birth of a Theater: Dramatic Convention in the Spanish Theater from Juan del Encina to Lope de Vega*. Princeton, NJ: Princeton University. Madrid: Castalia.

Surtz, R. 1983. *Teatro medieval castellano*. Madrid: Taurus.

Talavera, H. 1961. *Católica impugnación*. Ed. Francisco Martín Hernández. Barcelona: Flores.

Talavera, H. 2003. *Oficio de la Toma de Granada*. Granada: Diputación de Granada.

Tavarez, D. 2011. *The Invisible War: Indigenous Devotions, Discipline and Dissent in Colonial Mexico*. Stanford, CA: Stanford University Press. https://doi.org/10.11126 /stanford/9780804773287.001.0001.

Thomas, K. 1971. *Religion and the Decline of Magic*. New York: Charles Scribner's Sons.

Tomas, D. 1996. *Transcultural Space and Transcultural Beings*. Boulder, CO: Westview Press.

Torquemada, J. 1943–44. *Monarquía indiana*, Mexico City: S. Chávez Hayhoe.

Torquemada, A. 1983. *Jardín de flores curiosas*. Ed. Giovanni Allegra. Madrid: Clásicos Castalia.

Torre Villar, E., and Ramiro Navarro de Anda. 1982. *Testimonios históricos guadalupanos*. Mexico City: Fondo de Cultura Económica.

Turner, V. 1982. *From Ritual to Theatre: The Human Seriousness of Play*. New York: Performing Arts Journal Publications.

Urbano, H. 1987. "El escándalo de Chucuito y la primera evangelización de los Lupaqa (Perú) Nota en torno a un documento inédito de 1574." In *Cuadernos para la historia de la evangelización en América Latina*, vol. 2., 203–28. Cuzco: Centro Bartolomé de Las Casas.

Valera, B. 1945. *Las costumbres antiguas del Perú y La historia de los Incas (siglo XVI)*. Lima: Ed. Francisco A. Loayza.

Valera, D. 1934. *Una fuente contemporánea de la Conquista de Canarias: La Crónica de los Reyes Católicos*. La Laguna, Canary Islands: Curberlo.

Valiente, D. 1973. *An ABC on Witchcraft Past and Present*. New York: St. Martin's Press.

Vargas Ugarte, R. 1963. *Historia de la Compañía de Jesús en el Perú*. Burgos: Imprenta de Aldecoa.

Vigil, M. 1986. *La Vida de las mujeres en los siglos XVI y XVII*. Madrid: Siglo Veintiuno.

Vilches, E. 2004. "Columbus's Gift: Representations of Grace and Wealth and the Enterprise of the Indies." *Modern Language Notes* 119:201–25.

Vitoria, F. 1946. *Relecciones sobre los indios y el derecho a la Guerra*. Buenos Aires: Espasa-Calpe Argentina.

Vitoria, F. 1991. *Political Writings*. Ed. Anthony Pagden and Jeremy Lawrence. Cambridge: Cambridge University Press.

Wade, M. 1988. *La mujer en la Edad Media*. Madrid: Nerea.

Weaver, Mary Lewis Dewey. 1974. *"Magic and Witchcraft in the Narrative Prose of Cervantes."* PhD Diss. Stanford University, Stanford, CA.

Weckmann, Luis. 1992. *Constantino el Grande y Cristóbal Colón: Estudio de la supremacía papal sobre islas (1091–1493)*. Mexico City: Fondo de Cultura Económica.

Weckmann, Luis. 1994. *La herencia medieval de México*. Mexico City: Colegio de México, Fondo de Cultura Económica.

Wiesner, M. 1993. *Women and Gender in Early Modern Europe*. Cambridge: Cambridge University Press.

Wilson, D. de Armas. 1991. *Allegories of Love*. Princeton, NJ: Princeton University Press. https://doi.org/10.1515/9781400861798.

Zumárraga, J. 1928. *Doctrina breve in fac-simile*. New York: United States Catholic Historical Society.

Zwingli, U. 1981. *Commentary on True and False Religion*. Ed. Samuel Macauley Jackson and Clarence Nevin Heller. Durham, NC: Labyrinth.

About the Author

Born in Málaga, Spain, MINA GARCÍA SOORMALLY earned her bachelor's degree in English philology from the Universidad de Málaga in 1995. After completing her undergraduate degree, she continued as a student at the Universidad de Málaga, pursuing doctoral studies in Spanish philology. While working on her Spanish dissertation and teaching Spanish language at Duke University in Durham, North Carolina, Dr. García Soormally realized a growing interest in transatlantic studies and began a second PhD program in the Romance Studies Department at Duke in the Fall of 2000.

In 2003, Dr. García Soormally successfully defended her dissertation, *Magia, hechicería, y brujería: Entre La Celestina y Cervantes* at the Universidad de Málaga. She was subsequently awarded a PhD (*sobresaliente cum laude con unanimidad,* "with highest honors") in Spanish philology. In the following years Dr. García Soormally continued working under Dr. Margaret Greer at Duke, taking her research to archives in Lima, Peru; Madrid and Seville, Spain; and Mexico City, Mexico. In 2007, Dr. García Soormally successfully defended her dissertation "Idolatry and the Construction of the Spanish Empire," earning her second PhD, this time from Duke University.

In 2011, Renacimiento Press of Seville, Spain, published Dr. García Soormally's first book, *Magia, hechicería, y brujería: Entre La Celestina y Cervantes.* In an article in the Spanish national newspaper *ABC,* literary critic and permanent member of the Royal Academy of History, Luis Alberto de Cuenca listed this work among his five recommendations for the best undiscovered books of 2011.

Mina García Soormally joined the Department of World Languages and Cultures of Elon University in Elon, North Carolina, in the fall of 2007, where she is now an associate professor. At Elon, in addition to pursuing ongoing research in Early Modern Spanish Theater and transatlantic studies, Dr. García Soormally teaches Spanish language and literature. Outside Elon University, she serves on two executive boards, the Association of Hispanic Classical Theater and BRIDGES, a professional development program for women in higher education.

Mina García Soormally lives in Greensboro, North Carolina, with her husband, Clark Geddie, and their two daughters, Amanda and Olivia. For fun, she enjoys swimming and playing piano.

Index

Moon, worship of, 14, 14n19

Moors, xi, xiii, 34, 36, 37, 37–38n1, 53, 54, 58, 58n39, 59, 60, 61, 61n45, 68, 69, 70n59, 71, 73, 74n65, 75, 84n83, 91n5, 97n21, 107, 108n41, 118n65, 119, 120n70, 135, 137, 143, 145, 148, 149; baptism of, 90; Christians and, 38; cruelty of, 110n46; defense by, 106; evangelization of, xiv, 44n16, 114n59; fighting, 18, 109, 110, 117, 118, 166; idolatry and, 166; indigenous peoples and, 84, 109; as infidels, 151; Jews and, 39, 59, 59n42, 60, 112, 113, 120, 147; New Spain and, 108–17; signs for, 62n47; Spaniards and, 38, 88; as threat, 64n48

Moses, 25n32

Motolinía, Torbio de Benavente, 38, 38n2, 40, 40n5, 49n27, 90n4, 104, 104n35, 105, 106n38, 135, 167; on hell, 89; pagans and, 89; records of, 90

Moya de Contreras, Pedro, 52n31

Mudejars, Jews and, 111n47

Nahuatl, 95, 96n19, 138n7

Nativity, 18n25, 158

Navarro, Miguel, 46n21

Navidad, 66, 66n53

nazarenos, 3, 3n2

Nebrija, A., 58–59

necromancy, 10n11, 83, 83n81

Netanyahu, 119n67

New Jerusalem, 111, 111n48

New Laws, 116, 127, 127n81, 130, 131n87

New Spain, xiii, xiv, 30, 36, 41, 51, 52, 93, 91n11, 94, 97, 105, 106, 109n43, 125, 131n87, 132, 134, 141, 145, 149, 156, 162n38, 164, 164n42; chronological development of, 135; colonization of, xv; first impressions of, 77–88; idolatry in, 166; incongruities in, 38; indigenous population of, 99; Moors/Christians in, 108–17; *otherness* in, 39; transition in, 135, 153–54

New Testament, 21, 136n5

New World, xi, xii, xiv, 7, 7n8, 16n23, 40, 43, 44n18, 46, 46n22, 47, 49, 50, 51, 53, 56, 72, 94, 97, 109, 116, 117, 121, 125, 130, 135, 136, 137, 138n7, 143, 145, 148, 149, 166; Canary Islands and, 72n62, 77; Catholicism and, 19; Christianity and, 81n77; conquest of, 138; discovery of, 166; Franciscans and, 93; Garden of Eden and, 64; hegemonic power in, 39; idealized version of, 66; idolatry in,

11–20, 30; incorporation of, 53; indigenous populations of, 52; political power in, 47; portrayal of, 88

Nican Mopohua (Laso de la Vega), 134n2, 136n6, 143

Niña (ship), 66n53

noble savage, 64, 66

Nuestra Señora de Guadalupe, 144

Oaxaca, 91, 128, 136

"Obedience, The," 50

Ocean Sea, 39, 71

Ocelotl, 125, 126

Oficio de la toma de Granada (Talavera), 110, 111

O'Gorman, Edmundo, 142, 154, 155, 156, 161, 162n37, 164

oidores, 44, 44n17, 44n18, 103n34

Old Testament, 12, 60, 116, 136n5

Olid, rebellion of, 131n87

Olmos, Andrés de, 41, 94

omens, 10n11, 141n10

Ordenanzas, 99, 100

Ortiz de Madienzo, Juan, 44n18

other, xv, 18, 20, 24, 30, 58, 84, 112, 113, 167; American, 73; attitude about, 121; coexistence with, 117; converting, 163; covering over of, 64; demonic, xi, 18; integrating, 166; Jews as, 61, 62, 63, 72; modern state and, 68; repression of, xiv; self and, 61n45; Semitic, 113n53; transatlantic, 36

otherness, xii, xiv, 39

Our Lady of Antigua and of the Remedios, 155n24

Our Lady of Atocha, 137

Our Lady of Guadalupe, 133n1, 134, 140n9, 142, 144n15, 151, 157n28, 159n29, 159n30, 160n31, 160n32, 160n33, 162n38, 184; as black madonna, 137; chapel of, 156n27; feast of, 158; God and, 158n29; image of, 156n27

Our Lady of Monserrat and de la Peña, 155n24

Our Lady of Otrio, 155n24

Our Lady of Tepeyac, 183, 184

Our Lady of the Reyes, 155n24

Pachamama, 4

paganism, 32, 81, 83, 87, 99, 124, 168

pagans, 9, 12n14, 29, 43, 43n13, 52, 84, 89, 92n8, 95, 108, 116n61, 122, 124, 125, 128, 138, 140, 148, 160, 164; habits of, 141; idolatry of, 159;

sacrifices and, 85; superstition of, 22, 83;
temples of, 31–36, 90, 90n3, 92n7
Palos, Juan de, 49n27
papacy, 20–21, 47, 58
Papal States, 107
Papalotl, 125, 125n77
Parada, Alonso de, 44, 44n18
parallel paths, 29–36
Partidas, 117, 118n65, 120, 120n70, 145
Paul, 25n32, 26n34, 184
Paul III, Pope, 92, 93, 107
penitence, 69–70, 69–70n58
Pérez de Guzmán, Alvar, 120
Peter I, 119
Peter III, 45n19
Philip II, x, 5, 47, 52n31, 122, 132n89, 156
Pizarro, Francisco, 138
Pliny the Elder, 72n61
plurality, heterogeneity and, 60
Point of Cotoche, 78n72
politics, 7, 47, 55, 58, 74, 132; baptism and,
117–22; conception of, 112; goals in, 59n42;
religion and, 53; tribal, 39
Politics (Aristotle), 12n17
polygamy, 93, 128
Pontifice, 92n7
Poole, S., 143, 151, 152, 154
Porras, Diego de, 131n87
poverty, 21n28, 185
power, 54; colonial, 32, 75; ecclesiastical, 7;
political, 7, 47
Prescott, William H., 40n5
Primer Coloquio, 69
Primera Audiencia, 44
Prince, The (Machiavelli), 53
Protestantism, 29, 34n38
Pulgar, F., 88n89

racism, 61, 61n44
Real Audiencia, 44n18
Real Monsterio de los Jerónimos, 137
Reconquista, xiii, xiv, 34, 38, 39, 47, 48, 53, 58n39,
70, 70n59, 84, 87, 110, 116, 122, 135, 137, 143,
163, 164, 166; helping hands during, 145–54
Recuerdo de Sevilla, ix
Reformation, 30n35, 58, 166; Catholic, 20, 29,
136; Protestant, xii, xiii, 20, 21, 23, 29
religion, xv, 55n34, 76, 80, 86, 99, 107, 153; abandonment of, 6; auspices of, xii, xiii; Christian,

5, 154; destruction of, 92n7; external forms of,
22; goal of, 58; independence from, 55; indigenous, 90, 92n7; politics and, 53; popular, 5,
5n5; rejection of, 16; Spanish, 101n28; theory/
practice of, 23; true/false, 5–10, 22, 25, 26, 30,
32, 34, 87
religiosity, x, 34; Early Modern, 20–29; multi-
layered, 5
Renaissance, 21
Reprobación de las supersticiones y hechierías
(Ciruelo), 10
resistance, 49, 75, 112, 113, 130, 167; indigenous,
xii, xiii, 16, 32n37, 91, 101n28, 126, 153
"Revelation of Saint John the Divine, The"
(Revelation), 144
Ribadeneyra, Pedro de, 54, 55, 112, 117
Ribas, Juan de, 49n27
Ricard, Robert, xiv
rituals, 7n8, 24, 38, 39, 43n15, 111n48, 127;
Catholic, 27, 30; Christian, x, 44; native, 5, 8;
pagan, 33; pre-Christian, 5
Rivera Carrera, Norberto, 183
Rodas, 104, 105
Rojas, parallel society and, xv

Sabbaths, 8, 9, 41n6, 41n7
sacraments, 7n8, 8n8, 29, 51, 90, 93, 95n17, 97,
108, 128, 134
sacrifices, 89n2, 90n3, 91n6, 102, 140n9; human,
67, 79, 85, 85n84, 87, 90; pagans and, 85, 125;
prohibiting, 82
Sahagún, Bernardino de, 81n77, 100, 140, 141,
142, 142n11, 154, 159, 162, 164n42
St. Anthony, 30n35
St. Augustine, 24
St. Brendan, 74n64
St. Edmund, 30n35
St. George, 59n40
St. Hipólito, 107, 108
St. Hippolytus, 108n41, 109, 109n43
St. Isidore, 57n37
St. James, 37–38n1, 107, 108, 108n41
St. John the Baptist, 139, 139n8
St. Lawrence, 156n27
St. Mary, 141n9
St. Michael, 107
St. Peter, Virgin Mary and, 149
saints, 109n42, 114n57, 159; indigenous, 133;
worshipping, 21, 24

Salazar, Bachiller, 157, 161n34

Salazar, Francisco de, 142

Salazar, Juan, 155, 155n24

Salle, Gadifer de la, 72n61

salvation, 12n16, 50, 56, 57, 68, 78, 79, 86, 87, 117, 119n67, 168, 184

Sánchez, Ana, xiv

Sánchez, Miguel, 144, 150n20, 162n38

Sánchez de Cisneros, Alonso, 157, 160

Sandoval, Gonzalo de, 138

Santa Ana, 139

Santa Madre Iglesia, 42

Santa María, 66n53

Santa María de Guadalupe de Extremadura, 137

Santiago de Compostella, 38, 147

Santiago of Tlatelolco, 98n23

Santo Domingo, 106

Santo Oficio, 112

Saracens, 34n39, 109, 116n61

School of Salamanca, 56

self, *other* and, 61n45

Sepúlveda, Juan Ginés de, 12n17, 56, 98

Seville, ix, 51, 119, 120, 121, 121n72, 126, 137, 155n24

slaves, 12n17, 17n23, 44, 67, 77, 119n67; natural, 56, 105

Soldán, 37n1, 106n40, 108, 109n42, 117, 117n63

Son, 34, 34–35n39, 50n29, 66n52, 115n60

Songs to the Virgin Mary, 145

Soto, Francisco de, 49n27

Spaniards, 107, 109n43, 152; as gods, 81; identity of, x; indigenous peoples and, 63; Moors and, 38, 88

Spanish army, 105, 106, 106n40, 107

spirituality, 19, 21, 22, 79, 81, 97, 99, 103, 109

Sprenger, Jacobus, 9, 12

Stars, worship of, 14, 14n19

Summa Theologica (Aquinas), 10

Summis desiderantes affectibus (Innocent VIII), 9

Sun, worship of, 14, 14n19

Super Illus Specula (John XXII), 9

superstitions, 5, 21, 24, 91n6, 141n10; fighting, 9, 27; idolatry and, 15; ingenious, 22n30; Jews and, 28; listed, 10n11; pagan, 22, 83; species of, 10

syncretism, 5, 5n5, 141, 142, 159

Tabona, 151

Taki Onqoy, 16, 16n22, 101, 101n28, 129

Talavera, Hernando de, xiii, 48, 49, 50, 58, 97n21, 109, 110, 111, 111n48, 113–14; Catholicism and,

112, 116; idolatry and, 114; Jesus Christ and, 115; Moors/Jews and, 113

Tecto, Juan de, 47

Tello de Sandoval, Francisco, 52n31, 126, 127, 127–28n81, 130, 132n89

Telpuchtli, the Youth, 139

Temple of Solomon, 35n40

temples, pagan, 31–36, 90, 90n3, 92n7

Templo Mayor, 138

Tenerife, 72n61, 75n67, 76, 76n70, 77, 151

Tenochtitlan, 84, 104

Tepeyac, 133, 136, 138, 139, 142, 143, 149, 154, 157, 160, 161, 168; miracle at, 156; shrine at, 134

tilma, 134, 135, 143, 151, 160

Tlatelolco, 97, 97n22, 124, 125

Tlaxcala, 38, 40n5, 91, 93, 106, 107, 139n8; conquest/assimilation and, 104

Tlaxcaltecans, 104, 105, 106, 107, 109, 109n43

Toci, cult of, 139

Tonan, cult of, 139

Tonantzin, 134, 138, 139, 139n8, 140, 140–41n9, 141, 142, 148, 153, 159, 162, 164

Toronto, apostolic visit to, 183–85

Torquemada, Tomás de, 9, 95n16, 138, 139, 140, 159, 162

Torre, Bernardino de la, 49n27

Torre Villar, E., 161

Torres, Antonio de, 67, 67n56

Torres Naharro, Bartolomé de, 93

Tortosa, siege of, 147n18

transubstantiation, 26, 29

Traslado de ciertas Ordenanzas fechas por el Audiencia Real insertas en un provisión sellada con el sello real, 169–73

Tratado (Ribadeneyra), 54, 54n33

Tratado muy sotil y bien findado de la supersticiones y hechizerias y vanos conjuros (Castañega), 10

Treatise on Superstition and Witchcraft, 7n8

Treatise Reproving all Superstitions and Forms of Witchcraft, A (Ciruelo), 5

Treaty of Tordesillas (1494), 46n23

Tribunal of the Inquisition, 118n65

Trinidad, María Santísima de la, 3n2

Tula, lord of, 101n30

Tupac Amaru, 16, 101n28

Valencia, Martín de, 49n27

Valera, Diego de, 74, 74n66, 75, 76

Valladolid Controversy, 12n17, 56

Varón, Aracil, xiv, 39
Velasques, Diego de, 78, 78n72
Vera, Pedro de, 74n65, 77
Vicente, Gil, 93
Vide verbo hechizera, 42n11
Vila-Sirga, 148
Vilches, E., 67n56
Viracocha, 75
Virgen de Candelaria, xiv, 75, 135, 149, 151, 152, 153
Virgin Mary, 26, 32, 32n37, 73n63, 114, 115, 133n1, 137, 138n7, 142, 147, 150, 152, 159, 162n38, 164, 184; adoration for, 29, 33, 143, 160; appearance of, 136, 153, 157; cult for, 139; Devil and, 149; images of, 4, 135, 151, 155; intercession by, 138, 145, 147n17; materialization of, 149; miracle by, 134; power of, 146, 148; presence of, 73; St. Peter and, 149; songs to, 145
Virgin of Guadalupe, xiii, xiv, 132, 133, 134, 136, 138n7, 139, 143, 144, 144n15, 154, 160, 161, 162, 163, 167; cult of, 137; devotion to, 158; Diego and, 156; idolatry and, 135; image of, 157; living properties of, 151, 151n21
Virgin of Montserrat, 137
Visconti, Galeazzo, 9
Visconti, Matteo, 9n9
Vitoria, F., 13

Wisdom of Solomon, 11, 11–12n13
witches, xv, 5, 7, 7n7, 8, 9, 9n9, 9n10, 10, 41, 43, 43n12, 94
Wittenberg Castle's Church, 23
worship, x, xi, 5, 7, 8n8, 10, 11, 11n13, 12, 12n15, 14n19, 16, 19, 20, 21, 21n28, 22n29, 22n30, 24, 25n32, 26, 27, 29, 30n35, 34, 47n25, 99, 102, 113, 114, 129, 129n83, 140, 153; false, 13, 14, 22, 24n31, 26, 29, 33, 34n39, 35, 35n39, 41n7, 43, 43n15, 76, 101n28, 115; images in, 28; pagan, 94, 94n13, 122; places of, 31, 77, 78, 79, 84n83, 91, 91n6, 92n7, 129

Yanhuitlán, 128, 130n85, 131, 138n88
Yucatán, 50n29, 78n72

Zumárraga, Juan de, xiii, 40, 40n5, 41, 43, 45, 45n45, 51, 51n8, 52, 88, 89, 91, 92, 94, 97n22, 98n23, 120, 121, 126–32, 128n81, 133, 138, 143, 152, 156, 157, 158, 162; caciques and, 103n33; campaign of, 122, 124–26; Carlos and, 103; challenges for, 135; death of, 154; idolatry and, 42, 136; ministry of, 167; polygamy and, 93; schools and, 97; trial by fire of, 99–103; Virgin Mary and, 134
Zwingli, Ulrich, 113n56; Calvin and, 27; idolatry and, 26, 33; Luther and, 26, 27–28; reform and, 29; true/false religion and, 30

QUOTES IN SPANISH

CHAPTER 2 : NOT FOR THE UNINITIATED
WITH SOME ASSERTIONS THAT
ARE PROBLEMATIC IN LIGHT
OF RELEVANT SCHOLARSHIP
ON THE CONQUEST OF MEXICO
& ITS PRIMARY SOURCES